READING C. S. LEWIS

READING C. S. LEWIS

A Commentary

Wesley A. Kort

OXFORD
UNIVERSITY PRESS

OXFORD
UNIVERSITY PRESS

Oxford University Press is a department of the
University of Oxford. It furthers the University's objective
of excellence in research, scholarship, and education
by publishing worldwide.

Oxford New York
Auckland Cape Town Dar es Salaam Hong Kong Karachi
Kuala Lumpur Madrid Melbourne Mexico City Nairobi
New Delhi Shanghai Taipei Toronto

With offices in
Argentina Austria Brazil Chile Czech Republic France Greece
Guatemala Hungary Italy Japan Poland Portugal Singapore
South Korea Switzerland Thailand Turkey Ukraine Vietnam

Oxford is a registered trade mark of Oxford University Press
in the UK and certain other countries.

Published in the United States of America by
Oxford University Press
198 Madison Avenue, New York, NY 10016

Library of Congress Cataloging-in-Publication Data
Kort, Wesley A.
Reading C.S. Lewis: a commentary / Wesley A. Kort.
pages cm
Includes bibliographical references and index.
ISBN 978-0-19-022134-8 (cloth: alk. paper)
1. Lewis, C. S. (Clive Staples), 1898–1963—Criticism and interpretation. I. Title.
PR6023.E926Z7486 2015
823'.912—dc23 2014036645

1 3 5 7 9 8 6 4 2

Printed in the United States of America
on acid-free paper

CONTENTS

Preface | vii
Works by C. S. Lewis Cited | xi

Introduction | 3

PART ONE

1. *Surprised by Joy: The Shape of My Early Life* (1955) | 21
2. *The Problem of Pain* (1940) | 41
3. *The Screwtape Letters* (1942) | 66
4. *Mere Christianity* (1952) | 85
5. Some Reasonable Assumptions | 109

PART TWO

6. *Out of the Silent Planet* (1938) | 121
7. *Perelandra: A Novel* (1943) | 140
8. *The Abolition of Man* (1944) | 154
9. *That Hideous Strength: A Modern Fairy-Tale for Grown-Ups* (1945) | 167
10. Some Cultural Critiques | 189

PART THREE

11. *The Lion, the Witch and the Wardrobe* (1950) and *Prince Caspian* (1951) | 203
12. *The Four Loves* (1960) | 220
13. *The Magician's Nephew* (1955) and *The Last Battle* (1956) | 236
14. Some Principles Applied | 252

Conclusion | 265

NOTES | 275
INDEX | 295

PREFACE

I should declare at the outset that, as to the person and work of C. S. Lewis, I am neither a devotee nor a detractor. My attention to his work was occasioned some years ago when a group of undergraduates asked me to offer a course on Lewis. More interested in their enthusiasm than in Lewis himself, I obliged. I was aware of the existence of correspondingly strong negative appraisals of his work, some of which I encountered in my own department. From my reading of him I began to draw the conclusion that these pronounced opinions about Lewis were not based on what I began to see as basic and sustaining elements of his work but rather on his specific turn to Christianity as a move separable from that larger project. I have tried in my teaching and in my previous book on Lewis to assess his work more broadly. That intention lies behind this book as well.

A major reason for the sharply focused and divided reception of Lewis is that both ends of the opinion poll take his advocacy of Christianity as defining his work. Those favorably disposed take the rest of his work as valuable primarily because it enhances the visibility and academic standing of his apologetic efforts. His detractors, on the other hand, see Lewis's religious advocacy and apologetics as compromising whatever value his scholarly or imaginative work might otherwise have. As an alternative to these contrary but similarly based readings of Lewis, I hope to bring into view the stable, basic, and even controlling constants in his work. An overarching intention behind this book is to suggest this sense of the whole and to see why his broader project led him to give attention to religion and to value Christianity so highly.

At its more obvious level, this book is a commentary on and guide to representative and important texts by Lewis, a guide that can be used by individuals, groups, or classes that work through all or some of the texts discussed. Individual texts are treated separately, but they are also placed in three separate parts according to their helpfulness in granting access to what I take to be the structural components of his larger project. I have called the three components or strategies "reasonable assumptions," "cultural critiques," and "applied principles." The first of these includes assumptions, largely concerning philosophical anthropology and moral theory, that Lewis thought were shared or potentially sharable by reasonable people generally. The second, cultural critiques, comprises his analyses and questionings of modernity, especially the impact of modernity on personhood, personal identity, and personal relations, and the threat to human well-being posed by it. The third component, applied principles, relates to his distinction between principles and their embodiments and, second, to his constructive application of moral and doctrinal principles to delineate a worldview that he sees as preferable to its modern, particularly nonreligious, alternatives. He offers these applications not as final or universal but as modeling the kind of views that he would encourage others to form. I conclude each of the three parts of the book with a chapter that gathers some examples or indications of the component or strategy that texts in that part are most helpful in making available.

My overall goal, then, is to give attention both to particular texts and to a structural wholeness or coherence in Lewis's work.

Not all of his interests and accomplishments are addressed. Some obvious professional and personal investments, including those that identify him as a poet and a literary or cultural historian, are not taken into account. So when I refer to a view of the *whole* I do not mean *all*.

My task would be easier and clearer if Lewis had directed at least some explicit attention in his work to a description or defense of the three constitutive components or strategies that I have identified. As it is, the individual texts on which I comment do not coincide perfectly with the organizing interests that I discuss in relation to those texts. For this reason, in dealing with each text, I have chosen not to focus primarily on its relation to the component of his method that is the organizing principle of that part of the book, but to treat the text as an individual whole. It is my hope that the three aspects of the book—individual texts examined separately, a proposal that the texts in each part contribute to the formulation of a structural component, and the argument that the three structural components constitute the framework of Lewis's project—will do justice to his own strong interest in the relation between the particular and the inclusive.

I begin with an introduction that draws attention to some aspects of Lewis's context, setting the stage for what follows. I conclude the book with some final comments on his project and on why I am appreciative of it.

Before beginning, I want to thank my editor at Oxford University Press, Cynthia Read. It is fitting that her name, however cryptically, appears in the title of the book, since she offered numerous suggestions for making this book more readable than otherwise it would have been.

WORKS BY C.S. LEWIS CITED

Editions of works by C. S. Lewis cited by page references in this book are listed below in order of their appearance:

Surprised by Joy: The Shape of My Early Life. Boston: Houghton Mifflin Harcourt, First Mariner Books ed., 2012 [1955].

The Problem of Pain. New York: HarperCollins paperback ed., 2001 [1942].

The Screwtape Letters with *Screwtape Proposes a Toast*. New York: HarperCollins paperback ed., 2001 [1942].

Mere Christianity. New York: HarperCollins, 2001 [1952].

Out of the Silent Planet. New York: Scribner, 2003 [1938].

Perelandra: A Novel. New York: Scribner, 2003 [1943].

The Abolition of Man or Reflections on Education with Special References to the Teaching of English in the Upper Forms of School. San Francisco: HarperColllins, 2001 [1944].

That Hideous Strength: A Modern Fairy-Tale for Grown-Ups. New York: Scribner, 2003 [1945].

The Lion, the Witch and the Wardrobe. New York: HarperCollins, 1994 [1950].

Prince Caspian. New York: HarperCollins, 1994 [1951].

The Four Loves. Boston: Houghton Mifflin Harcourt, First Mariner Books ed., 2012 [1960].

The Magician's Nephew. New York: HarperColllins, 1994 [1955].

The Last Battle. New York: HarperColllins, 1994 [1956].

The Pilgrim's Regress. Grand Rapids, MI: William B. Eerdmans, 2014 [1933].

READING C. S. LEWIS

Introduction

Although not an obvious choice for sketching in the context of C. S. Lewis's work, one point from which to begin is his "Englishness." He was born on November 29, 1898, in Belfast, Ireland, but soon after his mother's death in August 1908, he was sent to English schools. With only a brief interlude, he was educated there. In the summer of 1917 he began his career at Oxford University, where he studied philosophy, classics, and English, served as a tutor in philosophy for one year, and became a tutor in English literature at Magdalen College in 1925. Except for some return trips to Ireland, his war experience in France, and a trip to Greece late in his life, he spent his days in England. He took a position at Cambridge University in 1955, but maintained his residence in Headington Quarry just outside Oxford until his death there in the late fall of 1963. He spent his free time largely in England, often on walking tours with friends over the countryside. His interest in things English was substantiated, of course, by his profession as a scholar of English, especially medieval and Renaissance, literature and culture, and the attachment to his English location, his vocation, and his personal identity seem to have much to do with one another.

However, while personally and vocationally engaged by and identified with England, Lewis remained an outsider who retained identification with Ireland. Although they were not close, his father, who continued to live in Belfast until his death in 1929, and his brother, Warnie, who lived with Lewis after retiring from a military career, also identified with Ireland. In addition, Lewis maintained during his life a regular correspondence with his boyhood friend in Ireland, Arthur Greeves. The most influential teacher in his early education, William Kirkpatrick, was Irish, as was also a very important woman in his life, Mrs. Janie Moore, of whom more later. The landscapes of Ireland and Irish love of storytelling, folklore, myth, and poetry had an appeal and resonance that continued, it seems, to exert a hold on him.[1] Given his attachments to Ireland, it is important to note Lewis's awareness of William Butler Yeats, whom he met in the early 1920s. What Yeats may well have represented for Lewis was identity with a particular location and culture and, at the same time, involvement in the cultural breadth of literary modernism.

Mention of Yeats opens a second matter related to Lewis's context, namely, his interest in myth, an interest Lewis cultivated and carried over from his youth into his later work and that he shared with many other modern literary figures. Perhaps one of the things that distinguish Lewis from his readers today, especially Americans, is this deep and developed fascination with myth. It accounts for his early and continuing admiration for such nineteenth-century writers as George MacDonald and William Morris. It also supports his orientation toward and understanding of such traditional cultures as medieval and Renaissance England and ancient Greece and Rome. And it relates him to many of his contemporaries who, like Yeats, were also interested in myth, people otherwise very different both from Lewis and from one another, such as James Joyce, D. H. Lawrence, Robert Graves, and T. S. Eliot.[2]

It is interesting to note that when they met in the early 1920s Yeats was more of a believer in unseen realities and their powers than was Lewis. Like many others at the time, Yeats thought there was something behind myths and fantasies that drew or affected human imaginings and feelings. In the closing decades of the nineteenth century and the early decades of the twentieth, there was strong interest in the occult, mystical, spiritual, and magical, and this was felt in Oxford as elsewhere. When Lewis met Yeats, he was, unlike his countryman, a materialist, and, consequently, a nonbeliever in all of that. Consequently, Lewis suffered, if that's the right word, a gap or tension between his deeply rooted attachment to myth and the mystical and his sense of what is real or true. Readers in contemporary America, influenced as they often are by literary realism and naturalism, must adjust to reading the fanciful and mythlike in Lewis's work, which was part of his culture. What he underwent, during his protracted conversion or return to Christianity, was an adjustment not to the wonders of mythic narratives and their unusual or supernatural features but rather to the possibility that there was something to these stories, that they represented responses to or intimations of realities behind them. He came to the conclusion, largely under the tutelage of Christian friends at Oxford, that his long-standing fascination with myth, which he knew to be shared by people in all places and times, was due not only to the recurring themes of myths across cultures, their breadth and starkness, but to the fact that myths gave testimony to something elusive but real beyond them. For Lewis, biblical and Christian narratives share in the world of myth, but he came to believe that they do so with unique completeness and veracity.

The play between Lewis's identification with and distance from his English context and the interplay of myth and reality went into making Lewis an engaged outsider in his academic vocation. They supported the combination in his work and manner of a sharply critical stance and an equally strong affirmation of his immediate context. Had he identified fully either with his vocational location or with an alternative or contrary to it, he could not have fused affirmation and critique in his scholarly work and personal manner so consistently as he did.

His less than full acceptance both of and by his Oxford colleagues may have been one of the reasons for the eagerness with which Lewis developed close friendships and group relations that were continuous with but also alternatives to his relations with academic colleagues. The most famous of these was with the members of the Inklings, a group that began in 1933 and met regularly until 1949. He also moved between his academic residence in college and his personal, more "Irish" life in Headington. His lack of full acceptance at Oxford also contributed to his move, after some thirty years of professional life there, to a position at Cambridge University as professor of medieval and Renaissance literature in 1955.

Lewis became, in the early 1940s, a celebrity. His visibility and even popularity rose both among students and among the population beyond university walls. While he had some public standing prior to the outbreak of the Second World War, it was in the early '40s that he developed a wide following. The radio addresses that he gave on the BBC between 1941 and 1944 were widely received. *The Screwtape Letters*, which began to appear in serial form in 1941, greatly extended his reading audience. The Socratic Club, a debating society founded in 1942 and in which he remained until 1954 a principal participant, sponsored meetings well attended by students. Issues of a religious nature regularly influenced the agenda. This visibility and popularity did not enhance his standing among academic colleagues, since it smacked of catering to popular tastes. Moreover, Lewis at the same time was publishing in areas outside of his and even any academic field, science fiction and topical essays on religious subjects, for example. I do not think that Lewis sought or was gratified by this popularity, but it must, at least to some degree, have offset the lack of recognition that seems to have been characteristic of his academic life in Oxford.

The complex relation of Lewis to his location and cultural context is not only interesting in itself but is significant for his work because it served to bolster the strong value he placed on holding particularity and inclusiveness, parts and the whole, together. Like living at once both on an island and within an empire, the dual stress on both the specific and the inclusive seems deeply embedded in his work. He saw the general and the particular not only as mutually affecting and illuminating but as also occasionally and significantly coincidental. This capacity or even habit is basic not only to his scholarly work but to his poetic and religious interests and identity as well. The relation was not unidirectional, as though he approached culturally specific things universally and in an intellectually imperialistic way. Indeed, he was very sensitive to the need to understand and appreciate cultures different from his own. He also was not so enthralled by the riches of English culture as to take them as an occasion of pride or superiority. Indeed, while he obviously identified with "Englishness," especially its literary traditions, at important and critical points he was willing to favor other times and places, both real and imagined.

It is noteworthy that someone so complex and ambiguously related to his context, a person of such diverse interests, should evince the continuity and consistency that we find in Lewis's work. This is underscored by the fact that in cases that have elicited sharply contrary positions among his readers, Lewis often chooses to locate himself between clear alternatives. As we shall see, instead of taking a side in a sharply divided field of opinion, he regularly locates himself in a less clear and more complex position somewhere in between, leaving him often with unresolved tensions. But this complexity does not detract from the sureness or sense of grounding that one finds in his work. Part of its consistency or continuity is a matter of style. There is in his written work a directness and even an informality that, combined with his erudition and insight, is engaging and compelling. His autobiography, sprinkled as it is with multiple references to texts the ordinary person is likely not to have read or even to have heard of, might not be much read were it not for the style of its writing, which could be called a respectful and thoughtful immediacy, even intimacy. Lewis was immensely learned, seeming not only to have read almost everything but to have read major texts numerous times, to remember almost all he read, and to be able to recite large portions from memory. He is not shy about displaying these acquisitions and abilities, but he also does not dominate or alienate the reader with them. He is never aloof, dogmatic, or, especially, arrogant. He has his feet on the ground even when referring to the stars.

This continuity in his work, which offsets his diverse interests and his engagements with various genres and kinds of audiences, has also to do with the continuity between his rational, historical, critical, imaginary, moral, and religious interests. Indeed, that continuity is central to his project. Lewis seems to counter an academic context in which interests or acts of diverse kinds are compartmentalized. It is not so much that he undertook to argue for the relations between various human interests as that he simply embodied those relations in his work and, one would think, in his manner and daily interactions. This does not mean that he ends with a kind of mush or confusion. The reader knows when a move has been made from a rational to an imagined or from a historical to a religious discourse or point. Distinctions are retained, but there is also ease of movement between them.

Relations are more assumed than conflicts, continuities more than separations.

The continuity or consistency in his work also rests on or arises from the primacy he grants to personal encounters with natural objects, texts, and other people. He does not explain or defend this attribution of primacy to encounters; he seems more to assume it. This means that he does not subject his encounters to or absorb them within some explanatory theory. This also means that his test for theories and explanations is their ability to take seriously and fully into account the encounters that we have in and with our world and their consequences for our being who we are or are becoming. This means that, while some theories and accounts are certainly more adequate than others, encounters are for him more particular, complex, forceful, and even mysterious than any account of them can be.

Given his strongly "English" identity, his erudition, and the complex position he holds in English modernity, it may be surprising that Lewis is better known and admired by Americans than by readers in Great Britain. Interest in Lewis burgeoned during and after the Second World War in American college departments of English, especially among faculty at conservative Protestant institutions. Lewis would not have been accepted in this context if his work had been of less scholarly merit or was less appealing to a general audience. However, he gained the recognition and even devotion that persist in the United States to the present day primarily because of his willingness to identify himself as a Christian, to take seriously the Christian aspects of the literary tradition with which he worked, and to include religious interests in his interpretation and evaluation of literary texts. This was inspiring and enabling for faculty working in academic environments that had seen, until midcentury, a growing gap, if not antagonism, between scholarship and religious identity and thought. Lewis became a kind of hero for a generation of teachers and scholars, especially in English literature, who were trying to apply the more appreciative cultural attitudes toward religion that emerged after the Second World War to academic work generally and to the study of literature in particular. His high standing among a large number of American readers depends on his self-identity in public and academic arenas as a Christian.

It could be said that Lewis played for American Protestant faculty a role similar to that played for their Catholic counterparts in philosophy by Jacques Maritain (1882–1973). Like Lewis in Oxford, Maritain initially identified with the secular and materialist assumptions of the culture of the Sorbonne. Dissatisfied with that culture, he converted to Catholicism and studied Thomist philosophy. At the beginning of the war he emigrated to America and taught first at Columbia and then at Princeton, where he was professor of philosophy from 1948 to 1960. His work was influential not only because it revitalized interest in medieval philosophy but also because he applied Thomistic insights to current debates in moral philosophy, politics, and aesthetics. What Maritain was for Catholic philosophers in this country, Lewis was for their Protestant counterparts in literary studies. Given the Anglophile attitudes commonly found among Americans teaching English literature, Lewis's standing was enhanced by his "Englishness." The influence, even the authority, of both scholars for their colleagues in America was due in large measure to their religious identities.

Particular aspects of Lewis's religious identity may also be important for an account of the high esteem in which he is held in America. Wheaton College in Illinois hosts the Wade Center, a depository and study center for Lewis and associated writers. Close ties between Wheaton College and C. S. Lewis would seem unlikely, given the fact, for example, that Lewis was a heavy drinker and Wheaton College, at least until recently, prohibited the use of alcohol not only by students but also by faculty. But Wheaton is an institution of strong academic standing that is firmly Evangelical, and the heart and soul of American devotion to C. S. Lewis is Evangelical. I shall have more to say later about this somewhat curious relationship between Lewis and American Evangelicalism. For now, let me point out a couple of things that may account for Lewis's attraction for American Christians of this kind. First, he was not church specific. He became a regular participant in the liturgies of the Church of England, but Lewis does not give the church in general, and certainly not a particular denomination, centrality in his work.[3] This lack of ecclesiastical specificity appeals to Evangelicals, who like to identify with fellow Christians without regard to denominational affiliation or tradition. There is a kind of essentialism, idealism, and elevation above institutional location and historical specificity in both Lewis and his American admirers. Second, Lewis, as we shall see, is sharply critical of modernity, and Evangelicals generally articulate a clear contrast between their own identities and those shaped by the surrounding culture. While I think Lewis is commonly misread or overread in his cultural critique, Evangelicals like this side of him. Third, in his moral theology or ethics Lewis's focus is more personal than social or political. This is not to say that Lewis lacks a social or political perspective, but he was far more oriented to personal than to wider problems. This orientation is consistent with Evangelical interests. Finally, Lewis was insistent that doctrinal and moral principles should be maintained even when they became difficult to apply or understand in current conditions. While I shall raise questions in my conclusion about this aspect of his work, it makes him attractive to Christians who bring to their reading of him a desire to have their certainty confirmed. I should add, however, that, for reasons I will mention later, I do not think Lewis was an Evangelical, although there are points of similarity and connection between his work and this prominent, even controlling, part of his audience.

It should also be said that Lewis's standing in America has been gradually enhanced by changes in academic literary culture. Earlier and more rapidly than in England, American literary studies became broader in scope and inclusive of genres. It is not surprising now to find an interest in cultural criticism, philosophical and theoretical issues, personal narrative, popular literature, and even religion among both American and English literary scholars. Consequently Lewis's versatility finds a larger real or potential arena of appreciation among American academics and among their English counterparts than was likely half a century ago.

Another important matter to take note of concerning his context is that Lewis emerged as a scholar in English literature at exactly the time of the discipline's rise and establishment. While English literature had important cultural and educational roles from the eighteenth century on, it was not part of the curriculum of Oxford and Cambridge until the early 1920s, just when Lewis was completing his education and beginning his professional academic life. As Terry Eagleton puts it, "In the early 1920s it was desperately unclear why English was worth studying at all. In the early 1930s it had become a question of why it was worth wasting your time on anything else."[4] He emphasizes his point: "English was not just one discipline among many but the most central subject of all, immeasurably superior to law, science, politics, philosophy or history."[5]

The question arises as to why this radical reorientation of cultural and scholarly interest and emphasis occurred. One reason was nationalism. There was long-standing cultural competition between England and the Continent, especially France and Germany, and England is known not as much for its music, as was Germany, and not as much for its visual art, as was France, as for its literature. The growing prestige of literary studies owed much to postwar national and cultural pride.

It was also a social and political movement. Many of the early movers, such as I. A. Richards and F. R. Leavis, were the sons of middle-class families. Classics, perhaps largely because of its distance from and possible irrelevance to ordinary and immediate conditions, was frequently the major subject of Oxbridge's upper-class students. English literature arose as the poor man's classics, more closely in touch with the ordinary experiences and lives of people but also elevated culturally above them. In addition, it granted a content to English culture that held unifying possibilities offsetting the potentials for disunity in a society divided by regions and class and that was threatened by political and social changes occurring after the First World War in other parts of Europe.

It was also a moral movement, a reinstatement of the nineteenth-century emphasis, epitomized by Matthew Arnold (1822–88), on poetry and literary criticism as giving to culture the shared moral content that religion earlier had provided. The period after the First World War was a time of accelerated cultural and social changes and one with a sense of discontinuity with the prewar period, and literature provided continuity with the past. More, it gave a sense of cultural and moral stability and shared values, and Richards and Leavis were, as was also C. S. Lewis, involved in applying the force, prestige, and values of English literature to contemporary problems and uncertainties.[6]

It was, finally, an idealist and spiritual movement. It drew heavily on the nineteenth century, on the idealism of figures like Samuel Taylor Coleridge and Arnold. Literary culture developed as a stable and elevated alternative to the growing mobility, urbanization, and industrialization of English society, and that spirit of uplifting the culture, of setting alternative, even contrary, values for the material, mechanical side of English life, was very much a part of the movement. Redeeming the culture from its increasingly brutalizing consequences was embedded in the study of English literature, in its mission. The constant emphasis in Lewis on raising things up, of countering the tendency to reduce everything, has, in addition to its religious and Christian sources and supports, this cultural warrant as well.

Lewis participated in this cultural context. He was influenced by it, and he contributed to it. His literary work, while it had a specifically Christian side or emphasis, was part of larger cultural and social movements in England, and it needs to be seen in that context. While he stands apart from his cultural and academic setting, he was also very much a part of it.

A final point worth clarifying at the outset is that Lewis expects a few things from his reader, and reading him will be enhanced by keeping these things in mind. For example, Lewis has a high regard for what he took to be ordinary experience. He prizes attention to present time and the everyday. Equally important and consistent is his high regard for feelings and personal responses. He counts on and attends to them both in himself and in others, and his interest in personal internality is profound. He believed that people, although also different from one another, experience things in similar ways, and he thought of literature and of religion, among other things, as revealing such continuities and similarities. Things are right for him when they are so morally and rationally, of course, but things that are right also feel right. Sensibility, the coordination of what we perceive with how we respond to it, and awareness of right relations and responses, why they occur and should be honored, are important for him. If something doesn't feel right it may well not be right. And how you feel about something, how you experience it, and its actual value have much to do with one another.

Another thing he counts on, something as important as feeling, is the ability to reason. Literature, religion, and philosophy consort with one another. They are differing aspects of one project, although each also has a life, so to speak, of its own. But they are not in conflict. If something does not make sense, is not rationally and intellectually appealing, it will also not have much religious or aesthetic potential. This is true for all three. Religion that is resistant to the rational or aesthetic also lacks resonance and potential. Reason, then, is not a contrary either to art or to faith. As we shall see, Lewis had as high a regard for rigorous thinkers as for artists and people of faith.

Along with experience and reason, Lewis has—and counts on in his readers to have—a high regard for imagination, and he has it for a number of reasons. One of them is that imagination enables us to live in a world that is larger than what we can see or touch. It opens up to us not only the realm of possibilities but also of realities that we cannot directly encounter. The stronger our imagination the larger is our sense of the world in which we find ourselves. Carl Sagan urged his hearers to live in a world that contains billions and billions of stars. Just so, Lewis wants his readers to imagine themselves as living in a world far bigger than the one that confronts them immediately.[7] Also, the imagination augments our identities by extending us into the future. We are persons not only by virtue of our memories and present interests but also in terms of our aspirations. What is it we long for and are striving to be? What is it that we most desire? Who I am and what I desire to be or become have much to do with one another. My imagination and who I am, then, are inseparable. Finally, the imagination has an important moral function. By using it, I can imagine situations in which the present ills and wrongs of our world are altered. We can think of a better way of arranging or of doing things. By means of our imaginations we see why present attitudes and actions can and perhaps will lead to unfortunate results, and by means of our imaginations we can project alternatives to present conditions and behaviors that are morally more robust and promising. Lewis calls on his readers' imaginations to enlarge and complicate the world, to allow them to have better desires and to desire better things, and to project a kind of world in which evil and destruction have less a say than presently they do.

Finally, it should be said that Lewis was not only very much a part of the context in which he lived and worked but also that he took the particularities of cultural context seriously. He lived in a different world from our own, and we should not expect that what seemed obvious or good to him, as he tried to understand himself and his context, will appear with the same force or adequacy for us today. As he himself would have been quick to acknowledge, he and his culture had their limits as well as their resources, and we are in the same position, with similar but also differing limits and resources. So reading Lewis must be a critical as well as an appreciative act. There are also religious and theological things that some readers will not like. For example, Catholic readers and Protestants who emphasize the centrality of the church and its disciplines and sacraments as crucial to the Christian life will be puzzled by a person who reveals a Christian identity without giving such matters centrality. Evangelicals will not like the lack in his work of a clear and strong doctrine of Scripture. While the Bible is important for Lewis, he usually does not defend what he says about Christianity and the Christian life by appeals to biblical warrants or authority.[8] More liberal Christians will be concerned about the lack in his ethics of a strong social, political, and economic emphasis. Finally, morally sensitive people of various persuasions will be put off by the assumptions and categorizations that he brings to his discussion or depictions of people who are female, of color, and gay or lesbian. Much of this can be chalked up to the cultural context of which he was a part, and it can be argued that he was less insensitive on these matters than many of his contemporaries. However, these are not minor lacks or lapses. The politics of gender, sexuality, and race are more basic to many people than are their beliefs, including religious beliefs, and their beliefs may well operate primarily to warrant their commitments to views relevant to their social, political, and economic locations. I am, frankly, sympathetic to this response, and I view much that gives rise to religious fervor in America today as closely tied to a self-serving advocacy of political and social views regarding gender, sexuality, and race. However, I also think that it would be excessive to attribute all of Lewis's work to his unacknowledged desire to warrant his political and social position and views. One should read Lewis, along with appreciation, with a degree of suspicion and should not dismiss slights and caricatures when they occur as minor slips or as extrinsic to who he is. Among other things, readers of Lewis should be thankful that they live in a time when there is more cultural and social awareness of and sensitivity regarding issues such as these than was the case in his own time and place.

Having said this, I need to add that Lewis was a surprisingly inclusive and generous person. He not only tolerated, he sought out and embraced people with whom he differed and disagreed. While he is critical of his culture and sharp in his points of disagreement with others, he did not easily separate people into groups, especially into camps of allies and enemies. We shall see, for example, that while he spent a good portion of his time and energy in arguing that a religious and, even more, a Christian way of being in the world was superior to its nonreligious alternatives, he was not simply tolerant but was understanding of people who religiously differed from him or were even not willing or able to be religious at all. Living as we do in a culture largely attentive to identity formation, including religious identity, by means of difference, opposition, and hostility toward others, it is remarkable, sobering, and perhaps healing to encounter someone as affirmative, appreciative, and understanding of others as he was while also being forthright about what he believes and thinks is or should be the case.

PART ONE

1

Surprised by Joy

The Shape of My Early Life (1955)

C. S. Lewis's autobiography grants access to a formative portion of his life and thus to some of the groundings of how and why he thinks the way he does. Because it is a conversion narrative it has an hour-glass shape, but far more attention is given to the preconversion period of his life. The book was written in his maturity, and his understanding of why he turned away from Christianity and then returned to it is affected by who he was when he wrote it, although the narrative is also partly based on his journals.[1]

Lewis was a very introspective person. Feelings, experiences, and other internal matters helped to ground his views of things. It is surprising that he should write about himself, however, given the kind of Christian he was. He was suspicious of self-consciousness and the risk of self-preoccupation it carried. Why would Lewis write a book about himself despite being so aware that self-attention can easily lead to pride?[2] I think at least three answers can be given to this question.

First, there is the matter of precedent. St. Paul, St. Augustine, St. Bernard of Clairvaux, John Bunyan—one could mention many others—wrote accounts of themselves as Christians. Lewis could justifiably feel that he was in good company. Second, he gives far more attention to his non-Christian phase and why he entered and departed from it than he does to his life as a Christian, so that the exercise is unlikely to be an occasion of spiritual pride. Third and, perhaps, most important, he thought that his life was similar to those of many others living at the time. By configuring his life as a movement from a Christian upbringing to a rejection of it, Lewis was not making himself exceptional but relating his own experiences to those of many of his contemporaries and even to English culture as a whole. Probably he does not draw attention to these similarities because they were obvious to him, as they would be to his readers. Western culture in general and English academic culture in particular were moving away from religious attachments and identities. While English institutions, including the universities of Oxford and Cambridge, remained officially Christian, from the middle of the nineteenth century on academic culture edged away from religious ties, producing a growing gap between intellectual maturation and religious identity. The pattern of Lewis's own life, then, was representative of the recent history of English, especially academic, culture. One reason he presents his conversion almost exclusively in intellectual terms, which may seem unusual, is that he lived in a culture that increasingly assumed that intellectual sophistication and religious belief were incompatible. Lewis wants to make clear, as he does in much of his other work, that this incompatibility is not obvious or inevitable, that Christian belief does not require the sacrifice of rigorous intellectual standards.

While we are on the topic of autobiography as a genre, a few things are worth pointing out. First, conversion narratives tend to draw a sharp line between the pre- and postconversion parts of the author's life. Often the author not only looks back at earlier years but down on them. Relative to the past, the present is usually shown as a better time. Indeed, the difficulties of the past are often exaggerated in order to emphasize the improvement identified with the time of writing. It may be partly for this reason that Lewis offers a rather bleak account of his youth. Early on he says that, with few exceptions, his youthful years were humdrum and prosaic (8). He associates his youth not with friends and playmates but with solitude (11). As a teenager, he thought of himself as "a great lout of a boy," inept at games, with a face that seemed always to convey something objectionable to others (94). His youth was marked by a number of difficult events, chief among them the death of his mother when he was only eight. That traumatic loss was closely followed by his being sent to school in England and the very unpleasant experiences he had there. Loss and dislocation were aggravated by his growing alienation from his father; their relations became distant and lacking in significant content or warmth.

A second characteristic, often found in male autobiographies, is that the author's self-account is largely concerned with individuation, how he became the person he now is, rather than with how important relationships were in his formation. Although some of this is due to a lack of close relationships at home and at school, when he does mention friends they have their place more in terms of their contributions to his development than in terms of the values of the relationships themselves. An example of this is his friendship with Arthur Greeves, which began when Lewis was sixteen. Arthur became a lifelong friend, but their relationship is described primarily in terms of what Arthur contributed to Lewis's development, especially an appreciation for the ordinary in life and for the value of the "Homely" (152).

Finally, autobiographies are not only objective accounts but also interpretations of the author's life, as Lewis admits. He says that diaries can be unhelpful, because it is only in retrospect that one can sort out what was important from what was not. An autobiography is also always selective; some parts of a life are left out because they are not suitable for public airing or easily explained. Lewis noticeably refers to such a part of his own life, which he calls "huge and complex" (198).

I

Now that we have looked at a few general qualities of this text, we should turn to its principal foci, the most obvious being Lewis's conversion or return to Christianity. We should first look at the reasons he gives for abandoning his Christian upbringing.

It is worth noting that Lewis had come to a more conscious and mature sense of himself as a Christian while a student at Oldie's school. He attributes this to his exposure to clergy and others who were thoughtful and convincing in their presentation of the "doctrines of Christianity" (33). But soon after, on his entering the school he calls Wyvern (actually Malvern) at the age of thirteen, he begins to move away from all of that. He gives several reasons for this. First, he always felt at odds with the physical world. He is an unathletic and unhandy person, which alienated him from his physical environment. Also, he absorbed from his father the belief that life is basically a struggle, especially against poverty or the threat of it. He admits to viewing the universe around him as not only distant but hostile. Later on his negative attitudes extend to cities, the increasing importance of automobiles, and newspapers. He was not, then, naturally or by upbringing, in William James's terms, at home in the universe. Lewis implies that his return to Christianity provided a new sense of relation to the world around him. Second, he had come to think of Christianity and its requirements as burdensome. Life seems to have been for him difficult enough without adding the obligations of religious observance and belief. Third, there was the problem of other religions. He was attracted to the myths of other cultures, and he found it difficult to discredit them as he thought Christianity required him to do. It was difficult for him to accept that all the religions of the world were false and only Christianity was true.

These attitudes set the stage for him to be influenced by the matron at Malvern, with whom he had a close relationship. She was a spiritualist, involved in a variety of the popular religious interests and activities of the time. Notable among these was a movement springing from the work and teachings of Helena Blavatsky, who, beginning in 1875 in London, gave the name Theosophy to teachings she claimed to derive from the spiritual masters of the world, especially from Tibetan Buddhism. The matron of Malvern was representative of a wide cultural fascination with various forms of spirituality, personal religious experience, and mysticism. This resonated with Lewis's ingrained emphasis on personal feelings and internality; this woman's influence fell on fertile soil. A question arises: how does Lewis's return to Christianity relate to the importance he gave to personal internality? We shall see that the two were closely tied.

His gradual return to Christianity can be dated roughly from 1926 to 1932,[3] but Lewis does not tell us much about how his non-Christian attitudes and convictions affected him from his time at Malvern, 1911–14, to his return to Christianity beginning well over a decade later. Given that conversion narratives usually emphasize the negative qualities of the period of disbelief, this omission is rather remarkable. His attention is turned, when treating this period of his life, largely toward his negative impressions of the world around him, particularly the culture of English schools.

Some factors that contribute to his conversion, however, have roots in his earlier life. One of these is the importance he attached to his imagination. He recounts the imaginative adventures he pursued as a young boy with his brother in the attic "study" of their large new house, especially the early stories of Animal-Land. Lewis assigned a high place to the power and work of the imagination. He posited a major distinction between acts of imagination and acts of fantasy. Fantasy produces fictions in which the author plays a central role in the fictive world. Works of imagination, such as Boxen, which combines Animal-Land with India, although created, stand outside of the author. Also, works of imagination can be continuous with experiences of reality. While Boxen is purely fictional, the sense of "Northernness" is real (82). A great stimulus to his imagination occurs during his youth when he encounters Arthur Rackham's illustrations for *Siegfried and the Twilight of the Gods*. They give him a new sense of what he calls the vast, a new appreciation for nature, and a more focused regard for myth. He depicts his imaginative life as a constant throughout his early years and as largely disconnected from his external or quotidian existence.

Another factor contributing to his conversion in an unusual way is the instruction he received from William Kirkpatrick or "the Great Knock." Kirkpatrick was not a believer, but this formative tutor attacks imprecise language and unsupported assumptions. This was not only good preparation for university life but also equipped Lewis to challenge unexamined assumptions, his own and those of others, regarding spirituality and religion. Being a Christian or not, then, depended on which option was better able to stand up to rigorous interrogation. Lewis elevates what he learned under "the Great Knock" to a general principle, namely, that "anything whatever that is good" will contribute, even if it is not Christian, to "training for the Christian life" (146).

A third contributing factor, also rooted in his early life, is the powerful recurring experience of what he calls "joy." It obviously holds an important place for him, as seen from the title of his book, which is taken from a sonnet by William Wordsworth, and I shall have more to say about it later.

Lewis's return to Christianity is a deliberate and quite intellectual process that reflects his growing discontent with philosophical naturalism, realism, or, to use a term more common today, materialism—the belief or theory that all that exists and occurs finds its source and explanation in matter and energy. Lewis relates his conversion, then, to his high valuation of personal matters for which materialism seems unable to provide an adequate account, self-awareness, agency, imagination, and reason. He had also encountered texts that gave support to his discontent with materialism. William Butler Yeats and his belief in magic and spiritual realities made Lewis realize that there were non-Christians who also rejected materialism as an adequate account of the world. Crucial as well is his encounter with George MacDonald's *Phantastes*, which he credits with adding to the spiritual the quality of holiness; Lewis's indebtedness to MacDonald is deep and lifelong. Engagement with the spiritual no longer alienated him from the physical world and everyday life. This opens him to the work of the French philosopher Henri Bergson, who imparted to Lewis a new appreciation for life and vitality. He also learns from Bergson that what exists is not arbitrary and alien to personal internality but necessary and related. And his friend Owen Barfield helps rid him of his snobbery about the modern as contrasted to earlier cultural times and helps him to recognize the inherent determinism of materialism and the attractions of the philosophical idealism that was prominent in Oxford at the time.[4]

Lewis's crucial move is from philosophical idealism to Christianity. This occurs in two steps. The first is to move from the Absolute, which he eventually sees as pallid, to God.[5] This move is not described as logically coerced. It is, rather, based on a free choice that Lewis also thinks of as a necessity. It is, in a word, an intuition, which came to play an important role for him. Intuition was supported by its prominent place in the academic culture of Oxford, especially as expressed in the work of philosophers like H. A. Prichard and W. D. Ross. His move from theism to Christianity, allegiance to the person and work of Christ, seems also to have been based on intuition, a freely chosen insight that is also a necessary conclusion.

I have traced, however briefly, the course of Lewis's turn away from and then toward Christianity. It would be good now to say what his conversion was not, before going on to say what it was.[6]

We tend to think of conversion as accepting something. We often hear of people talking that way about becoming a Christian, accepting Christ into their lives. But Lewis does not talk that way. Rather than accepting something or taking something in, he thinks of becoming a Christian as being accepted, as moving out into something. One begins to live in a different world or to live in the world differently. The new world becomes larger and more engaging than the one left behind.

The second thing to notice is that he does not become a Christian out of fear that he will go to hell or out of the hope that he will go to heaven. While Lewis does not deny the realities of heaven and hell, they are not primary reasons for becoming a Christian (233). For him, hell and heaven are more logical extensions of what it means to be a Christian in this life, and he sees preoccupation with heaven and hell as a form of self-concern. When we think of the great awakenings in American history or of American Evangelicalism today, we think of a strong emphasis on the threat of hell and the reward of heaven. Lewis does not employ that kind of rhetoric and its incentives to describe his change of mind.

The third thing to notice is that his conversion has little to do with the church or becoming a participant in its life and its sacraments. While he began, during his conversion, to attend worship services both in his college chapel and in the church near his home in Headington, and while he later preached in church and wrote about church life, church does not have a prominent place in his depiction of the difference it makes to live as a Christian. While the church has a role in his life and while he identified with it, he also admits to being "antiecclesiastical" (234). He was not opposed to what is often referred to these days as "organized religion," but he did not emphasize the church, its sacraments, and preaching as crucial for becoming or for living as a Christian.

Finally, becoming a Christian is not for Lewis related to accepting the Bible as authoritative. While Lewis had high regard for the Bible and was a student of it, he did not assign it a central or determining position. Questions of truthfulness and value were not for him settled by reference to the authority of the Bible. It should be added that he seems to have taken the seamless interweaving in the Gospels of the mythlike with the historical as a correlative to Christianity's ability to sustain the idea that the otherwise separated aspects of his own life, the spiritual or ideal and the material, are interrelated.

If becoming a Christian is not for Lewis the result of accepting something into his life, fear of hell or expectation of heaven, participating in the life of the church, or recognizing the authority of the Bible, what is it? In my opinion, what counts most in his conversion to Christianity and the difference it makes is that Christianity offers a more adequate account of things than is available in alternative accounts, especially nonreligious ones. Adequacy is important for him. There is a comprehensiveness and complexity to Christianity that allows persons to take into consideration the multiple aspects and dynamics of the world in which they find themselves. When one becomes a Christian, one enters a larger and more complicated world. This is why it is crucial to Lewis's project to point out that modern culture, because it is largely shaped by materialism, is more confined and confining than is a religious, especially a Christian, culture.

This understanding of Christianity as providing a commodious, complex, and inviting world points to the importance of place and spatial orientation for Lewis. His autobiography reveals how spatially oriented he is. This may seem a strange thing to say, given that he was in his professional work primarily a historian. In addition, some philosophers who were influential for him, such as G. W. F. Hegel and Henri Bergson, were strongly oriented to history and temporality. Indeed, modern academic culture, from the late eighteenth century on into the time Lewis is writing, was dominated by a sense of time, history, and process. A turn toward spatiality and spatial theory is a distinguishing mark of late modernism or postmodernism, and to say that Lewis was primarily spatial in his way of thinking and imagining is to place him somewhat outside or ahead of the academic and cultural currents of his time.

Lewis remarks on how significant an event it was for him, at the age of seven, to move into a new and more spacious house. He says that this house "is almost a major character in my story" (10). He tells us that he soon "staked out a claim to one of the attics and made it 'my study'" (12). Gaston Bachelard in his book *The Poetics of Space* comments on the importance of houses for the development of childhood identity.[7] Early memories, he contends, are structured not temporally but spatially, and the form of that structuring is provided by the house in which the child grows up. The various spaces of houses have distinctive qualities. Bachelard is particularly interested in attics and the sense they provide of removal from the bustle of daily living, a place where children are free to construct their own world. Attics, not only by being above the house but also because they reveal the geometry of the house's structure, are attractive, while basements, being underground, are forbidding. Houses stimulate the imagination and invite exploration and reinvention. The image of a child finding and creating a world within a house is for Lewis, I think, a close analogy to what it means to live in the world as a Christian. This is also why, it would seem, houses and attics figure significantly in the Narnia Chronicles.

The products of Lewis's imaginative life are primarily spatial. Boxen, the locus of many imaginings, was a combination of Animal-Land and India. Narnia also is a place, and Lewis conducts us to other places in his science trilogy, notably Mars and Venus. His fictions are spatial, and much in them is given over to exploration of the places to which the reader is transported. Although a historian, he viewed literature spatially: "it does not matter at what point you first break into the system of European poetry" (53). And he laments the effects of modern transportation because it "annihilates space," and space is "one of the most glorious gifts we have been given" (159). The imagination constructs alternative worlds, and it seems very much a part of Lewis's project to show that Christians and nonreligious persons live in differently constructed and interpreted spaces.

Lewis's spatial imagination supports, if it does not ground, his understanding of Christianity. What he seems most to emphasize about Christianity is that it is capacious enough in its account of things to include the complexities and contraries of life, the spiritual as well as the material, the passing as well as the lasting, the particular and the universal, and both good and evil as other accounts of our world cannot. He thinks of Christianity, then, as providing a house, a complex world both inviting and unpredictable.

II

As we have seen, in his treatment of this period of over a dozen years as a non-Christian, Lewis devotes less attention to his own attitudes and behaviors than to the attitudes and behaviors of other boys in the schools he attended. This shift of focus can be partially explained by his belief that English public schools provide the environment in which the future leaders of English society are reared. Lewis retains a lifelong concern about schools and education because he is concerned with the future of English culture.

It is not so much what is taught in these schools that bothers him as it is the attitudes that they seem not merely to allow but actively to encourage. This does not mean that he lays the blame for his non-Christian phase at the feet of Malvern or of its students, although there is an implied relation. Attitudes allowed or encouraged by the school are incompatible with the nurture of faith, and Lewis worries that the future leaders being trained there will bring into their adult life assumptions that are not reliable groundings for morality and faith.

The first of these attitudes is indifference to the imaginative life. The imaginative life for Lewis is expansive, upwardly directed, and open to options more commendable than those available in the ordinary world. The atmosphere of the school supports not an upward and expansive orientation but, rather, a reductive and disdainful attitude toward the world. When Lewis, as he writes his autobiography, looks at his Oxford location, he concludes that "for the last thirty years or so England has been filled with a bitter, truculent, skeptical, debunking and cynical *intelligentsia*" (107). This way of being in the world begins already in early schooling. Rather than the allure and excitement of imagined possibilities, the attitudes allowed or inculcated in the schools are dismissive and derisive toward the imagination and its visions. Lewis does not make the connection, although it is implied, that materialism tends to discredit the importance of the imagined because it grants primary authority to material causes and explanations. The pervasive habit of the ironic mind is to reduce things to something less than they present themselves as, to look behind for more basic motives or causes. Negative and cynical attitudes are inhospitable to the life of the imagination, and for Lewis the life of the imagination and learning are intimately connected.

Second, the atmosphere of the school promotes self-serving attitudes: "to get on, to arrive, or, having reached the top, to remain there, was the absorbing preoccupation" (108). Affectation and social competition produce an interest in relationships based on what grants advantages and are characteristic of academic life not only in the schools but also, by implication, in Oxford and the broader academic world. This life is a struggle in which the fittest, that is, the most self-centered and ruthless, are most likely to win out. Lewis places himself as an outsider relative to the culture that nourishes such attitudes and behaviors. He develops strategies of avoidance and spends his free time in the library.

It is interesting that Lewis neither singles out for condemnation the homosexual relationships and practices that dominated the social life of the school nor interprets them as consistent with the attitudes and behaviors that he questions. One might think that, if nothing else, he would object to the predatory and power-based attitudes supporting these behaviors, especially the exploitation of younger boys by older boys. But I think that he is eager as an adult to emphasize the importance of sins, so to speak, of the spirit and not of the flesh. Also, as he says, he did not address the morality of these behaviors because he himself was not drawn to them. He further suggests that these liaisons formed at least somewhat positive alternatives to the pervasively brutal relations among the boys. But the crucial reason is that, standing where he is while writing this account, he is aware of how many of those boys did not come out of the First World War alive. The only intimacies they experienced, then, were of this kind.

Lewis does not associate the teachers or the curriculum so much as the students themselves with what he dislikes in the general atmosphere of the school. Later, however, in the lectures that make up his little book *The Abolition of Man*, he does relate the behaviors and attitudes he deplores to the general philosophy behind what is taught in the schools. There is no mistake about Lewis's intense and continued interest in education, as there is no mistake about his evaluation of it.

III

Finally, there is the experience of "joy." Its importance is suggested not only by its appearance in the title of the book but also by his recurring references to experiences of joy throughout his life. The title, taken from Wordsworth, also makes clear the importance of Romanticism for him and his work. But first of all, what is "joy?"

Lewis distinguishes joy from pleasure. This is because he wants to emphasize the pain that is associated with joy. This pain arises from a sense of not being included in something expansive of which a person is aware but cannot define. More positively, joy is the sense of something expansive and appealing that evokes a strong sense of longing, as toward something that summons and completes. It is a vastness with an elusive content and wholeness. It is something that stands ahead or above, something toward which a person aspires. The experience of joy is not simply passive, although awareness of it comes from outside, and it is not something the experiencer projects. While the experience of joy can come unmediated by other things, it often is associated with exposure to vastness in nature, to mountains, horizons, and seascapes, for example.

Joy is related to the imagination—both direct attention away from the person to something more or something other that the person would like to be part of but stands apart from. Joy is also related to becoming religious because a religious way of being in the world directs attention to something above and beyond in which the person can be included. It is not surprising, then, that Lewis should tie occasions of joy to the Absolute in idealism and later to the longing for God. What is also important about this for Lewis is that joy is a response to something real. The lingering importance of joy is that it seems responsible more than anything else for his conclusion that materialist explanations are not adequate to account for all that we encounter in our lives. He cannot accept the explanation, for example, that joy is really a form of sexual desire. Lewis knows what sexual desire is, and he writes about it often enough. But joy is something else, and this something else is prized by him and calls on him to take it seriously. Experiences of joy, like experiences of the sublime, to which we will turn in the next chapter, are intimations of something real but unaccountable that human beings can and want to be related to. They reveal or testify to the capacity that humans have to reach out toward the transcendent.

It may be difficult for readers to take Lewis's descriptions of joy and, even more, the significance he imputes to joy seriously. He seems to be making a lot out of something that is fairly flimsy or elusive. But there was much in Oxford, especially during Lewis's early years there, and in English culture more broadly after the First World War, that was deeply attuned to spiritual things and attentive to religiously significant experiences. Magic, the occult, various spiritualist philosophies and religious movements, and séances and communications with the dead were far more part of that world than they are of our own. Philosophical idealism and theories of intuition were part of academic culture as well.

Lewis's attention to joy also reflects his attachment to Romanticism. There is much in the Romantics for which Lewis has sympathy, and in this regard he differs from at least some of his major literary contemporaries. In addition to the importance of the sublime and the internal life, Lewis shares with the Romantics an interest in myth. A myth for Lewis is not relevant only to the time in which it arose, because it seems to transcend history and to be universal rather than particular and parochial in its appeal. Myth also deals with the great issues of life, with good and evil, with suffering and deliverance, with wrongs righted, with death and delivery from death. Finally, myth relates the transcendent world to the everyday. Figures appear and events occur that we do not expect to encounter in our ordinary life, but they also are figures and events related to ordinary life. Myth, then, gives a more expansive, more unified, more upward-directed world than that in which ordinarily we live. It is clear that Lewis relates joy, myth, and the imagination closely to one another. Myth is also related to religion, and Lewis was not above referring to the biblical and Christian stories as myth. He could do so because he did not think, as we tend to do, that myth is untrue. Myths can be true, although their truth is not the same as the truth of history. For Lewis, the Christian myth is true.

Lewis draws on the Romantics not only because of the importance they placed on experience, especially the experiences of joy and the sublime, and on myth but also because of the high regard in which they held nature. The Romantics were thinkers and artists who responded to the growing urbanization and industrialization of English life by turning to nature. Nature seemed more related to the particularity and spiritual quality of personal life than did newly constructed urban and industrial environments, massive, external, and anonymous as they were. Lewis was well aware that the nature to which the Romantics were drawn was not something they encountered, so to speak, in the raw. Nature is also a cultural construction, and the English Romantics were indebted to a number of cultural sources, such as Italian landscape paintings. But nature offered an alternative to the environment that was becoming increasingly prevalent in England. It is not surprising to find Lewis expressing distaste for cities, as when he says of Belfast, "Noises come up from it continually, whining and screeching of trams, clatter of horse traffic on uneven sets, and, dominating all else, the continual throb and stammer of the great shipyards" (154). Lewis never seems to lose his dislike of cities, and he preferred to spend his leisure time not visiting London or the great cities of Europe but walking in the English countryside.

It is important to say, finally, that Lewis appears intent on avoiding a tendency, found if not so much in the Romantics themselves as in those influenced by them, to focus attention on the internal, on the capacity for or awareness of experience. Repeatedly, Lewis cites reminders of the distinction between the experience of something and a person's attention to the experience itself. He says, for example, that "of primary importance for an experience is what is other or outer. The experience is a 'by-product'" (168). Introspection can threaten experience. From A. K. Hamilton Jenkin, his friend at Oxford, he learned, as also from Arthur Greeves, the importance of being "receptive" (199), of being outwardly oriented. This basic attitude permeates the account: his boyhood interest in science and the planets, his growing interest in nature and art (146), and his sense of what reading requires. While there may be equally important distinctions in Lewis's work, this one, between a primarily external and a primarily internal orientation, is unsurpassed. A person's internality, indeed personhood itself, is a consequence of a person's encounters and relations with what lies outside. Like the distinction between experiencing something and attending to the experience, and like the distinction between philosophy as something one studies and philosophy as a way of life, as it was for Plato, so Christianity became for him not something primarily to think about or to be conscious of but something within which to live, of having been, as he says, "taken out of myself" (233).

IV

I have brought into focus aspects of his autobiography that are important for understanding how and why Lewis construes and views things as he does. Now we turn back to a matter to which he refers in passing, that "huge and complex episode" that he deliberately omits. This, without doubt, refers to his relationship with Mrs. Janie Moore. This part of his life often comes up in discussions of Lewis and his work. As is well known, this relationship came about because she was the mother of his friend Paddy Moore, with whom Lewis went into the war. They vowed to one another that, should one of them be killed, the other would attend to the bereaved parent: Mr. Lewis, who was a widower, or Mrs. Moore, who was separated from her husband and caring for her young daughter. As it turned out, Paddy did not survive the war, and Lewis made good on his vow and began not only to attend to Mrs. Moore but to live with her until her death in 1951.

The question arises concerning the nature of this relationship. Lewis partisans tend to dismiss the notion that it was an intimate or sexual relationship. They will consistently and emphatically refer to Mrs. Moore as Lewis's "adopted mother." And there is a good bit of support for this opinion. She was in her forties when Lewis was barely twenty. Lewis felt deeply bereft of his mother. Returning from the war traumatized by physical and mental wounds, being mothered would certainly be of benefit and comfort to him. Lewis knew her as Paddy's mother, and her young daughter, Maureen, lived with them, underscoring her motherly role. Indeed, it seems somewhat unlikely that she would have had intimate relations with Lewis in these circumstances. Finally, Mrs. Moore is depicted, especially later, as a fairly unpleasant and increasingly burdensome person, so that it is easy to assume she was never sufficiently attractive to be of interest to the young Lewis.

However, there are also reasons to think that there may have been more to their relationship than "adopted mother" suggests. Prominent among them is this passing reference in his autobiography. If she were his "adopted mother," why not say something about that? Why does he characterize it as something "huge and complex"? Lewis was secretive about his living arrangements, and few of his friends and colleagues knew of them. Again, it seems that if it were only a mother-son relationship, why conceal it? Lewis's father expressed his concern about the relationship. To his friend, Arthur Greeves, Lewis confessed that he loved Mrs. Moore. He bore with her not only through more than thirty years of life together but through her final illness and death. Lewis did not court other women or marry until after Mrs. Moore died. Almost immediately after her death he begins his relationship with Joy Davidman, whom he eventually marries.

It is reasonable, then, to take a middle position on this question. Lewis, as a young man returning from the war, shorn of Christian identity and influenced by the experimental and innovative cultural climate of postwar Oxford, was vulnerable to an intimacy with an older, experienced woman in the security and confinement of his home. However, it is also likely that this relationship ended by the time he was reappropriating his Christian identity. His return to Christianity and, perhaps, also the death of his father in 1929 would have provided reasons to discontinue a relationship of that kind. However, the responsibility and commitment that stemmed from it would account for his continuing support of her and his avoidance of other female intimacy.

I bring up this matter not only to elucidate an otherwise enigmatic paragraph in the autobiography but to express my uneasiness about the divided camps that exist on the question of who Lewis was and the value of his work. On the one hand are those who elevate him to sainthood and to a religious and moral stature with few if any rivals in the modern period. On the other hand his detractors question his standing not only as a scholar and artist but as a person. I take a position somewhere between these contraries. I have no difficulty in exploring the question of his relation to Mrs. Moore as I have, but I do not want to use it to discredit him. It is an unusual feature of his life story, and it often is the elephant in the room when Lewis is discussed. So I think it is prudent to declare oneself on this matter.

2

The Problem of Pain (1940)

There is no better way to comment on this book than to follow its argument, since the book is closely and, I think, engagingly argued. First, however, it will be good to consider why Lewis wrote the book and what he seems intent on accomplishing in it. Whether he is deemed successful in his argument depends on what it is he set out to do.

The first thing to note is that the problem of pain and human suffering, closely associated with the problem of evil, is a perennial problem in the philosophy of religion. Keeping in mind that Lewis read philosophy at Oxford and for a year taught it at University College, it is not surprising that he would be drawn to this problem, especially because it is a problem in and for Christianity. Lewis takes on another perennial problem in his book of 1947, *Miracles*. Both books show that for Lewis the relations of philosophical to religious interests are basic.

We can also infer from what he writes in the preface that Lewis tackles the problem of pain because he has experienced it, although his statements about this are guarded. He says that he is not in danger of underestimating pain, anticipating the objection that those who talk about pain and suffering, especially in an attempt to reason away the associated problems, cannot themselves have suffered much. Although he does not go into detail, we can assume that he has in mind experiences like the early death of his mother, his time on the battlefield, being wounded in the war, and the deaths of many of his friends. Indeed, the First World War, because of its duration, barbarity, and intractability, created a climate of cynicism and despair concerning human life. Lewis can assume that, because he experienced the war firsthand, he could be recognized by his readers as knowing something of what suffering is all about.

Lewis goes on to distinguish between suffering and the problem of suffering. There are two kinds of suffering, then, suffering itself and the problem that suffering creates. Both suffering in itself and the questions it raises about the meaning of life can cause individuals to form a negative view of the world in which they find themselves.

Pain and the problem of pain had long established themselves as obstacles to religious, especially Christian, faith. They still have that force today, and it is not uncommon to meet people who justify their nonbelief by calling up the problem of suffering, especially the suffering of children and other undeserving victims. Belief in God seems incompatible with all the suffering in the world, much of it baffling. Most of us have faced this dilemma in one form or another. When we witness the suffering of a child, for example, our response is grave: the sadness of seeing a child in pain, the feeling of helplessness, and the offense at the injustice of undeserved pain. The idea of a God who is able to prevent such suffering and does not can easily become objectionable, and the problem of pain continues to be a major obstacle to belief in God. I think Lewis takes up this problem in part because during the modern period, and after the First World War, human suffering was frequently invoked as an obstacle, even a moral objection, to belief in God.

We should notice that his other major work of this kind, *Miracles*, addresses another problem that often forms an obstacle to belief. In an age of growing knowledge of natural causes, people find difficulty with Christianity because it requires belief in miracles. Modern people live in a culture of explanations and the urge to find them. Many things that in the past were thought to be unexplainable are now scientifically understood, and this gives rise to the assumption that anything still outside our understanding will eventually succumb to explanation. Belief in miracles goes against the direction of modern culture and the expectations that science creates. It is important to notice that these two causes for rejecting Christianity, the problems of pain and miracles, fortify and complement one another. The first finds fault with a God who does not intervene in the human world, and the second finds fault with a God who does.

Lewis therefore addresses the problem of pain not only because it is an intellectually challenging and recurring philosophical and theological problem but because it prevents some, perhaps many, people from becoming Christians. There is, one could almost say, a pastoral tone to the work. Lewis takes the problem seriously because it is experienced by many people, as it was by him. Of special concern to him, we can assume, are people who would like to believe but find it impossible or even indecent to believe in God when there is so much undeserved and unexplained suffering in the world.

It is important to state at the outset that Lewis does not set out to solve or explain away the problem raised by human pain and suffering, especially undeserved suffering. Rather, he sets out to reduce its enormity, to make it less of an obstacle to belief than it is taken by many people to be. This is also true of his book on miracles. He does not try to argue people into accepting miracles as possible or actual but rather to remove at least some of the basis for rejecting their occurrence out of hand. It's possible at this point to make a general observation regarding the relation for Lewis between argumentation and belief. I do not think that Lewis tries to persuade his readers, by means of rational argument, to become believers. However, he thinks there is a relation between reason and faith. Rather than espousing one of two clear alternatives—reason validates faith or faith is irrational and immune from rational inquiry—Lewis turns to reason and argument primarily to create a level playing field, challenging the presumed rational advantage of nonbelief over belief in modern culture. He takes away the privileged position nonbelief enjoys in the culture, primarily because of its attachments to science, and he goes on to argue that a religious, and even more a Christian, view is reasonable and indeed superior to its nonreligious alternatives. He challenges the privileged position of nonbelief by showing that it is often based on misconceptions of what religion and Christianity are. He does that in this book, too.

I

By rehearsing Lewis's argument, I do not want to imply that I can put it more clearly than he did. Indeed, it is remarkable how simply and directly he advances his thoughts so that people without sophistication in such matters can follow him. But I justify retracing his steps by saying that I give particular attention to assumptions that he considers to be reasonable, sharable, and supportive of his project.

In his introductory chapter Lewis addresses a basic question, namely, the origins of religion. Principally, he wants to separate himself from Christians who ground religion and belief in deity on an appeal to the design of the world. Lewis thus aligns himself with David Hume, who, in his *Dialogues concerning Natural Religion*, argues that evil in the world discredits arguments for God based on design. Lewis denies that religion arises as a result of people's observation and assessment of the world in which they live. He admits that if belief in God depends on conclusions drawn from observation of the world, people easily could end up rejecting God because of all the suffering they see. Lewis takes a card out of his opponent's hand by agreeing that, based on observation of the world around us, one could easily conclude that there is no God. He says that he once was an atheist, and that his atheism was related, either as a cause or as a result, to his viewing the world in terms of the distressingly negative things he observed in it. The emptiness of the universe, the isolated position of life in relation to the vast, cold, surrounding lifelessness, the history of human warfare and destruction, the sickness, pain, and cruelty in human life: all these can easily warrant atheism, misanthropy, and a despairing view of the world. Indeed, it is very difficult to move from observation of the world to the conclusion that a benevolent God is responsible for creating and overseeing it. The corollary is clear: if belief in God is not an inference drawn from observation of our world, the negative qualities of our world do not establish a case against belief in God.

Having dismissed the assumption that religion is based on observation of the world, Lewis is left with the burden of saying on what it is that religion is based. How shall we account for all the religion in the world if it is not a conclusion drawn from observation? Lewis points to three factors.

The first factor is a certain feeling or experience that people have. Borrowing from a book published in England in 1925, Rudolf Otto's *The Idea of the Holy*, he calls it the experience of the "numinous." Otto's book was widely read in England because there was, as we saw in reading Lewis's autobiography, widespread interest in religious experience and feeling. This interest goes back to the Romantic period. In fact, Otto bases his theory of the numinous on the work of Friedrich Schleiermacher

(1768–1834), who made religious feelings, particularly the feeling of absolute dependence, grounds for understanding what religion is and why it is important for people. Lewis, by turning to the experience of the numinous, taps into a strong and highly valued current of thought in his own time. This experience or feeling also has behind it Romantic attention to the experience of the sublime, and Lewis himself placed a high value on that experience.

One problem with arguments based on feelings and experiences is that they are difficult to pin down. This problem is aggravated when the task is to distinguish feelings and experiences from one another. One can describe the numinous only by comparing or connecting it to other more familiar experiences, but it must also be differentiated from them. So the experience of the numinous is like fear, but it is different, too. In the experience of the numinous one feels uneasy as much as afraid. Unlike Otto, who depends heavily on Schleiermacher, Lewis turns for clarification to another Romantic, William Wordsworth, and to the experience of the sublime. The text Lewis chooses is the stolen boat scene from *The Prelude*. In it Wordsworth describes how one evening he came upon a boat tied up by the shore of a lake and decided to borrow it for a little ride. While rowing out onto the lake, he is looking back at a mountain on the shore. As he moves farther away from the shore, another mountain behind the one he initially saw suddenly looms up, dark and ominous, and the young Wordsworth is so unsettled by it that he quickly returns the boat and heads home. Lewis uses this example to clarify what he is trying to pinpoint as a kind of experience that can occur and recur in human life.

It is as important for Lewis as it was for Otto to see the experience of the numinous as unique. While it is similar to other experiences, it neither depends on them nor is a composite of them. It has its own standing. This is established on the basis of the experience itself, an experience of something powerful that cannot be fully accounted for. All of us at times find it difficult to convey to someone else an experience we have had, something unusual that has occurred. We say it was like this or that or unlike anything else. Lewis is making something that is very difficult to describe basic to his argument. But in response to the complaint that the basis of his argument is elusive and inexpressible, I think he would say that the force of this complaint is blunted by the fact that many of our experiences and feelings are inexpressible and that the experience of the numinous is a response to what by its very nature is not definable or fully describable.

It is important to keep in mind that for Lewis experiences are experiences of *something*, especially when validated by other witnesses. So the experience of the numinous is not simply the result of some chemical event in the brain or some psychological phenomenon arising from something quite different from what it projects. Indeed, to experience the numinous is to experience something that presents itself as the contrary to anything that arises from within a person. Its force derives from its not having its source within the person but from being something other.

The second factor that goes into constituting religion is morality. It is interesting that Lewis gives the role of morality in human life an independent status. It is not the case for him that morality and religion inevitably and clearly coincide with one another. Morality arises not primarily from religion but from the question people ask about who they are; and when they raise that question they seem to be led inevitably to a further question, namely, whether who they are is who they ought to be. When people become self-conscious, either at a certain stage in their lives or at a certain stage in human development, they begin to ask these questions. This questioning gives rise to two things. First, it raises the possibility of a goal or norm to which humans should aspire in order to become the persons they ought to be. Second, people seem to be aware that they do not, perhaps even cannot, attain that goal or norm. While all of this may seem highly conjectural, it is not an unusual way of proceeding. Lewis contends that consciousness carries with it the capacity freely to perceive what is necessary. That is, people can intuit truths. They recognize that there are norms and goals for human life toward which they should aspire. Lewis, as we will see when we look at other texts, believes that individuals, even in differing cultures, come to surprisingly similar conclusions concerning what these norms or goals are. Indeed, Lewis takes the proposition that human beings share not only a moral awareness but also moral norms as a reasonable assumption.

Lewis's argument departs from Otto's. Otto combines the numinous with the moral in his concept of the "Holy." Lewis argues that the experience of the numinous and the intuition of moral norms and goals are not always and certainly not necessarily related. In fact, he suggests that it is unusual and unexpected to see the two as related. I think he suggests this because the numinous is oriented to something outside the individual and to the unexpected and indescribable, while awareness of moral norms arises from people's consciousness of themselves and is more reasonable and more easily described. He contends that it is common to find religious experience and practice detached from morality and morality detached from religion. He finds it unusual, if not unique, that ancient Israel combined the numinous and the moral, particularly in the Mt. Sinai narrative. This combination of the numinous and the moral is the third stage in the development of religion, and it has special relevance to Judaism and Christianity.

Keep in mind two things. First, by establishing the numinous as basic to religion, Lewis is preparing the ground for his discussion of the problem of pain. He implies that to solve the problem of pain would be to dissolve the numinous. While the enormity of the problem of pain can be reduced, especially as an obstacle to belief, it cannot be removed. This is because God is, among other things, dreadful. Second, by depicting the relation of the numinous to the moral as unusual and even strange, he anticipates the problem of pain as he will address it, namely, as a problem that arises from the combination of contrary factors, God's power (the numinous) and God's goodness (the moral). The problem of pain, he is suggesting, arises with particular force in biblical faith because Judaism and Christianity to an unusual and perhaps unique degree unite God's power and God's goodness. Rather than being a source for an answer to the problem created by pain, then, Christianity, by its affirmation of a God who is both powerful and good, creates or at least aggravates the problem.

The final factor, crucial to Christianity, is the Incarnation. The power and the goodness of God come to expression for Christians particularly and most fully in the life, death, and resurrection of Jesus Christ. What is unusual about these Christological paragraphs is that Lewis wants as much as possible to present the Incarnation as shocking. Jesus's claims to be the son of, or to be one with, God are so extreme and so out of the blue that we must conclude that he either was "a raving lunatic" or was precisely who he claimed to be. This kind of argument is called an exclusive disjunction. It is a favorite of debaters, since it presents two alternatives, one of which, by being unacceptable, compels acceptance of the other. Lewis liked this kind of move, and he employs it several times in his works. Many of his readers like it too. Probably no other sentence from Lewis is quoted more often than this one. It deserves some comment.

First, Lewis is addressing readers who very likely have been influenced by interpretations of the Gospels that try to distill the moral, that is, reasonable, teacher from the more than human figure that the Gospels and the rest of the New Testament construct. In the nineteenth century and still in Lewis's day there was a strong current of theology that tried to rescue the Jesus of history from the Christ that the church was thought to have made him out to be. Lewis with this comment is opposing that effort. When you are dealing with the New Testament, with the Gospels, and with the person of Jesus, he implies, you are dealing with something that cannot be divided in that way. Jesus and what he claimed to be or what others claimed him to be cannot easily be separated.

Second, in this line of argumentation Lewis has been relying a great deal on intuition, and he wants to play that card again. He wants to stress that the Incarnation is not a logical conclusion or something that could be anticipated. However, it is also, or for those reasons, susceptible to being recognized not only as possible but as necessary. It's the kind of thing one would not have thought up on one's own. Once intuited as axiomatic, its rightness and necessity become obvious. It not only fits; it clarifies everything.

However, I think that Lewis overplays his point. True, the Gospels present Jesus in relation to his claims or the claims about him by others as shocking and even offensive. But what was shocking and offensive was not so much the claims in themselves as that this particular person should be making them, one who seemed to lack all the necessary credentials for being who he or others say he is. The claim itself was not so shocking. The prophets identified their words with the Word of God, and the kings were representatives and extensions of God's power on earth, even sons of God. The contemporaries of Jesus were looking for the appearance of someone who would conform to or build on those precedents, who would also speak for or extend the power of God. They were not prepared, however, to take Jesus as filling such a role. Indeed, few things are more crucial for the Gospels and the New Testament than the need, in recognizing

Jesus as the Messiah, to alter expectations of what such a person would be like. And the work of doing that is partially handled by appropriating texts from the Hebrew Bible, particularly the Suffering Servant passages in Isaiah, to effect a radical change in understanding the nature and work of the Messiah. Consequently, this move by Lewis, his exclusive disjunction, is among the weakest in his argument, however much he, and many of his readers, liked and repeated it.

Finally, I am surprised that in his Christological section Lewis does not refer back to his epigraph for the book, a quotation from one of George MacDonald's sermons. MacDonald says that the Son of Man suffered not that human beings would no longer suffer but so that they could make their sufferings like his. Suffering is associated with feelings of loneliness and, in relation to those who seem free from suffering, inferiority. MacDonald's point allows for what, in other places, Lewis calls "transposition." This would have been both a logical conclusion to this section and a meaningful one. Since he emphasizes that Christians above all are saddled with the problem of pain, it would make sense to point to this defining characteristic of Christianity as providing, while not a solution, at least a meaningful response to the problem.[1]

II

Having clarified that the problem of suffering arises in Christianity because of the dual affirmations that God is all-powerful as well as good, Lewis takes up each side of the duality. Most attempts to mitigate the force of the problem of suffering do so by placing limits on God's power. Lewis has put himself in a position that keeps him from moving freely in that direction; he has made the august and awesome nature of deity basic to religion.

Modifying it would threaten that foundation. On the other hand, he does want to place limits on what it means when Jesus says that with God all things are possible.

The first qualification concerns "possible." Lewis distinguishes between contingent and intrinsic impossibilities. That distinction is clear when related to human possibilities. There are some things that cannot be conceived of as within the range of human possibilities. It's a little more difficult to erect that category in relation to God. I think Lewis's argument is not grounded on this distinction but on an implied interpretation of the Gospel sayings, namely, that to say something is impossible for someone may imply that it is possible for someone else. And, indeed, Luke's version of the saying (18:27) can be read as meaning just that: the fact that some things are impossible for humans does not entail that those things are also impossible for God. Lewis seems to press the matter further. Mark and Matthew do not rule out the conclusion, he implies, that some things are flat out impossible, even for God. Since no list is provided of things that are intrinsically impossible, we do not know what they are. In other words, there may be a less than perfect match between what we assume to be and what actually is possible for God. Consequently, we should not assume that if something we want to happen does not, it is because God has the power to do it but refuses. Whatever is not possible for God is intrinsically impossible; we cannot be certain how to distinguish between what is possible for God and what is not. Another way of saying this is that we cannot erect categories of what is possible and impossible for God to which God is subject.

The second qualification we should place on our sense of God's power has to do with the natural and social contexts in which we live. These contexts resist divine intervention for at least three reasons. The first is that as humans we come to an awareness of ourselves not in isolation but in relation to our surroundings, and we distinguish ourselves and others as persons because of the particularity we experience in relation to our social and natural contexts. The constancy, predictability, and uniformity of our natural and social contexts allow for our sense of freedom and our ability to change. Second, these contexts mediate our relations to other persons. Rather than know people immediately, the way, perhaps, we know ourselves, we know them in relation to things we share. The common world is not only a stage on which human relationships are enacted; it also provides the means by which we know one another. For example, we know people by what they do and what they make of things. It is good that these contexts resist divine intervention or disruption. If they became, by virtue of frequent divine alterations, unsteady and unpredictable, we would no longer so fully understand who we and other persons are. Third, the conditions, both social and natural, under which we live do not and cannot benefit all of us at all times equally. It may be good for the farmer that it is raining, but the roofer is out of work until it stops. Interventions that would benefit us might well do harm to others. Lewis implies a fourth factor: people, because they tend to be self-serving, will want to alter the shared context, both natural and social, to advance themselves without thought for the well-being of others.

Lewis closes this part of his argument by anticipating the rejoinder that if the natural and social conditions under which we live are partly to blame for suffering and God created these conditions, it might have been better for God not to have created the world. There are two forms of this argument. The first is that it would have been better for God to have created a world in which such conditions did not exist. However, such a world would be so different from what is actually the case that it most likely would not give rise to and accommodate human life. The second is that it would have been better for God not to have created a world at all. But this begs the question of the norm by which the nonexistence of something could be judged to be preferable to its existence. While we can assess the relative value of differing existent or possible things, we cannot compare something that exists to nothing, as though they shared a common status.

This chapter on God's power would be more successful, I think, if Lewis had made more of considerations he reserves for the next section, especially the idea that God withholds power in order to create room, so to speak, for human agency. As they stand, Lewis's arguments—that our idea of what is possible for God needs to be qualified and that there are requirements for an orderly natural and social context that limit the range of divine interference—seem less than fully adequate. I think he is content with this inadequacy because he does not want to posit a limited or emerging God, since doing so would also lessen God's augustness and the experience of the numinous on which Lewis bases the origin and essence of religion.

III

Lewis approaches the question of the goodness of God in a way similar to that in which he approached God's power. Just as there is less than full congruence between what we think is possible and what actually is possible for God, there also is less than full congruence between what we think is good for God to do and what actually is good for God to do. Here too he is careful not to posit total disconnection between the two. What we think is good and what is good for God, while not the same thing, are related. This is demonstrated by our ability to recognize some behaviors and principles as morally superior to others and even to our own.

Lewis is eager to attribute reliability to human reason and morality; a crucial component of his argument is the assumption that humans share an ability to know what is true and good. He notes, in passing, that he opposes the Calvinist doctrine of total (human) depravity, one of the canons that came out of the Reformed synod of Dordrecht in the early seventeenth century. Lewis actually misreads that doctrine, which has more to do with the extent of the consequences of human evil to include all aspects of human life than with the extent of the corruption itself. But the point is clear and important to him. Lewis does not want to posit a discontinuity, much less a contrary relation, between human reason and intuitions concerning the good and what actually is good. However, this does not mean that what we think is good and what actually is good are in full congruence with one another.

Somewhat abruptly, Lewis alters the terms of the problem by moving from the goodness of God to the love of God (31). Generally the problem of suffering is related to morality. If God is good why does God not intervene to prevent or alleviate undeserved, that is, unjust, suffering? But Lewis turns the question from the goodness of God to the love of God, related matters, to be sure, but not identical. I think that, as when discussing the power of God Lewis is commenting on the saying of Jesus that with God all things are possible, here too he is implicitly commenting on a well-known biblical passage, the saying in the Epistle to the Hebrews that whom God loves God also chastens (12:6).[2] In this way he moves the discussion from a general or abstract level to a more personal one. Now it is not so much a question of the goodness of God but of how a loving God can allow or even cause suffering for creatures he loves.

The ensuing argument is quite clear. We tend to think of loving as associated with being kind or nice, being lenient and indulgent. But for Lewis, love seeks the well-being of persons, which leniency and indulgence may not promote. In addition, Lewis argues, the love of God for us and the relation that we have with God, while very much like our relations to other persons, are also different from them. We are far more like other humans than we are like God. So there always is both continuity and discontinuity between what counts in our relation to other people and what counts in the relations, including love, between God and us. Lewis goes on, however, to select moments in human relations that seem to illuminate God's relation with humans. God's love for us is "persistent as the artist's love for his work and despotic as a man's love for a dog, provident and venerable as a father's love for a child, jealous, inexorable, exacting as a love between the sexes" (39). These examples may not be wholly convincing, but they serve his point, namely, that love at its purest is an intense interest in the well-being of the other and this interest is not limited to or determined by leniency and indulgence.

Lewis's next move follows smoothly. We tend to think of God's love for us as acceptance of us because we like the way we are. We tend to think that we and our interests are good and that God should support and promote them. But God, as in the examples given above, acts toward us primarily to promote or refine our relations to God first of all by diminishing or subverting our self-assessment. The objection arises, then, that God, in countering our self-regard, is no less self-regarding. But while our relations to God are necessary for us to be fully human, our regard for God is not something that God needs in order fully to be God. Relation to God is crucial for human well-being, including our freedom, because God by definition is a freeing God, a God who, by being complete, has no need of anything. Problems arise for our relation to God through our wanting to be godlike or self-warranting; the solution, the relation that God makes possible, is to make humans godlike, which means making humans not self-seeking but loving, as God is.

Lewis then launches into an extended consideration of human sin. He thinks this is necessary not only because it is relevant to the discussion of human suffering but also because moderns do not take sin seriously. This is due, he suggests, primarily to psychoanalytic theories that make guilt and shame pointless and even damaging for human actualization. This puts moderns in the West at odds not only with most other people in history and the world today but, more important, with the culture in which Christianity arose, which assumed human wickedness. Unless this changes, Christianity will appear irrelevant to the present culture, offering an answer to a need that has been discredited or is no longer felt.

This does not mean that we have altogether lost the awareness that at times we do objectionable things. But the cultural tendency to disparage guilt and shame promotes habits by which the relation between an objectionable act and deeper, questionable moral qualities is broken. I can claim that my act is uncharacteristic of me, that it can be chalked up to my having "a bad day." I can take refuge in the claim that many people do things far more reprehensible than what I have done. I can blame the social system that has conditioned me or encouraged my objectionable behavior. I can also think that time will erase my misdeeds. I can argue that humans are by nature prone to do bad things and that objectionable acts should be thought of as normal and expected. I can minimize my misdeeds by insisting that they are outweighed by the good things I do. And I even can think of Christianity in a nonmoralistic way, as higher than morality. These strategies for avoiding the inference that objectionable acts are signs that something deeper and more pervasive about us is amiss deprive us of the potential benefits of guilt and shame, namely, the impulse to look for rectification outside ourselves. Shame and guilt can trigger the recognition that we want to and can be other and better than we are.

Wickedness is not an essential but a secondary human characteristic. This is the principal message of the story of the Fall. Lewis wants to avoid the question of why the Fall of our ancestors at the beginning of time should have an effect on us, why we suffer the consequences of actions so remote. Lewis interprets the Fall as establishing that wickedness, while a part of human life from the beginning, is unnecessary and freely chosen. However, wickedness in humans is not surprising because of what gives rise to it. Lewis turns to St. Augustine and the primal sin of pride, and he points to that stage in human development or in the maturing of a person when self-consciousness arises. Becoming self-conscious is a crucial stage because it can allow the valid event of becoming a person in relation to other persons and to God to become instead the falsifying turn toward trying to be a person by means of a primary relation to oneself, of thinking that the basis or potential for personhood lies within. It is only true of God that God's personhood is based wholly within who God is, and when humans assume that this is true of themselves they are attempting to become gods. In the process of becoming self-conscious, we tend to become self-possessed. Rather than, so to speak, looking up, in their self-consciousness humans tend to look down on the rest of their world as subservient to their belief in their own inherent importance.[3]

In this discussion Lewis points to two problems, but avoids addressing them directly. The first is the fact that God could not have been taken by surprise when humans acted as they did. God's foreknowledge and God's omnipotence in the face of human free will and sin pose a perennial problem in Christian theology, and Lewis, while acknowledging it, does not attempt to solve it here, although he touches on it in *Miracles*. The second problem is that both the Bible and Christian theology depict human sin as a corporate condition. Lewis emphasizes personal identity and individual self-consciousness and self-idolatry, but the tradition also emphasizes groups, nations, and humanity as a whole. Lewis does not try to resolve the tension between his own emphasis on personal self-consciousness and this tradition.

Lewis turns from the primal error in human life to the human experience of having to endure things we dislike. He implies that such experiences can counter our primal error and dethrone our deified selves. If we are to be humans as we are meant to be, this dethroning must always occur, and it will be neither easy nor pleasant. Indeed, the tradition refers to it as a kind of death. Pain, when viewed as part of a process, while still an evil, will also be or become meaningful and productive.[4]

Lewis names some generally understandable benefits that can arise from setbacks. For example, they can deliver us from the illusion that we can count on events to accord with our wishes. Pain can make us aware that our lives are not in our own hands and that we do not live in a world of our own making and control. Pain arises from the fact that we do not live in conditions under which what we want to do or be and what we can or ought to do or be are the same thing. In fact to some degree they are contrary. Indeed, under present conditions, what we need and ought to be and do is often what we do not want or like. This point may obscure the fact that sometimes what we enjoy doing can be the same as what it is good for us to do. However, Lewis wants here to keep the other side in view, namely, that we are often required to do things that are good but that we do not want to do, the chief of them being, according to Lewis, acknowledging that God, and not we, is God. When we do acknowledge that God is God, however, we thereby are enabled to become ourselves. Lewis contends that this truth about life, which is basic to Christianity, is widely known even in pre- and non-Christian cultures.

Lewis's position, then, is that pain is evil but can have good consequences. This allows him to argue that we should try to alleviate pain because it is evil. To put it differently, pain is, to a degree, both a consequence of human sin and a means by which the consequences of human sin can be altered or reversed. The continual need for humans to have their primal situation altered means that pain can never be entirely eliminated from life. Does this make efforts to improve human existence futile? Lewis's answer seems to be that some forms of pain are not needed for the changes that suffering can produce, and these forms and their causes can and should be addressed.

Lewis does not identify submission, which is basic to Christian formation, with political or social subservience. Domination by powerful people or institutions does not coincide with submission to the will of God. The kind of relation a person has with God is unique. Lewis also implies a Protestant principle here, namely, that people do not reveal their submission to God by submission to Christian clergy any more than by submission to kings and magistrates.

Lewis's insistence on the necessity of pain should not overshadow the genuine and legitimate pleasures and joys of life. There is much pain in the world, but we should not make it a basis for describing our world and our places within it. Also, we should not aggravate the problem created by pain by taking it as an aggregate. Pain is always particular, and it is experienced under specific circumstances. Finally, it is necessary, while relating sin and pain, also to distinguish them; pain, when it has passed, should be forgotten, while sin, when passed, should be redressed.

IV

It may seem strange that Lewis includes discussions of hell and heaven in his treatment of pain and suffering. But he feels compelled to talk about hell because it also evokes the problem of pain. How can a merciful God allow people to suffer eternal torments, as the damned are thought to do? Lewis, while admitting that he detests the doctrine (120), asserts that the problem created by the doctrine of hell arises from confusion between forgiving evil and condoning it. It is necessary to accept forgiveness: refusal to do so leaves the sinner without recourse. A person ends up in hell because that is where he or she wants to be; it is the logical termination of a path that has been chosen.

A second problem raised by hell is the contrast between the shortness of life and the eternal extent, so to speak, of hell. Eternal punishment seems disproportionate for the crimes of a single, brief lifetime. Lewis responds that the temporal and eternal are not to be compared in terms of length, since they are very different states. It is the finality of this consequence that should be stressed more than its endlessness. In addition, the traditional images of hell—fire, darkness, and deprivation—seem to suggest conscious suffering. But, Lewis contends, hell is a place of nonpersonhood. It is a place where people cease to be people, and it is not appropriate to think of it in terms of unending human punishment. A further problem is that it seems indecent that some people should enjoy a heavenly state while knowing that others are suffering so horribly in hell. But, Lewis again argues that this suggests some kind of coordinate existence between the two. The last problem associated with hell is that God's power appears compromised by the fact that some people have their own way and reject God. But for Lewis, this reflects God's willingness to allow people to have agency, to be persons.

Lewis includes a discussion of heaven in this study of pain for quite different reasons, principally because of the connection many people make between suffering experienced in this life and the reward of heaven. He admits that there is a "pie in the sky" element in Christian doctrine, and he is uneasy with it because it can become a preoccupation and distraction from the realities of this life. Heaven is a logical culmination of a direction already inherent in the move away from self-idolatry toward God. Heaven is not for everybody because not everybody would want to be there. There is a kind of match between what people desire when they desire a relationship with God and what heaven is like. It is interesting that Lewis places so much emphasis in this section on desire. Drawing on St. Augustine, he implies that our valid desires in life are really instances of desire for God. Desire is enormously important for Lewis, and he wants us to desire good things. There is a fit or continuity between a person who desires God and what heaven is like. It is a fit that also matches the human desire for a combination of individuality, which is a part of our self-awareness, and unity, a unity with one another and with God. A metaphor for this relation of the individual and the whole might be music, in which many particular and differing instruments or voices go into producing a unified, though complex, sound.

V

It may seem surprising that Lewis adds a chapter on animal pain, but it should not. The suffering of animals is often cited to support the conclusion that no good God could have created a world in which it occurs. In the modern period, bleak depictions of the natural world were increasingly prominent in the culture, and Lewis wants to address the question raised by the harsh conditions and brutality that characterize the lives of animals. He was especially aware of the unnecessary pain inflicted on animals by human beings. Lewis had high regard for animal life and passed harsh judgment on humans for their disregard and abuse of animals.

Lewis wants, first of all, to place this problem in a separate category from that of human pain. While stressing continuities between human and animal life, he also makes a clear distinction between them. Christianity primarily addresses human life, leaving animals largely on the periphery. Why there are so many different kinds of animals and what role they play in the larger scheme of things are questions that do not find answers in Christianity, beyond the fact that animals are part of divine creation and sources of wonder and wisdom for humans. Lewis is not content to leave it at that. He takes on the risky task of relating the question of human identity to animal awareness. This move is risky because, while we know what it is like to think and feel as humans, we do not know what it is like to think and feel as a dog or porpoise. Lewis says that the so-called higher animals are aware, so that humans and apes have more in common with one another than either of them has with a worm. But humans, he posits, are different from higher animals in that humans are self-conscious. People not only are aware of what is happening to them; they can reflect on it. They can observe themselves. He thinks that animals are capable only of successive perceptions and feelings and not of conclusions drawn from or interpretations given to them. He wants to discredit what is sometimes called the "pathetic fallacy," that is, attributing human attributes to nonhuman objects, and he places limits on animal intelligence. He admits the difficulty of establishing that higher animals have no awareness of themselves, no sense of individuality. Equally, however, there is no evidence that they do. Perhaps we should, especially in light of human cruelty to animals, place the burden of proof on the skeptics and assume that higher animals are to some degree self-conscious. Lewis's ambivalence regarding human self-consciousness and its relation to disobedience and pride may at least to some degree diminish its value as an attribute that elevates humans above animals.[5]

The second question Lewis raises is the relation to evil of killing and other painful aspects of animal life. Although he does not say so, this is also a problem in Christianity, because depictions of the actualization of God's intention in and for the world found in the prophets, particularly Isaiah, remove violence from the relationships between animals and between animals and humans. Lewis suggests that, due to the introduction of evil into the world prior to the creation of humans, animals were already adversely affected before humans came on the scene. This allows him to make a point that recurs in his work, namely, that humans have redemptive functions to perform relative not only to animals but also to the whole of nature. The effect of human sin on animal life is due in part to the failure of humans to fulfill their mandate to raise animal life to states of greater harmony with one another and with humans.

Lewis maintains that humans can help to bring animals to a higher level of awareness, so that they may even develop rudimentary selves. Since what defines a person is consciousness, can it then be said that some animals also have a potential for immortality? Lewis seriously considers this question. But he suggests that animals have their immortality as an aspect of the immortality of the person or people who brought them to the higher state of awareness. He leaves this possibility open, but he ventures no further, pleading that, if it is difficult to imagine what heavenly life is for humans, it is much more difficult to imagine what it would be for animals. Complicating the picture is the fact that Christianity offers two different forms of eschatology. One, more important for most Christians, promises the spiritual continuation or reconstitution of human life, which, although it includes bodies, characterizes them as spiritual bodies and seems to disregard animals completely. A second version looks for a new heaven and earth, a reconstitution of the world as it was before the arrival of evil. Lewis is drawn to this second vision, as we shall see in *The Last Battle*.[6] But the two forms of eschatology do not easily combine, which prevents this otherwise interesting discussion from reaching a conclusion.

We should keep in mind that relating animal life to the problem of pain is an interesting addendum for Lewis because it is relevant to a basic set of alternatives. We saw in his autobiography that as a young man he developed a very negative view of the world in which he found himself. This attitude was certainly not exceptional in his culture. The assumption of a contrary relation between our personal well-being and the natural and social conditions under which we live is prominent if not dominant in modern and recent Western culture. In Lewis's return to Christianity he exchanged this negative for a more positive assessment of the conditions under which we live. That exchange, while not described by him, is important for his worldview. It sets Lewis apart from most influential Christian spokespersons not only of his own day but also of ours. His comments on animal pain, then, must also be seen as a part of this larger interest, namely, the development of more positive evaluations of and relations with the larger world in which we find ourselves.

3

The Screwtape Letters (1942)

The year 1942 was eventful for Lewis. He was engaged in his BBC broadcasts, which had debuted in 1941, and the Socratic Club at Oxford, which featured Lewis, began its highly successful run. He was lecturing at Oxford on the work of John Milton, which formed the basis for his book *A Preface to Paradise Lost*. *The Screwtape Letters*, which owes a great deal to Milton, appeared serially beginning in 1941 and a year later was published as a book.

The Screwtape Letters belongs to the English tradition of the epistolary novel, of which Samuel Richardson's popular *Pamela; or, Virtue Rewarded* of 1740 is a prime example. The text also had a personal context; the life of the Patient resembles that of Lewis in that, like Lewis, he has fallen away from his Christian identity and is returning to it. So Lewis was drawing on firsthand knowledge of the kinds of distractions and obstacles that can arise to impede that process. When readers asked Lewis about which studies in human psychology he had read, he replied that he had simply looked at himself.

I

Before turning to the novel, we should look at some things about evil that are important for understanding the text. The first is that for Lewis evil is derivative or dependent and not original or self-sustaining. Evil and depictions of evil should always be constrained by the primary status of the good. Evil has no existence of its own but is a distortion of or parasite on something good. Lewis is emphatic that he is not a dualist. Following such theologians as St. Augustine, he is eager to put evil in its place.[1] We can best recognize the evil form of something by contrasting it with a form that is freed as far as possible from evil's distortions and corrosions. This means that Satan and the subordinates of the "Father Below," especially Screwtape, have no existence of or on their own. They are all dependent on a being that once was part of the good Creation but has been distorted and is gradually being absorbed by evil. It gives Satan too much credit to say that he exists. This is the obverse of what one should say about the "existence" of God. Because God is the *source* of all that exists, it cannot be said that God "exists." In other words, "exist" is too much to say of Satan and too little to say of God.

This is why beings below, like Screwtape, are always hungry. By necessity, he is a devourer. His primary goal is less to foil the work of God than to perpetuate himself. He is wholly self-preoccupied with his own survival and expansion. This makes him the precise contrary to God, whose attitude toward humans is both puzzling and repugnant to Screwtape. Rather than wanting to possess and devour, God releases people, frees them, and allows them to be themselves. Screwtape cannot imagine a way of relating to others that is not self-serving, that is not aimed toward sustaining and expanding oneself. He thinks of his "Enemy's" way of relating to people as a grand deception, as also basically self-serving, although in a concealed and deceitful way. This allows Screwtape to take the moral high road, so to speak, since he is honest and forthright about his desires and motives while his "Enemy" is deceptive.

What kind of being is Satan, then? He is a fallen angel. Angels are of great interest to Lewis, as they were to Milton. In the opening books of *Paradise Lost* Satan appears as recently fallen, trying to rally his co-conspirators to make their own heaven below. In his *Preface* to Milton's work, Lewis takes up the interesting question of whether angels have a material or only a spiritual nature. This question is not settled by the tradition. Lewis had already engaged this question in his *Out of the Silent Planet*, and he pursued the solution that "angels" have a material nature but of an elusive kind. When it comes to Screwtape and his ilk, however, perhaps because of the devouring habits of these fallen angels, Lewis seems to suggest more of a physical nature than for the "eldila" in his science fiction.

Lewis is aware of the cultural standing of evil inherited by his readers from the nineteenth century, as he was aware of the Romantic perception of Milton's Satan as a more interesting character than his Christ. This idea that evil is more interesting and creative than goodness is one source of the fascination with nonconformity, self-assertion, and rebellion in modern culture. Lewis does not want to feed this fascination with evil. His task is to treat Satan seriously and not simply as a comic figure, but also to show him as less interesting than God and the good. This is a difficult assignment. We know that it is easier to write interestingly about evil characters than about good ones. Evil seems colorful and various. We can conclude that Lewis thinks this is a grand deception. Here and elsewhere he wants to make the point that evil, while it may appear to be various and creative, is really repetitive, monotonous, and derivative. The "Father Below," the great devourer, is also the great homogenizer. Good, meanwhile, does not draw attention to itself so easily because it is not deviant. Good is how things ought and want to be. There is, for Lewis, a kind of "natural" feel to goodness. This is why the conversion of the Patient is presented as "natural" (146). For Lewis, it is good rather than evil that distinguishes people from one another, particularizes them. Evil simplifies, reduces, and homogenizes them.

In what I think is a very clever move, Lewis casts hell as a bureaucracy. He uses the same tactic in other places, particularly in *That Hideous Strength*. As Max Weber made clear, bureaucracy is the typical form of authority in late modernity. It also serves Lewis's aims because bureaucracy has a homogenizing effect, which supports Lewis's argument about evil. A "bureaucrat" is, almost by definition, someone whose personality and distinctiveness have been absorbed by the system. Finally, casting hell as a bureaucracy supports Lewis's aims because he wants to take evil seriously, but not too seriously. We generally share a dim view of bureaucracy and of bureaucrats in our society, and we both complain and joke about our difficulties dealing with them. There is something comic, then, about Screwtape's sense of importance and his jealousy about his position while we know that he is a cog in a system that works against his sense of distinctiveness. Finally, Lewis's use of bureaucracy is effective because it parodies heaven, which is also hierarchical. But the heavenly hierarchy, we are left to assume, does not confine its members but rather is constituted by their full participation in, one could say their creative particularization of, the positions they hold.

Finally, we should notice the important role of subtlety in the novel. In the tradition, subtlety is primarily associated with evil, because the serpent in the story of the Fall is called the most subtle of all the creatures that God made. Evil is traditionally tied to craftiness and insinuation. In this novel, evil is not expressed in vivid and powerful actions like homicide or larceny but appears in attitudes and acts that may be difficult to distinguish from their wholesome counterparts. Screwtape's advice to Wormwood often requires fine distinctions. On many occasions Screwtape must take something Wormwood has proposed and show how it can be seen differently. The evils to which Screwtape wants Wormwood to lead the Patient are often seemingly minor matters. Evil gets its reputation of being more interesting than good because it often is represented in its most egregious and vivid forms. Lewis wants to avoid making evil look interesting and, at the same time, to make clear why it is so insidious. It looks so much like the good, and the distinction between them is often very difficult and fine. Indeed, because evil is attached to a good and therefore always has at least some good in it, it is always possible to frame a defense of an evil. In this novel, Lewis often takes us upstream to the point where the good and evil forms of something begin to distinguish themselves from one another, where they begin to diverge.

II

Lewis himself was an inveterate letter writer, and he and his brother were assiduous in answering the many letters he received, an influx that began to grow at this point in his career. I think that in this book he has in mind the distinction between official and personal communications, which is what makes the personal references in Screwtape's letters sound so insincere. The expressions of affection when they appear resemble the efforts of the manager of a bureaucracy to convince the lower ranks that together they are part of a "family."

Addressed as they are to specific circumstances and problems and recommending appropriate responses and tactics, each letter is complete in itself. But the book also has a structure, although it is somewhat loose.[2] Lewis may have wanted a more vivid structure, but that might have given Screwtape's program a rationality he did not want to accord to it. There are three distinguishable groups of letters. After the first letter, a kind of introduction, letters 2–16 deal mainly with social and political matters. Letters 17–22 focus more on personal interests, primarily those having to do with the "flesh." In letters 23–30 attention shifts to personal matters of the "spirit." Letter 31 concludes the action; Wormwood loses the Patient. While these divisions are not watertight, they do give some structure to the work.

The plot behind the letters directs action toward the goal of seducing the Patient and keeping him from returning to Christianity, a plot of failure. Paralleling this plot is the process of Screwtape's degeneration, his descent from his status at the beginning as an officer eager to pull rank to the ignominy of a centipede wholly dependent on others. The more tacit, contrasting plots are readily inferred: the return of the Patient to Christianity and the "success" of the "Enemy." This plot structure resembles that of *Paradise Lost*, which recounts the rise of the Son and the degradation of Satan, who at the outset is grand and eloquent but in the end is reduced to the condition of a hissing snake.

III

Having mentioned things that lie in the background of this work and pointed to its structure, I turn to commenting on the contents of the letters. This could be approached topically, but it seems best to tackle the letters in the order in which they appear.

1. The reference to the Patient's friends as "materialists" reminds us that Lewis, when he turned his back on his Christian

past, embraced materialism. Materialism is the view that everything that exists or occurs can be explained in terms of matter and energy. Lewis thought of materialism as a view that was deeply embedded in modernity, could not sustain scrutiny, and was even self-refuting.[3] This is why Screwtape urges Wormwood not to present materialism as intellectually convincing but as fashionable, and to treat rival positions as old-fashioned or soft-headed. Lewis thought of worldviews current in his time as based on unexamined assumptions spread, among other ways, by journalism. Indeed, he suggests that materialism, because it is not rationally defensible, undermines the value of rationality itself and thus science. Screwtape implies, an idea strange to hear in Lewis's time, that there may be a more positive relation of science to religion than generally thought. This view has at least two supports. The first is that scientists are more aware than ordinary people of the vastness and complexity of the world in which we find ourselves. They are not as likely as their nonscientific contemporaries to be narcissists. Also, they see a close relation between what they think and what is the case and between their ideas of things and their actions because theory, especially mathematics, and application are closely connected in their work. Lewis wants to make this point about science, along with his point about reason, to undermine the common equation of religion with anti-intellectualism.

2. It may surprise the reader to learn that Screwtape sees the church as an ally in his efforts. Lewis was not strongly oriented to the church or participation in its life.[4] A church is an actualization that can challenge as much as it supports personal faith. Church people have their peculiarities, some of them off-putting, and one has to adjust to these realities when participating in the life of the church. Primarily, however, the church is an ally for Screwtape because many people, especially recent converts, will find the church's life a bit humdrum compared to the novelty and

intensity of their newly adopted Christian identity. Such people are likely to see churchgoing as compromising or confining.

3. Attention here is drawn to the relationship of the Patient with his rather annoying mother, a detail that may reflect the often difficult relations that existed at home between Lewis and Mrs. Moore. Notice the subtleties that creep in, the annoying forms of communication and how people who live together and know one another well can direct barbs so subtle that the person responsible can plausibly take offense when the victim protests. Human relationships, especially close ones, were for Lewis both important and difficult to sustain. He was by temperament not a gregarious person but, on the contrary, reclusive.

4. The topic of prayer is important for Lewis. In his autobiography he refers to the burdensomeness of prayer as one of the reasons for turning his back on his Christian identity. The Patient, then, should be led to associate praying with obligation. Prayer can also be off-putting because it requires a certain physical posture. Further, prayer can allow attention to be drawn away from the one to whom prayer is addressed and redirected toward the praying self, especially to personal feelings, which are otherwise important and positive aspects of the religious life for Lewis. Finally, an object of the Patient's own making can be substituted for the Enemy. Since humans cannot have a conception of God that is unrelated to the ordinary, it is possible to allow proximate things to displace the one to whom they should point. Prayer, which for Lewis was a, if not *the*, principal form of Christian practice, was also for him vulnerable to distortions.

5–6. These two letters allude to the Second World War, which was raging as Lewis wrote, and they reveal Lewis's position toward the war, which was in line with his response to the First World War. Lewis did not give war the same weight that many of his literary contemporaries did. He did not think the wars altered the course of history, were revelatory of what human beings are really like, or separated English culture from its past. Writers like T. S. Eliot, Virginia Woolf, Graham Greene, William Golding, and many others drew far more radical conclusions from the wars, as though they revealed the truth about human nature generally and European culture particularly, and many drew a sharp line between the prewar and postwar culture. Lewis is more restrained.[5] War of course rivets the attention, but Screwtape reminds his underling that war, rather than helping the tempter, can divert people's attention away from trivial things and those they can control to more important and powerful things; this can easily create a susceptibility to faith. In the face of this possibility, Wormwood is urged to use the war to create self-concern. This includes directing the Patient's attention away from the legitimate causes of the fears that arise in time of war and toward fear itself so that, rather than a response to reality, fear becomes a state of mind. This gives fear an inward status, a place in the heart, where the virtue of courage would otherwise reside. It is good to recognize how subtle these distinctions are. Note especially the subtle principle regarding self-consciousness put forward by Screwtape: "in all activities of mind which favour our cause, encourage the Patient to be unself-conscious and to concentrate on the object, but in all activities favourable to the Enemy bend his mind back on itself" (26). Lewis was deeply ambivalent about self-consciousness. It was both crucial to the moral life and threatening to it, and Screwtape reveals himself here to be an astute moral theorist in reverse.

7. The question here is whether it is helpful to the tempters' purposes for humans to believe that devils exist. Devilish pride would dictate that people give them their due. But believing in devils threatens the adequacy of materialism, which is a great ally in their efforts. It is best, then, to discourage belief in devils, at least for now, so that beliefs in the high value of other things such as vitality, sexuality, and psychoanalysis can lead to unrecognized dependence on the realm below.

8–9. These letters turn to the question of "undulations" in personal life, the reality and effects of changing moods, the troughs and peaks to which humans are subject. Screwtape can give no straightforward answer to the question as to which of the two is the more fertile ground for temptation. Troughs, when experienced by the Christian as the absence of God, can be fertile ground for faith. No one is less amenable to Screwtape's purposes than the person who continues to be faithful during times of uncertainty and trial. But troughs can also favor the tempter. Periods of emotional emptiness or discouragement can be exploited with an appeal to sensual pleasure as a distraction or relief. This is not to say that physical pleasure is itself inimical to faith; the opposite is true. Pleasure and the Enemy's purposes are closely tied, a very important point for Lewis, which he takes up later, especially in *Perelandra*. What must be done, Screwtape directs, is to make the experience of pleasure a goal and the trough appear to be a state that will not change of itself but that requires deliberate alteration. Notice that here and elsewhere Screwtape deals not with individuals so much as with "types" of persons. This is an important, if subtle, distinction for Lewis. I shall have more to say about it later, but it is enough to see that the Father Below deals not with persons but with types while the Enemy above deals with individual persons who must be treated as such.

10–11. In these letters Screwtape addresses an important quality of English life, especially after the First World War, namely, social sophistication—what used to be called "worldliness," a preoccupation with the fashionable and striking. This is associated, for Lewis, with the skepticism and cynicism that became pervasive in the postwar culture. Affectation and a sense of disdainful superiority separated the social classes, an elevation based not on something worthy or substantial but on a superficiality of style and attitude. Lewis knew that we are expected to present ourselves in ways adjusted to the situation and occasion. However, there is always the danger that we may come to identify with what we present ourselves as being. And while it may sometimes be necessary to pretend, this role playing can be detrimental to our character. The tempter can also encourage the Patient's vulnerability to seduction through the centripetal dynamics of social groups, especially those that offer an identity in opposition to others viewed by the group as inferior. Enjoyment is important to social groups; Screwtape analyzes various forms of enjoyment and identifies those that serve his purposes. Chief among these is flippancy, the act of making light of good and honorable things. Flippancy, a hallmark of the sophisticated society that Screwtape promotes, is always useful to him because it does not discriminate among its objects according to their value and sets those who practice it above the objects of their scorn. Jokes are more complicated. Sometimes a joke can alter the way in which something is seen, especially something—sex, for example—that has been freighted with too much seriousness. But jokes can also undermine healthy reserve and modesty, and that is helpful for tempters. Fun lies further from the tempters' interests. It suggests a kind of playfulness, of not taking oneself too seriously, and tends to be inclusive and affirmative. Joy is even worse. It implies an attitude toward life, a sense of mirth and of being delighted. It rests on an orientation that is basically other directed. In joy a person is taken up by something larger.

12. In this letter, Screwtape wants to build on Wormwood's apparent success in leading the Patient away from his recently renewed Christian orientation. The plan is to distract him from religion. Soon it should no longer be necessary to provide distractions; the Patient will seek them for himself. These distractions must not be inherently interesting, because directing the Patient's attention outward could easily lead to a renewal of interest in Christianity. Screwtape remarks that those who successfully are

brought into the orbit of the Father Below are apt belatedly to realize that "'I now see that I spent most of my life in doing *neither* what I ought *nor* what I liked'" (60). Lewis draws a close connection between what we enjoy doing and what it is good for us to do; that is something we shall have to look at more fully later. It is enough now to emphasize how for Screwtape (and for Lewis) "the safest road to Hell is the gradual [that is, unconscious] one" (61).

13. The sense of progress is short-lived. The Patient has done things he genuinely enjoys doing: reading a book and taking a walk in the countryside. Lewis distinguishes genuine from vain, self-serving, or exploitative pleasures. Genuine pleasure arises from the delight taken in something that comes to a person from without. This is a setback for the forces below because it could lead to giving oneself over to God; the two actions are linked. In the realm below, pleasure, if that's the right word for it, takes the form of consuming, of taking things into the self. This is the point behind Screwtape's discourse on what the Enemy wants, namely, for people to become themselves by first of all losing themselves.[6]

14. Screwtape is growing increasingly concerned because the Patient, it seems, is becoming humble, a bad sign because humility makes it possible to regard the worth of others. Screwtape recommends trying to turn humility into something else, such as self-contempt, denigration of personal abilities and gifts, or pride in the profundity of his own humility. Loving oneself and loving others are clearly related; Screwtape points out that what should be avoided is the process by which one comes to love oneself through loving others. Self-preoccupation of any kind, even preoccupation with one's faults, serves the interests of the Father Below.

15. A lull in the war brings up the question of present time. Screwtape thinks that attention to present time should be avoided.

It is better to orient the Patient to the past or, better still, the future. This is because present time is real. Even more, present time, because it seems not to move, suggests the eternal. Preoccupation with the past distracts attention from the present. And the future can be a focus of lust and ambition. Screwtape's views of time mirror those of Lewis, who privileged the present over the past and future. It can be argued, I think, that this emphasis in Lewis owes more to his philosophical idealism than to Christian theology or to biblical texts that so often focus attention on the past and future.

16. Ground is being lost by the return of the Patient to church. This needs to be spoiled. One method is to create a sense of connoisseurship with respect to churches and their liturgies. This may be a particularly fruitful point for congregants in the Church of England, since care is so often given to the aesthetics of liturgy. Taste and critical awareness radically alter the position of the participant, and it can become tempting to judge and look down on what is occurring. Encouragement to sample different churches also serves this purpose. Screwtape has interesting recommendations about two local parishes whose pastors are bound to help the cause of tainting the Patient's attitudes toward church.

17. Turning to more personal matters, especially physical desires, Screwtape begins, perhaps oddly for most readers, with gluttony. Odder still is the shift of attention from excess, which we normally associate with gluttony, to delicacy and fastidiousness. The principal example offered is the Patient's mother, and one can hardly avoid the thought that Lewis again has Mrs. Moore in mind. What Screwtape targets is the kind of self-preoccupation that lies behind the insistence that food be just so. It not only indicates a primacy awarded to the palate but also an insistence that the world conform to one's tastes and demands. Such delicacy is presented as a more female form of gluttony; its male

counterpart lies in mastery of the menu and knowing what are the best restaurants or the proper wines to choose.

18–20. Screwtape gives a good bit of attention to sex, emphasizing the prominent role played in modernity by romantic love. This topic leads Screwtape into his most extended and revealing exposition, which he calls "the philosophy of Hell," a philosophy pervasive in, if not defining of, modernity (94). A word must be said about it.

Lewis did not advocate a wholesale rejection of modernity. Rather, he singled out typical lines of thought and attitude that he found alarming or objectionable. He uses Screwtape's statement to clarify some of these, attributing them to hell itself. These include individualism, human relations as basically antagonistic and competitive, and the notion of life as a zero-sum game in which one person's gain is another's loss. Ideas such as these come to clearest focus in social Darwinism, which, as promulgated by Herbert Spencer, was widely received and influential in England and in the United States. For Lewis it seems that love and sex must be freed from these assumptions. Love and sex, rightly understood, are based on regard for the well-being of another.

Screwtape is an advocate of romantic love. This is because romantic love is a feeling located within the individual. Romantic love draws attention away from the beloved and directs it inward. The intensity of the feeling of being in love makes it addictive. The corollary of romantic love, its intensity and the desire to experience it, is sexual desire, which is also potentially addictive. Romantic love and sexual desire, while they seem natural because they seem to arise spontaneously, are for Lewis largely socially and culturally constructed. The reader is asked to infer that sex and love in the context of a caring relationship are more natural than the modern culturally fashionable fascination for romantic love and sexual desire.

21. In this letter Screwtape draws out the necessary moral consequences of common ideas about ownership. He extends the language of possession from simple to complex matters so that the Patient's attitude to the whole world is one of possession: my boots, dog, wife, father, country, and God (114). A shift of meaning occurs when one moves, for example, from "my boots" to "my friend," since my friend, unlike my boots, is not exclusively mine and not subject to my whims and uses. The deeper problem is that people do not really own, in that sense, anything at all; "the word 'Mine' in its fully possessive sense cannot be uttered by a human being about anything" (114). Indeed, what Screwtape understands and what Lewis wants to make clear is that people do not own but are themselves owned, either by the Enemy or by the Father Below.

22. Major setbacks occur. The Patient has befriended a woman who poses a threat to the interests of hell. He is drawn to her innocence rather than repulsed by it. And he is easily moved by pleasure. Pleasures, Screwtape reminds Wormwood, do not necessarily serve devilish ends but need to be twisted. Worst of all, her house has music, silence, and a lovely garden, while Screwtape favors the noise and confusion of hell.[7] When the letter comes to a close, and with it the second part of the book, Screwtape has inadvertently allowed himself "to assume the form of a large centipede" (120). The change recalls the moment in *Paradise Lost* when Satan, who began so majestically, turns into a snake and "back on himself recoiled."

23. Having failed to lure the Patient by means of the "World" and the "Flesh" (123), in this third section of his correspondence Screwtape turns to possibilities for corrupting the Patient's spiritual life. One way to do this is to dilute or complicate the figure of Jesus, particularly by separating the Jesus of the Gospels from the historical Jesus. This can be achieved, for example, by seeing

behind the Jesus of the Gospels a great moral teacher or a social revolutionary. What is advantageous about this change of perspective is that the historical Jesus is a construction or conjecture and no devotional relationship with him results. Screwtape is enough of a New Testament scholar to recognize that the earliest writings of the New Testament are the epistles of Paul, and Paul is comparatively uninterested in the life of Jesus, focusing instead on his death and resurrection.

24. Spirituality can also be corrupted by means of pride, and Screwtape recommends inculcating a certain group identification, a sense of spiritual superiority relative to people outside the select group. This is promising because the Patient, through his girlfriend, has joined a sophisticated Christian group. This presents some possibilities for a religiously fortified snobbishness, the feeling of being part of "an inner ring" (132). Christianity then becomes a way of forming a clique, of differentiating those on the inside from those on the out.

25. This letter starts out along lines similar to those of letter 23, but it moves in a different direction, toward the enticing possibilities of novelty. Screwtape works with the contraries of continuity and change, noting that this duality is built into human life. Change has the potential to lead people astray through the particular pleasures of novelty. Such delights can lead to a desire for ever more novelty at the expense of stability and continuity, making the familiar look stagnant and dull. Thirst for the new and disdain toward the traditional make normative what is fashionable, groundbreaking, irreverent, and "cutting edge."

26. Here Screwtape makes one of his more subtle distinctions, between charity and unselfishness. Unlike charity, which makes the well-being of the other person primary, unselfishness turns attention away from the other person and toward the unselfish self. It easily turns into self-righteousness and makes the other person look, in contrast, selfish. The possibilities are

enhanced by the fact that, according to Screwtape, gender affects selfishness, so that men and women are unselfish in differing and mutually annoying ways.

27. Screwtape returns here to prayer, particularly petitionary prayer, and its corrosion by doubts about its efficacy. He says that people are vulnerable to this doubt because they think of the Enemy as having the same kind of relation to time as they themselves have, forgetting that the Enemy lives in an eternal "Now" and does not encounter things only successively. Citing Boethius as a thinker who makes this clear, Screwtape celebrates the fact that modern people do not take seriously ideas from the past, so that he and his kind need not fear their deleterious effects.

28. Wormwood must be alert to the status of death in human life because the Patient, who has come into a relationship with the Enemy, would escape the tempters were he to die now. Generally it is desirable that humans are given the opportunity to age, because over time they become increasingly at home in and attached to the world. Also, they should be led to think that this world itself can someday be turned, by means of science or politics, into a kind of heaven.

29. Virtues are the topic here, and Screwtape allows that it is difficult to corrupt or distort them. Virtues cannot be attacked directly. The principal virtue addressed here is courage, a virtue still greatly admired in modernity. Courage seems to affect all of the virtues, because it implies persistence in the face of adversity. Rather than attack courage, the thing to do is to encourage cowardice, a kind of fear that produces hatred of what is feared. The difficulty is that cowardice is disliked by the culture and therefore not easily cultivated.

30. The Patient, unfortunately, performs his duties under difficulty, displaying his courage. What could be cultivated, since cowardice is out of reach, is fatigue, which produces irritability and a tendency to make demands on the world. Another possi-

bility is to focus on the trauma of war, on carnage and death, matters very much in evidence at the time Lewis is writing. This can lead to the conclusion, as it did for many of Lewis's literary and theological contemporaries, that war reveals what the human world is really like and everything else is illusion or façade. What is ugly and troubling is real; what is edifying is sentimental and illusory.

31. Wormwood has lost the Patient. Screwtape, rather than becoming angry with him, uses the diminutive endearments of "poppet" and "pigsnie," expressing his love for Wormwood, albeit a love that is self-centered and devouring. Screwtape points out two important things. First, he notes how "naturally" the Patient went into that new life, "as if he'd been born for it" (172). The second is how strange the world of the Enemy is. These observations lead him to the conclusion that their work is severely hampered by their lack of intelligence regarding how these effects are generated, how the self-seeking motives of the Enemy can so effectively be camouflaged.

This last point is worth emphasizing. It is not the case that Screwtape and the interests he represents intentionally distort and dissemble. From their point of view, what they propose and hope to achieve makes sense, is even obvious and natural. However, Screwtape, while he also treats the aims and actions of the Enemy as puzzling and deceptive, takes them as genuine: "all the talk about His love for men, and His service being perfect freedom, is not (as one would gladly believe) mere propaganda, but an appalling truth" (38). We can assume that Lewis thinks his readers, although greatly influenced by the "philosophy of Hell," also still retain the ability to recognize truth, goodness, and even the divine as in some way "natural."

Perhaps because complaint and self-pity suit Screwtape, Lewis presents him as insisting that he is at a disadvantage: "Everything has to be *twisted* before it's any use to us. We fight under cruel disadvantages. Nothing is naturally on our side" (118–19). Lewis extends the point that the natural is good and needs to be twisted if it is to be useful to the interests of evil by creating, however implicitly, a category of matters in the human world that are neutrals: "Like most of the other things which humans are excited about, such as health and sickness, age and youth, or war and peace, it is, from the point of view of the spiritual life, mainly raw material" (103). The undulations or changing moods in human life are similarly treated. Both pain and pleasure are, for Lewis, among realities that can be viewed as or can be put to the service of good or of evil (64). It may be somewhat surprising to the reader that Lewis, while he considers aspects of modern culture as aiding and abetting the force of evil, presents the devilish case, even in his own day, as the more difficult one to make.

4

Mere Christianity (1952)

Mere Christianity is a collection and expansion of the published radio talks that Lewis gave over the BBC while England was suffering through the most difficult years of the Second World War. These talks made Lewis's name almost a household word, and it is not surprising that they did. The war against Germany, which seemed a battle between a Christian society and a barbarian regime, seemed to warrant the revitalization of England's Christian identity.[1]

The talks were part of an attempt by the BBC to consider the question of England's "national character," a topic that had enjoyed a recurring place in English consciousness since the end of the eighteenth century.[2] Lewis, as we have begun to see, had a strong interest in identity theory. The idea of "national character" suggests an extension of the philosophical question of personal identity to the identity of the nation and its culture. Is there some stable "essence" or shared quality that can give coherence and continuity to what it means to be English and also relate "Englishness" to a history that includes Christianity? This is probably why he spends a good deal of time in the talks on the question of "character," particularly what he takes to be its moral content. It is also not surprising that he relates this discussion of "character," both personal and national, to Christianity, which provides a major component in the continuity of English culture.

The idea of a shared English character lends support to Lewis's attempt to articulate the "essence" or shared qualities of being Christian—despite the fact that there are, even in England, many kinds of Christians. It is important for him to treat the relation of Christianity to English character and identity as providing unity and not as causing divisions and conflicts, as of course it frequently had in the past. This idea of Christianity as having a core or essence, what he calls "mere Christianity," also conforms to his idealist tendencies, which commonly entail the assumption of an essence, unified and complete, of which various manifestations are partial or compromised. Lewis is, then, a minimalist who wants to avoid differences by making what is essential as unencumbered as possible, in the hope that what is crucial can be shared.

Lewis's presentation of principles essential to Christianity also implies that these principles remain even when individuals, groups, or even generations of Christians fail to apply or even understand them. This position on Christian doctrine is similar to his position on the principles of morality. It is difficult to live consistently in accord with doctrinal and moral principles, but this difficulty does not diminish their value. At different times Christian doctrines and moral principles may be harder or easier to understand, affirm, or follow. What may now seem obscure or intractable may become more accessible or applicable at another time. I take the unchanging nature of principles and the need to apply them in various situations, as one of the three constitutive interests of Lewis's work. There will be more to say about this interest in the third part of this commentary.

The assumption that there is an essential or mere Christianity that sponsors a variety of manifestations gives rise to the question of what is essential and what is not. The religious conflicts that wracked English life were not waged over differences that were thought to be superficial. Can the differences between Catholic and Protestant or between Calvinist and Baptist forms of Christianity be transcended by attention to something essential on which all agree and to which all should defer? While I tend to give such differences more weight than Lewis does, I also think that he does an acceptable job of pointing to principles that most Christians would agree have been, are, or should be shared.

The principal division of the talks is traditional and appears in several Christian creeds and catechisms. Paul's epistle to the Romans can be thought of as organized along similar lines: the plight of humans due to sin, the response of God to that plight, and human life consequent to the grace of God. The three parts of the book, then, are Sin, Salvation, and Service, to use simple terms. The fourth part, which becomes more sermonic and parochial, deals primarily with the doctrine of God.

I

It is instructive to see that Lewis grounds his presentation of Christianity on what he takes to be reasonable and sharable assumptions. He starts out talking about human beings in general, staking the claim that to be human is to know that there is a right and a wrong way to live. This is not the same as saying that being human means knowing in every case what is right and what is wrong. People differ on moral questions, but when they do, especially when they quarrel over their differences, they do so with the conviction that there is a right and a wrong. One can put his point even more sharply; we are human beings to the degree that we have this sense that there is a right and a wrong way to live. Animals, by implication, lack this awareness. Even though humans often disagree on what are the right and wrong ways for humans to live, it is striking, Lewis thinks, that there exists across differing cultures surprising agreement on answers to that question, a point that he makes on several occasions and that we will encounter again later on.

The second point is just as important: while to be human is to know that there is a right way to live, humans also are aware that they do not conform to that way of living as fully as they ought. These two points do not depend, for Lewis, on religious teaching; they are part of human awareness, a part so crucial as to help define for him what it means to be a human being. The means by which humans know these things is intuition, and the results of acting on these principles produces "character." Lewis's appeal to intuition was supported by his cultural context because it was in good standing as a topic in philosophy. Henri Bergson, a philosopher to whom Lewis refers in these talks, valued intuition highly, and at Oxford there was a school of intuitionist ethics, particularly represented by H. A. Pritchard and W. D. Ross. It is an ethical theory that posits the existence of real moral principles that can be immediately apprehended, principles like those of geometry that, when understood, are taken as self-evidently true. Lewis's interest in the relation of morality to character and to virtue is set in play primarily by Aristotle; virtue ethics has a recurring role in the philosophical and theological tradition.

It is revealing to note, in his title to this part of the book, "Right and Wrong as a Clue to the Meaning of the Universe," the status Lewis accords to the knowledge we have regarding the role of "ought" in our lives. The ability to distinguish right from wrong, while it distinguishes humans from other creatures, does not isolate them from their natural context. Rather, it shows that their relation to that context is moral as well as physical, a conclusion reinforced by the fact that humans can intuit other norms and axioms, such as those basic to mathematics. Intuition reveals the continuity between our minds and the larger, natural world.

Lewis takes up objections to his position, the first being that our desire to do what we think is right is the result not of intuition but of instinct. He responds by distinguishing the instinct to help someone from the recognition that I really *ought* to help that person, even if I would rather not. Furthermore, instincts can easily come into conflict. The instinct to preserve my own life may collide with the instinct to help someone in distress, and it falls to a higher capacity to decide which option is the right one to choose.

A second objection to his position is that morality is a social convention, a result of conditioning. On this view, moral behavior, like good manners, is learned. He responds that, indeed, much that comes under the heading of moral and decent behavior is taught and learned culturally, but it is also the case that we do not think of all societies as equally moral. Indeed, we may even think that another society is more moral than our own. It can also be said that culturally based theories of human morality cannot account for the similarities between the moralities of different societies and for the emergence of moral order in societies rather than order based solely on power.

Lewis calls our awareness of the basic difference between right and wrong a "Law of Human Nature." This Law of Human Nature is not an inference we draw from human behavior; it is causal and not simply descriptive. The sense of "ought" is a reality that presses on us. This means that there is something real in our world, something crucial to our being human, which cannot be accounted for in materialist terms. However, I do not think that Lewis takes this "law" as solely intuited. Rather, he implies that it also comes to human awareness by means of experience.

Just as people learn over time that certain herbs are helpful in treating ailments while others do harm, so people come to awareness that certain behaviors support a good way to live while others do not. This is not to say that what is good and what is not are really only what people think they are. As with herbs that actually do promote health, some behaviors do actually promote a good way of living.

In all of this, Lewis's aim is to attack materialism as an adequate basis for an account of our identity as persons, of the world around us, and of our relations in and to it. There are for him only two views on such matters, a materialist view and a "religious" view, which posits something like mind as prior to, within, or behind the world as we encounter it. Implied here is that an English national character cannot be founded on theoretical materialism but needs a religious base.[3]

By distinguishing between materialist and religious views, Lewis does not want to pit religion and science against one another. Science is limited when it comes to the question as to whether there is more to our worlds than what we are able to observe or measure. One can be a scientist without being a materialist. Conversely, if there is a mind of some kind behind the world as we know it, we would not discover it by observing the world scientifically. Rather, we come to that awareness by taking seriously the human-defining awareness of the important distinction between what is morally right and what is wrong. As I know that I live under an ought that I have not myself produced and that does not come to me from society or my instincts, I can infer that the world operates under principles the presence of which cannot be fully accounted for in materialist terms.

Lewis ends by gesturing toward a third position on these matters, namely, a vitalism such as Bergson's belief in a life force, a force directing evolutionary processes toward their goal. Lewis sees this as a mediating position, a kind of religious naturalism.

The trouble with it, he thinks, is that it collapses the distinction between physical processes and some kind of mind that directs these processes toward their goal. Mind and matter, while not incompatible, are distinguishable. Thinking is not simply a natural event.[4] This is why answers to the question of how we ought to live cannot be based, as social Darwinism is, on observations of animal life. So also, mind and matter cannot be combined to form a third thing, a unity that is prior to the distinction between them.

Religious people have tried to argue from observation of the physical world to a kind of designing mind behind it. Lewis thinks a more reliable basis for such an inference is moral law. The inference to draw is that this mind is above all moral. In *The Problem of Pain* Lewis drew a sharp distinction between the numinous and the moral, but here he closely relates the moral to the numinous. God's morality, while attractive, is also terrifying because it confirms what we already know, namely, that there is disconnection between who we are and who we ought to be and how we ought to behave. This means that we are not only misaligned with the norm but also are misaligned with the mind behind that law, with God. One cannot begin to talk about Christianity without first establishing that people are not what they ought to be and know it (31). They thus not only shortchange who they are or could be but damage the relations they might have with their natural context, with other humans in it, and with the source of the good, with God.

II

Rather than argue that reflection on the moral character of human life leads to belief in God, Lewis begins this more explicitly Christian section with a second reasonable assumption.

Most of the people who have ever lived believed in a god of some kind. Those who do not believe form a small minority. Religion, or belief in a god of some kind, seems to be natural or reasonable. Lewis does not make either of his two arguments, the moral and the religious, dependent on the other, but allows them to stand as separate but mutually reinforcing.

Beliefs in deity differ. Some people posit a god that is not related to morality and others a god who is moral. Some posit a god who is continuous with the universe, and some posit a god separate from the universe. Beliefs that do not relate the god to the moral and see the god as continuous with the universe are pantheistic. Beliefs that relate the god to the moral and distinguish between that god and the universe Lewis calls Abrahamic.

Lewis must address the question of evil in the world; those who believe in a god that is moral face the question of why there is so much evil in the world. Lewis suggests two religious options concerning the origin and status of evil. The first is that good and evil are coeval and coequal. This is dualism. The other, which is the Christian view, is that evil is secondary to and dependent on the good. Human awareness of good and evil suggests that the standard by which they are judged transcends them. The source of this standard is God. So being good can be defined, ultimately, as being in a right relation with God. Evil has no corresponding consequence because evil is dependent on something good that it perverts. Doing evil leads to nothing; it has nothing of itself that sustains it. Choosing evil inevitably leads to or implies nihilism in both its moral and its ontological forms. Evil, although parasitic, is pervasive. Humans are inclined to choose evil because it is readily found in and extended by human pride, the inclination toward self-interest and the domination and exclusion of others.

Having operated so far with what he takes to be reasonable and sharable assumptions, Lewis shifts to matters more closely linked to Christianity. The first is that God responds to human evil and does so in four ways. The first two are general: that God preserves in humans the ability to distinguish right from wrong and that God keeps alive in our imaginations the prospect of divine help in the struggle against evil. The other two are particular: God revealed to the people of Israel what kind of God he is, and a man appeared who spoke as if he himself were God. Notice Lewis's use again of an exclusive disjunction to argue his reader into alignment with the conclusion that Jesus was what he and others claimed he was. He was fond of this kind of argument, but, as we saw in *The Problem of Pain*, it is questionable.

The doctrine of the atonement, that in and by the life, death, and resurrection of Christ human relations with God are restored, is a central Christian principle. Despite its centrality, however, it does not explain how this change occurs. Lewis makes a characteristic distinction between the principle and various theories about how and why it is consequential (54). It may be helpful to think of the various applications of the principle of atonement as versions of one of three options: those that direct the effects of Christ's life and death toward God, those that direct those effects toward Satan, and those that direct those effects toward human beings. The first of these has its most famous spokesperson in St. Anselm of Canterbury (1033–1109). He argued, to simplify a bit, that Christ's death was a sacrifice to God that satisfied God's demand for justice. The second option, directed toward Satan, is usually associated with the church father Origen (185–253) and suggested by the language of Mark 10:45, which describes the death of Christ as a ransom. On this theory, this is a price paid not to God but to Satan who, because Adam and Eve had sinned, had gained a claim on human souls. The third option, often called a moral theory of the atonement, is directed toward humans, and Peter Abelard (1079–1144) offers a good example. The death of Christ, because it is an act of self-surrender and obedience, has power to cause humans to act similarly. Lewis varies in his loyalties among these three options. Here he seems to favor the third: the remedy for sin lies in the ability and willingness to lay aside claims for oneself, and one can do this by participating in the death of Christ. That participation takes three forms, baptism, belief, and Holy Communion.

We should note that Lewis stresses in his description of atonement what is often called "impartation" rather than "imputation." That is, the alteration in human life is not simply declared; it is imparted. Sacraments and beliefs have the consequence of spreading "the Christ-life to us." They are "conductors of the new life" (61). This imparted life enters persons and begins to change them in such a way that they are increasingly able to undergo the kind of voluntary and obedient death that Christ himself accepted. Christians actually become the body of Christ in the world, reenacting or actualizing his death and experiencing the new life that it brings.

Lewis ends by looking at a difficult question, the doctrine of limited atonement. Are the benefits of Christ's death and resurrection confined to those who explicitly are or become Christian? Lewis argues that, while the new relation to God is made possible only by Christ, it is not clear that people must know that in order to be affected by it. On the other hand, Lewis is not a universalist, as was George MacDonald, a Christian author he greatly admired. However, he was inclusive. His earlier statements about truth in other religions prepare the ground for this move. Not only, one can infer, do other religions possess truths concerning human morality and the existence of deities: there is also soteriological truth in other religions, that is, truth having to do with overcoming evil and its consequences in and for human life.[5]

III

It is interesting that Lewis gives more pages to "Service" or practicing the Christian life than to "Sin" and "Salvation" combined.

This emphasis seems to reflect the orientation of his talks toward the topic of "national character." In this third part he spends much of his time talking about moral character. It is also interesting that he again turns away from a specifically Christian to a more general grounding, to what I am calling reasonable assumptions, when he addresses the topic of character. He comes to the Christian meaning of these matters only after establishing their relevance to the shared human situation. A good deal of what he says about character and the moral life, like what he said about moral intuition as constitutive of human identity, applies to all humanity.

Lewis starts out by reiterating a basic point, namely, that who we are as human beings and what it is good for us to be are not at odds. Here he wants to counter the widespread notion in modernity that what by nature we are or desire to be conflicts with moral law. Morality, for Lewis, rather than opposing us, has everything to do with our well-being. Morality is like the set of instructions that accompanies a newly purchased machine and directs its owner what to do and what not to do to ensure optimal performance. Morality is not an arbitrary imposition; it is the way by which human fullness can be realized.

The second thing to get clear is that morality is more complicated than moderns tend to assume. We tend to think of it in terms of our relationships with other people, especially concerning the infliction of harm. However, there are two other components of the moral life that are equally important, if not more so. One of them is the relation that exists within us between our various constituent parts. Personal integrity, unity, or balance—Lewis does not give it a name—is important because people who are rightly constituted are most likely to benefit rather than endanger the well-being of themselves and others. Another component is equally important, namely, the goals or aspirations of a person's life. As noted, we tend to think of morality only in connection with our relations to other people, because modern people can most easily agree on the passive principle of not harming other people. Lewis implies both that this is insufficient and that this component is not likely to flourish unless the other two are also in place. He ends with a look at this third component of morality, goals and aspirations. He affirms that this component directs a person's life toward its source. That is, he implies that the only suitable goal of human life is an ultimate one.

Lewis inserted into the published form of his BBC talks a chapter on the four "cardinal virtues." Although not much in his treatment of the virtues is novel, the topic is germane to his project. Note his assertion that "all civilized people recognize" these virtues (76). A few points about his treatment of the virtues deserve comment. For example, he is eager to rescue "temperance" from the narrow definition it has acquired in modern culture. While it denotes moderation, he also takes it to mean not allowing something to take over one's life. Under "justice" stands a very important matter for Lewis, namely, keeping promises. I will have more to say about this later, but keeping promises and being a person are closely related by him because the force of a promise has everything to do with the character of the person making it. Finally, the virtues are not advanced as ends in themselves. Rather, they form the way by which a person begins to take on a certain character, the way a person's life takes on a positive quality. As Lewis says, "right actions done for the wrong reason do not help to build the internal quality or character called a 'virtue', and it is this quality or character that really matters" (80). As an athlete's muscles have been trained to perform actions reflexively, so a virtuous person acts in a morally commendable way as if by second nature.

Since this discussion is related to the national character, it is fitting that Lewis should take up the question of social or national morality. He says that there is no specifically Christian answer to questions regarding social morality. Some general principles can be identified, but their application to specific social problems is dependent on the situation at hand. Such applications should be left to those who are well informed on matters of economy, politics, and social dynamics (83). There are, however, some characteristics of a society that Christians should advocate. People should have work, and the fruits of their labor should be worthwhile. People should respect one another and offer due obedience toward those in authority. Cheerfulness should be encouraged. Lewis also notes, without pressing the point, that return on investments—one of the basic principles of modern social economy—is specifically prohibited by Christian Scriptures. And he makes concern for the poor a major plank in any Christianly informed social ethic. The measure of help to the poor should be determined by the norm that giving to others curtails what a person or society might otherwise prefer to do for him-, her-, or itself.

Since the focus of his Christian ethics is on the individual person, the question of psychology and mental health naturally arises. Lewis thinks of morality as a means by which people become most fully themselves, a goal that he shares with Sigmund Freud. He wants to distinguish Freudianism as a medical practice from Freudianism as a philosophy. The first of these is unobjectionable; the second is mistaken or distorted. Very likely Lewis sees Freudianism as a form of materialism, and, as we have seen, he considers materialism an inadequate basis for an account of persons and their potentials. Also, Freud posits conflict, both internal and between persons and society, as inherent to human life. Lewis, as we shall see more fully later on, resists the notion that conflict is structural, basic, or inevitable. He also, in this chapter, puts emphasis on the will, what individuals do with the "raw material" each has to work with. He calls the thing that chooses the "real central man" (91). It is difficult to give will and agency their due within a materialist framework, since materialism generally implies determinism. This is no small matter for Lewis because will and agency affect personhood: "every time you make a choice you are turning the central part of you, the part of you that chooses, into something a little different from what it was before" (92).

When Lewis turns to the question of sexual morality, he has two broad objectives. The first is to counter the widespread belief that Christianity is antisexual. The second is to show that sexual morality is by no means the most important arena of human behavior for Christianity.

Lewis upholds the difficult Christian principle that sex should be limited to marriage. The principle is difficult to live up to because our interest in and need for sex today have divorced it from its primary role as the means of reproduction. As he points out, an excessive interest in sex may well arise not from need but from indulgence. Later he calls our appetite for sex "morbidly inflamed" (106). "Everyone knows," he says, "that sexual appetite, like our other appetites, grows by indulgence" (97). We are advised by experts to "just do it," as we commonly say today, because indulgence is healthy. But Lewis sees forces at work in this campaign that may not have our best interests in mind. It may well be that "people who want to keep our sex instinct inflamed" are motivated by the desire "to make money out of us" (99). Like all lies, the idea that sexual indulgence is good for us has truth within it, namely, that sex is a normal and healthy aspect of life. However, most people would agree that in sexual practice restraint is also a good thing. The only question is what those restraints should entail. The Christian principle is not wholly different from those held by other people; but it is more focused. The flip side of mistaken contemporary ideas about sex is that chastity is unhealthy and repressive. It need not be. Again, people generally agree that restraint is good; they differ concerning the degree of and reasons for restraint.

Questions of sexual morality are vexing in the United States because we are aware as Lewis could not have been that it is a very important site of the disestablishment of religion in our country. Restraints concerning sex and reproduction have, since the 1960s, gradually been removed from the control of religiously sponsored directives. It is more difficult today than it was in Lewis's time to discuss sexual morality publicly under the aegis of religiously based principles. The principle of restricting sex to marriage has been compromised even among Christians. Lewis would have us keep in mind that it is important to retain the principle even when we encounter wide divergence from it among fellow Christians. Moral principles are not in every time and situation easily understood and applied, but they ought not to be diluted or set aside in order to accommodate current ideas or practices. Lewis ends his discussion of sex by insisting that so-called sins of the flesh are not as vicious as sins of the spirit, and that "a cold, self-righteous prig who goes regularly to church may be far nearer to hell than a prostitute" (103).

A second principle he invokes is that persons should remain married. He justifies this principle by the role played by promises in the actualization of personhood. He then looks at some of the reasons people terminate their marriages, the principal one being that they are no longer "in love." He goes on to question the status of "being in love," that is, romantic love. Being in love is a state or feeling, and it is not the same thing as loving. Loving someone is not so much a matter of feeling as of will. When two people marry they are asked not whether they do love each other but whether they *will* love each other. Love as an act of will creates a unity between the partners that survives the time when feelings of being in love wane. If an individual makes *being* in love normative and, after marrying, meets someone new in relation to whom that feeling arises, that individual will likely abandon the wedded spouse for this new lover. So, however good and exciting being in love may be, it must yield to the other kind of love, that of will. When it does, the relationship is opened to new ways of appreciating and enjoying one another. However, Lewis goes on to emphasize that Christians should not legislate concerning the permanence of marriage for the society as a whole. In fact, he seems to suggest that there should be two kinds of marriage, one for religious people, in which promises and commitments of a lasting kind are appropriate, and another for nonreligious people, for whom another model may be more appropriate. He ends his discussion of marriage by defending the principle that the man of the household should be its head. He bases his argument less on Christian than on practical considerations, although he also thinks that there is "something unnatural about the rule of wives over husbands" (113).

Having dealt with morality concerning the flesh, Lewis turns to the spirit. This is his commentary on the two-part commandment to love God above all and the neighbor as oneself. He begins with the love of neighbor, addressing the mandate to pray for and forgive one's enemies. He thinks that the non-Christian world sees this commandment as at best puzzling. The point is that one cannot discriminate when it comes to loving the neighbor. Some neighbors are or become enemies. Should a line be drawn excluding them? No, Lewis says. In all cases there is a need to distinguish between things that are objectionable and those that are not. No one who exists is free from objectionable traits and actions, but no one is totally evil. While there is more evil in some people than in others, people cannot be cleanly divided between the good and bad.

The question arises whether love for neighbor, including enemies, is a recipe for pacifism. Lewis thinks not, although he acknowledges respect for the honest pacifist. He contends that killing people may be necessary, although we should not kill out of hate or for satisfaction. It can be argued, I think, that killing in defense of something good can be justified, especially in response to an attack; it is more difficult to defend, as Lewis seems to, killing people as punishment for crime.

The principle of forgiving enemies and loving others leads, for Lewis, to the topic of humility. On the way he must deal with humility's opposite, pride. Pride is, he says, the utmost evil, the "anti-God state of mind" (122). Pride pits us against one another; pride is essentially comparative and competitive, as St. Bernard of Clairvaux makes clear in his discussion of pride and humility in monastic life. Competition can lead to a desire for power, and the struggle for power leads to enmity and strife. Far from combating pride, religion often abets it, and for Lewis the combination of religion and pride is especially troublesome.

The antidote to pride is at the minimum to take seriously or, even better, to admire something outside oneself, something that does not reflect oneself or offer self-enhancement. Humility cannot be pursued directly—to try to cultivate humility turns the focus back on self. The only way to become humble is by taking a genuine interest in and having a real regard for something outside oneself. While this may apply to anything admired not selfishly but for its own sake, it has greatest promise when directed to other people.

This brings Lewis to his discussion of the theological virtues, which are possibilities only for people who have a genuine interest in and concern for others and thus are grounded in humility.

Charity is a form of love that is not first of all a feeling but an act of will, a direction or attitude of concern for the well-being of others. Such an act implies forgiveness, because we are dealing with far from perfect beings. It is easier to be concerned about the well-being of people who are likeable, but that should not be a condition for charity. When you *will* to take a genuine interest in people you may well end up liking them more than you did at the outset. Conversely, the more indifferent you are to the well-being of others the more you will grow to dislike them.

Hope also requires humility because it orients a person to something more, to something not fully realized. Rather than distracting attention from present conditions, hope enables one better to effect change, in the expectation of what lies beyond. Because our desires correspond to things in our world, our persistent desire for something beyond suggests that something of that kind potentially exists. Although hope makes our dealings with present realities more effective, when those realities fall short we may become cynical or angry. The conditions of our world always fall short of our desires, but it is also true that we can alter these conditions to bring them more in line with what should or could be.

Faith has two forms or levels. The first is belief. The principles of Christianity, while reasonable, can be difficult at times even for Christians to understand or hold as credible. Lewis is firm on this point. It is better, he thinks, that we fall short of understanding or even finding credible certain Christian doctrines rather than modify or dilute them to make them more palatable or easier to affirm. Faith is the will to affirm them even when doing so is difficult. He admits that he himself has times when "the whole thing looks very improbable" (140). Faith must be trained, must become a habit, and we must regularly be reminded of what it is we profess to believe.

The second or higher level of faith is more difficult to explain and cannot easily be explained to someone who lacks such faith. Faith at this level is the realization that it is impossible through our own efforts to become the persons we ought and want to be. That can only come to us as a gift. This does not mean that a person of faith abandons effort and waits passively. No, a person is released in trying to live virtuously from the anxiety and discouragement that otherwise may follow from falling short of that goal. Faith and trying hard are not contrary; when acting together, their mutuality is revealed. But moments when who we are and who we ought to be are aligned with one another are not so much moments that we achieve as they are moments when something has been given to us, moments of being received, moments, that is, of grace.

IV

Remember that Lewis has been structuring his moral theory in terms of loving one's neighbor, which depends on and leads to, among other things, humility. Having established the importance and nature of humility, he was able to talk about the theological virtues, since they come into play only for persons who are humble. But the theological virtues also point beyond themselves, since love, hope, and faith lead beyond to love of, hope for, and faith in God. The fourth section of the book, then, deals with God, who God is, and what a relationship with God entails.[6]

While God is different from ideas about God and from the feelings that people have relative to God, those ideas and those feelings are not unrelated or irrelevant to who God is and what it is like to love God. Ideas about and feelings for God are neither univocal, that is, identical or descriptively adequate to what God is like and how people are to be related to God, nor equivocal, that is, unlike what is actually the case. They are analogous. That is, there is a continuous/discontinuous relation between human ideas of and attitudes toward God and what is or should be the case. Lewis, in other words, agrees with Thomas Aquinas that there is a middle position between the two clearer options, namely, that there is full agreement or that there is full disagreement between human thoughts and feelings about God and what actually is true. Lewis is neither mystical nor doctrinaire, neither a fideist nor a rationalist concerning this matter.

There are two aspects, characteristics, or attributes of God, two principles that Lewis thinks must, above all, be kept in view. The first of these is that God is a *living* God. He uses this attribute rather than others, such as that God is supernatural in contrast to what is natural or eternal in contrast to temporal. Perhaps because of the prominence in his own time of various forms of theoretical vitalism, especially that of Henri Bergson, Lewis is eager to affirm that God is vital or living. However, when we say this of God we must also distinguish between what it means that we and other creatures are living beings and what it means to affirm a living God. Lewis distinguishes between two kinds of life or living and gives them differing names. God's life he calls *Zoe,* and the life that animates us he calls *Bios*. Now these two kinds of life, while distinct, are also compatible. Human beings can be animated, so to speak, by both kinds of life, both biological and spiritual. Indeed, in some people *Zoe* seems to be more important as an animating force than *Bios*. The Incarnation is a principle that affirms the compatibility or continuity between these two forms of life.

The second thing to say about God is that God is personal, and being personal needs to be understood first of all by means of the tri-personal nature of God. God is inherently personal because God is relational, relational first of all within God's self. The doctrine of the Trinity, then, indicates, among other things, the complex nature of God's being personal. God is also personal in that, by creating a world and human beings in it, God has a personal relation with that world and those beings and gives to them the ability to respond to that relation. When humans become aware of that relation, they recognize within it the action or being, so to speak, of the three-person nature of God. God's being active, personal, and complex comprises basic and interdependent characteristics of God.

One, if not a primary, form of the relation that humans and God have with one another is prayer, and Lewis turns to it, particularly to the question of how God can have a relation with so many people who may be praying at the same time. This question, along with other questions such as whether intercessory prayer can have an effect on the outcome of someone's illness, for example, Lewis answers by distinguishing our time and God's time or eternity. For Lewis the closest we can come to understanding these matters is to begin with present time, with "now." As is clear, "now" is the only kind of time that is real, since the past is no longer and the future is yet to be. So "now" gives us some idea of God's way of being because God is real and because God is not temporal, which means, among other things, that past and future do not have for God the standing that they have for us. The reader could ask whether "now" can, so to speak, be isolated, since it is so fleeting. Indeed, some theorists claim that there is no "now," that "now" is the name we give for the point at which the future turns into the past. "Now," in fact, tends to be atemporal, even spatial, and Lewis seems prepared to accept these implications. There is an implied relation in Lewis between present time, spatiality, and eternity.

On the matter of a person's relation to God, Lewis prefers, as we already have seen, impartation to imputation. That is, he affirms that in a relation with God something actually is given or imparted to the believer. What is given is God's own life, what earlier he called *Zoe*. That is, a person has a relation to God that is somehow continuous with the relation that God has within God's own personal life. Lewis calls this impartation a "good infection." He differs from those Christians who think that God's relation to people is more a matter of declaration, of a status imputed to them.

The new life that is given to people does not necessarily conflict with the person's *Bios*. If it does it is because people mistakenly define their lives in terms of their own centrality. When they do so, God's life will appear to be a hostile imposition. But there need not be antagonism between the two kinds of life, and in the person of Christ he sees, among other things, the continuity or compatibility between them.

For at least two reasons it is important for Lewis to make the point that people, at least potentially, are, at the level of *Bios,* already related and not isolated. However, this relational potential has been occluded by pride and its consequences, which affect all persons. The Incarnation, the joining of God's life to human life, affects, actually and potentially, human *Bios*. This means that the joining has already occurred and needs only to be appropriated or actualized in the life of persons. The result of this appropriation or actualization is that persons, by being relational, become particularized. They find themselves to be integers in an inclusive and meaningful mathematics, or, as Lewis following St. Paul puts it, particular organs in a complex but unified body.

But Lewis is not done with prayer and with the relation that people and God can have. He uses the language of pretending. Although he does not mention John Calvin, Lewis may have in mind the word that Calvin used when speaking about reading Scripture or receiving the sacraments, *sicut* or "as if." Pretending is not make-believe; treating something "as if" does not necessarily mean treating something as other than it is. Nor is it simply going through the motions. Pretending is aspiring or acting in hope. One puts oneself in the position, so to speak, of anticipation that the reality or truth of what is hoped for can be heard or seen. In prayer, as well, one addresses God as Father, as though one were already a child of God. This is not a presumption; it is an act of anticipation, hope, or aspiration.

Lewis adds two comments concerning this process by which, in and through our relation to others, we are transformed to become children of God. First, this is not an easy process, and there is much in us that resists it. It is also difficult because we have, perhaps mistakenly, a firm or clear notion of who we are by ourselves and we are not sure what we will be like when we love others and God. Also, we are deeply affected by the notion that we belong to ourselves, that our lives are our own. So it is not an easy thing for this process to occur; it will be slow, uneven, and often painful. The second comment is that this is what Christianity, finally, is all about. All the other things that go into constituting Christianity are subservient to this process. The process Lewis describes is not, for example, for the sake of the church; the church exists for the sake and as a result of the process.

This process, while uneven and vulnerable to setbacks, moves on toward the goal of completion. This completion means both inclusiveness—a person's life in its entirety is undergoing transformation—and perfection, the actualization of the personhood of that person. In addition, we cannot be certain, when viewing people, concerning the activity and extent of this process in anyone. For example, it is not possible clearly to distinguish Christian from non-Christian people, indicating thereby that in the first group this process is occurring and in the second group it is not. Finally, the process and what generally in the society we think of as good or nice people are related ambiguously to one another. That is, while a person undergoing transformation is likely to be viewed favorably even by people who have no knowledge of or interest in this process, it is also very possible that there may be some dissonance between what that person is like and how that person is viewed by others.

Lewis ends his discussion of the relation of God and people to one another in positive and expansive ways. Let me begin with his second point. Drawing out his recurring interest in personal identity theory, Lewis makes the point that not undergoing a transformation of the kind he has described is increasingly to lose personhood. The result is that what I assume to be myself turns out to be merely a "meeting place for trains of events which I never started and which I cannot stop" (225). This quite skeptical view is commonly found in personal identity theory today, namely, that the self, upon which so much philosophical and psychological theory depends, is an illusion. So the process Lewis has been describing is not the transformation of an already existing self; it is the creation of a self, a process based on or marked by an abandonment of the notion that one already has or is a self.

The other concluding point is worth emphasizing because it is so different from the preoccupations of many of Lewis's admirers with eschatology as imminent judgment and destruction. Lewis holds out a very different scenario, one in which transformed or newly created selves or persons in the world, related as they are, also have a transforming effect on their wider contexts. He holds out the prospect that human transformations may occur that outstrip the anticipations provided by evolutionary theories and technological projections. Lewis wants to affirm the truth that lies within such theories and projections, but he wants them to find their fulfillment in Christian hope.

5

Some Reasonable Assumptions

One of the planks in Lewis's platform is his assumption that some basic and important moral and religious matters are and have been generally agreed upon by reasonable people. The texts considered so far, while interesting and important for many other reasons, are suited to the task of surfacing some matters of this kind, particularly concerning persons, their relations to one another, and their relations to the whole. Lewis, in his presentation of Christianity, does not want to be arbitrary or dogmatic. He is basically a reasonable and inclusive thinker, and he takes his views of things as not only defensible but also as acceptable by and useful to people of many stripes. What he posits or clarifies as sharable is substantial, but it neither depends on nor compromises the distinctively Christian principles to which later he turns.

A good place to begin is with experience, a point that is particularly important for two of the texts looked at so far, his autobiography and the opening section of *The Problem of Pain*. Certain human experiences have for him a normative standing that requires not only that they not be ignored but that they be given their due. These experiences take various forms and are variously occasioned, but share certain qualities. The experiences of joy in his autobiography, his reference to the stolen boat scene in Wordsworth's *The Prelude,* and his reference to Wordsworth's sonnet in the title of his autobiography testify to the importance of experience for constructing a worldview. Further evidence is the critical moment in *The Screwtape Letters* when the Patient has done something simply for enjoyment. This emphasis in Lewis supports his reliance on Rudolf Otto's experiential account of how and why religion appears in human life and cultures. Clearly, he has confidence in the reliability and shared quality of human experience.

Central to that experience is the reception of something elusive, powerful, and attention deserving that comes from without, something that relates to a person but also remains unattainable and not fully comprehended. Experiences of joy, the sublime, the numinous, and of being drawn into something larger and more significant are recognizable and meaningful, and, while some may dismiss such experiences as too elusive, ephemeral, or occasional to provide a basis for an account of the world and our position in it, they occur widely and are sufficiently revealing to warrant a basic place in one's worldview. His affirmation of such experiences is supported by at least three factors. First, there is textual confirmation, going beyond Immanuel Kant's third critique and beyond the Romantics to other powerful and convincing testimonies. Second, he lived in a culture in which people took unusual experiences seriously, whether one thinks of other literary artists, of philosophical idealists and intuitionists in Oxford, or of mystical improvisers like the eccentric but widely followed Oxonian Aleister Crowley. Finally, and I think most importantly, these experiences confirm for Lewis an important component in identity formation because they evoke a response in a person that would not otherwise have occurred. The process of personal formation and identity is not first of all a matter of self-creation but is a consequence of what is experienced as received. Experiences of this kind can be extended outward to a general principle, namely, that we are in the world most fully when we anticipate such experiences as gifts basic to our becoming persons in the world.

A corollary of this point about experiences is that they require a positive or receptive attitude toward the world. This openness toward the world does not come naturally to Lewis and is not promoted by his culture. In his autobiography Lewis tells us that from his youth he lived with a generally negative orientation to and understanding of his world, which he identifies as inherited from his father. He was by nature reclusive, and this held him back from encounters with other people. At some point—he does not tell us when or how this occurred—he exchanged this negative view of and distance from his world for a more open and receptive attitude.

This positive attitude toward the world put him at odds with attitudes in his culture that arose in the Victorian era but became prominent after the First World War. War and other aspects of late modernity including industrialization and urbanization led many artists and intellectuals to move from open or positive to sharply negative views not only of modernity but also of human culture and nature more generally. For many, contemporary events had ripped away the appearance of human virtue and reliability like a false façade that had concealed a now exposed reality, the seediness, to use a favorite word of Graham Greene, behind the concealments. Lewis's newly acquired open and receptive stance put him at odds not only with other literary artists and critics but also with a postwar generation of Christian theologians, who exchanged theological liberalism for a new or radical orthodoxy that placed Christianity in opposition not only to modernity in particular but to the human and its cultural enterprises as such.

Lewis's open attitude toward his world did not lead him to construe it as evidence for a creative and providential God. Indeed, as is clear in *The Problem of Pain*, one can draw quite the contrary conclusion from observation of the evil and suffering in our world. In the concluding chapter of the second part of this study I will focus more directly on his critiques of modernity; they were sharp and deep. Lewis was well aware of the force of evil in the world, and he thought that evil, while not self-sustaining, was neither accidental nor occasional. Evil is embedded in everything we encounter and do, and it is superhumanly empowered. Nonetheless, Lewis continued to affirm the basic reliability of the world in which we find ourselves. He considered evil nonessential, secondary, and, because it depends on human history for its continuing sustenance, temporary.

Lewis does not clarify the relation between his positive orientation to the world and the next basic point, namely his positive assessment of human moral awareness, but we can assume that for him they were mutually supportive. It is clear, in any case, that Lewis affirmed that human beings are capable of developing positive moral norms and practices. He implies that moral norms are intuited and that moral practices develop as a natural process, that over time we learn that some attitudes and actions are beneficial to our well-being and others are not. The development of moral norms and practices is not necessarily tied to the role of religion in people's lives and cultures; religion and morality are not necessarily joined. Christianity does not, he contends in *Mere Christianity*, offer a "brand new morality" (82). This allows him to formulate in *Mere Christianity* a virtue ethics that posits the cardinal virtues as generally within human reach: as he puts it, a morality "which all civilized people recognize" (76).[1] It is not too much to say that for Lewis a positive basis in culture and in personal morality and behavior is necessary for viable and healthy religion (31). It can be inferred that he had doubts about a kind of religion, even a kind of Christianity, that neglects the firmness in persons and their culture that morality provides; such neglect, one might think, is seen among contemporary Christians who construct human nature and culture in a negative way. Finally, his more positive assessment of human moral potentials, standards, and practices ties morality to nature. Moral norms and directives do not stand first of all in opposition to human nature, to human needs or desires, as Freud posited, but enhance them. Who we are as human beings, even what we most deeply need or desire, and morality are not antagonistic but mutually supportive.

Lewis sees as his principal challenge not human nature or modern culture as such but a particular, although pervasive, error, namely, theoretical materialism. While it has appeared at other points in history, materialism plays for him a particularly powerful role in modernity, advancing during the last decades of the nineteenth century and becoming deeply embedded in modern assumptions, attitudes, and practices. One reason for setting himself against materialist ways of accounting for and relating oneself to the world is that they reduce to material explanations experiences such as joy and the sublime, which are so important for him as intimations of something higher and alluring for which humans long and to which they should aspire.

Materialism for Lewis provides a hopelessly inadequate account of who as persons we are. All the things that are important for us as persons, our rationality, intuitions, moral sensitivities, imagination, and will, are reduced by materialist views to something other or less than what they appear to be. Of special importance for Lewis in this regard is the role of will or agency in personal identity. In *Mere Christianity* Lewis presents human agency as pivotal for the "real central man" (91), making the will a principal if not defining characteristic of personhood. This does not mean that humans are agents or authors of their own personhood; but they are able to orient themselves toward their world in such a way as to be receptive to those gifts that evoke newness of being. The most consistent goal of Lewis's project is to show that the defining characteristics of personal life are not given their due by theoretical materialism or even by an idealist philosophy to which he initially turned in his dissatisfaction with materialism, but by religion generally and Christianity particularly. The clearest manifestation of the inadequacy of a materialist view is its inherent determinism.[2] It is reasonable and consequential to assume that, in order to give an adequate account of ourselves and our world, we are required to include the nonmaterial or spiritual. He finds this confirmed by the fact that most people who have lived or are living now are in one way or another religious.

Lewis, then, is in agreement with the father of modern anthropology, E. B. Tylor, who held that the two options in human cultures are religion on the one hand and theoretical materialism on the other and that modern religious persons have more in common with what Tylor called religious primitives than they do with their modern materialist neighbors. This is why Lewis is so affirming of religion in general and does not take as his principal goal advancing Christianity in opposition to other religions. This is especially clear in his treatment of classical paganism, about which he was so knowledgeable. This is also why he can identify with Rudolf Otto in locating the origin and essence of religion in the human experience or intuition of the numinous and the holy. And this is why he can argue that morality, as it is found across cultures, develops among humans as a natural progression by which intuition and discernment distinguish between what is good for people to be and to do and what is not, a process that reveals continuity between the natural and the moral and between different cultures.

These grounding and reasonable assumptions direct his emerging understanding and eventual reappropriation of Christianity and lead him from philosophical materialism through absolute idealism to theism and, finally, to Christianity. Christianity is able to account for both the material and the spiritual aspects of human life and especially for their compatibility with and relations to one another. In other words, Christianity does justice to what, for Lewis, is most immediately available to and important for us, namely, our personhood. Materialism renders problematic or necessarily discounts what is most important to us as human beings, namely, how we are or ought to be as persons.

However, it would not do to think of Lewis, despite all his emphasis on experience, intuition, rationality, imagination, and will, as anthropocentric. For one thing, he, like William James, thinks of experiences as experiences *of* something. Like James, he thinks our attitudes, beliefs, and goals are reciprocally related to our world. They have consequences for how we view the world, and our view of the world affects our experiences in and of it.[3] This means that the world in which we find ourselves has a moral or spiritual as well as a natural or material quality and that, as a consequence, we are in and should have full relations with it, first of all with other people.

The texts studied in the next part will direct us more to the power and effects of evil in human life and modern culture. It would therefore be good to consider why evil enters the process of personal formation and disrupts and distorts it. It is not philosophical materialism that does this, although for Lewis materialism is a deficient and distorting view of things. Rather, it is pride, which he takes as humanly shared and as producing a process of identity formation that is based on self-preoccupation, self-enhancement, and self-possession. This process is a false and falsifying one. Lewis thought of this form of personal identity formation as an understandable and almost inevitable consequence of human development, because children come to an awareness of themselves and stake their well-being on self-enlargement and protection—a process that also characterizes the development of the species as a whole. As we shall see, Lewis accounts for the widespread cultural role of materialism less in terms of the authority of science than in terms of the connection between materialism and self-preoccupation or pride. A materialist view opens the world to exploitation that serves the process of self-expansion. The almost unavoidable direction that personal identity formation takes, affected by self-interest and pride, does not mean that we must be resigned to evil. True, evil is deeply embedded in human life because its taproot is at the very center of the process of our becoming persons, namely, our becoming aware of ourselves. Self-preoccupation aggravates the potential, in our relations with other persons, of competition, that is, advancing ourselves at the expense of the well-being of others; there is good reason why Screwtape includes competition in his philosophy of hell. As Lewis says in *Mere Christianity*, "Pride is *essentially* competitive," and it conversely could be said that competition is driven primarily by pride (122). In addition, moral evil and human pride have superhuman support so that evil is not only something humans invent and perpetrate but a power that can have them in its grip. But evil, however pervasive and powerful, is not coequal to the good. Evil is derivative, secondary, and dependent. The real and the lasting is the good. This is why, for Lewis, the basic or grounding view of our world and our relations in and to it should be positive.

What Lewis assumes, then, is a commodious, complex, and basically positive sense of relational expectations and behaviors toward our world, which he thinks can largely be shared by people generally. It perceives a real mutuality between humans and their contexts, and it opens the way for continuity and positive relations between human beings and between humans and their larger world.

Another assumption not directly addressed by Lewis is that, while relying heavily on experiences and while holding to the reality of "raw feels," such as pain and pleasure, he located himself within what Martin Irvine calls a "textual culture." Irvine points out that medieval Europe, with its roots in late antiquity, became a culture anchored in and by *grammatica* and all that it entailed, primarily that learning and wisdom are through language and, more important, through texts and how they are read.[4] Lewis affirms this, and he implies a deficiency in modernity's relation to textuality. The medieval period was bookish and clerkly.[5] He assumes the necessity of a textual culture and therefore imputes textuality to the modern period, countering the popular assumption that the Romantics' experience of nature was raw and free from texts. For this reason, too, he takes materialism to be based not on facts but on a worldview. The role of texts in how people are in and relate to their worlds underscores the importance of that aspect of *grammatica* that calls for distinguishing between more worthy texts and those that are less so. His assumption of a textual culture also explains why he does not separate biblical texts entirely from all others. Finally, his critique of modernity, while not limited to his identification with a textual culture, is related to it because he attacks the modernist assumption that facts can be encountered in a positivist way, that is, as accessible without and understood apart from texts.

PART TWO

6

Out of the Silent Planet (1938)

There is no commonly agreed-on definition of narrative that clearly establishes how it differs from nonnarrative discourse. It is possible, however, to secure some characteristics of narratives that set them apart. Narrative discourse is a compound of distinguishable elements or languages. Four of these stand out. The first and perhaps most frequently noted is the language of character, personal characteristics attached to a name. The second is plot, the combination of events or actions with a developmental line or pattern. A third is the language of the teller, which appears by means of the material that the teller has chosen, the attitude that the teller assumes toward that material, and the style or voice of the teller. The fourth language of narrative is that of place and location.

Lewis has a very spatial imagination, so it is not surprising that the language of place should be prominent in his fictions.[1] We generally are transported to unusual places that are described in detail; that is certainly the case in this, the first novel of his science trilogy. The other languages are also developed in this narrative. Ransom is the main character, and readers are kept very close to him. We see things through his eyes, and we are made aware of his thoughts and his reactions to what he encounters. There are other interesting characters, although we view them from without, especially Devine and Weston. They are antagonists, although Weston has some characteristics that commend him in Ransom's eyes. The main plot has a "Jack and the Beanstalk" pattern: removal from this world, adventures in another, and return, with both departure and return marked by risks and obstacles.[2] There are subplots: the hunt for the Hnakra, the long journey to Meldilorn, and the trial of Ransom, Weston, and Devine in the presence of the Oyarsa of Malacandra. The teller of the story finally comes on stage when it is time, as he says, "to remove the mask" (150). The teller is a friend of Ransom, whose relationship with him is built mainly on their common interest in medieval studies. We learn that Ransom has shared with this friend the experiences that constitute the narrative. The story is told in a fictional mode, for fear of straining the credulity of the reader.

Lewis's imagination is spatial, but also moral and religious. Through the genre of science fiction he carries the reader not only to a different world but to a different society. This other world contrasts sharply with that of the reader. Grave moral and spiritual contrasts emerge only gradually because such things are so thoroughly integrated into the lives of the inhabitants of this other world that they are largely unaware of them. Lewis brings the reader to a world that morally and spiritually is a model of what society can and should be—a model in comparison to which modern societies are inferior, even objectionable. When contrasted with this model, characteristics of our own society seem odd and are difficult for Ransom to explain, while those of Malacandra seem natural and reasonable.

The principal achievement of the novel, then, is to throw into question what we assume to be self-evident and inevitable, while at the same time making a quite different way of living seem ordinary and natural. Lewis can count on his reader's thinking of earth as exceptional in the universe by virtue of its supporting life, especially, of course, human life. His readers will start out thinking that other worlds, however interesting, are lifeless and therefore inferior to our own. Lewis turns this expectation on its head by giving us a narrative in which earth is unique primarily in being problematic.

A second important achievement of the novel is to counter two modern assumptions, which are identified with the work of H. G. Wells and which Lewis earlier in his life accepted. The first is that space is cold, empty, and alien to us, that we are not only isolated in the universe but surrounded by something threatening. The second is that our relations with other beings are inevitably competitive and antagonistic. These assumptions Ransom carries with him into space, and he is amazed when what he finds there is quite different from what he expected. He first of all discovers that space, rather than dark and forbidding, is bright and invigorating. It is the birthplace of worlds. There are several reasons why this is important for Lewis. First, it conforms to his idealist philosophical orientation. Also important to Lewis is the idea that space is primary relative to matter and that the more inclusive and less dense precedes what is more specific and dense. The heavens are more enduring and generative than the planets to which they have given birth.

In addition, it is important for Lewis to retrieve earlier understandings of the world in which we find ourselves. In few other areas is the separation between modern and premodern understandings so clear as in relation to space. In the modern period astrology and a general tendency to "read" the heavens have been left behind, and the notion of a meaningless space with which humans have no real relation has taken their place. Lewis wants neither to abandon all that has gone into forming our modern understanding nor to revive the idea that planets affect human moods and behavior. He does, however, want to establish that modern understandings need not sever our sense of relation to what encompasses us. As we are told, Ransom "found it night by night more difficult to disbelieve in old astrology: almost he felt, wholly he imagined, 'sweet influence' pouring or even stabbing into his surrendered body" (33). We see from the change in Ransom that it is possible, faced with the vastness and wonders of space, to exchange a sense of alienation and fear for connection and appreciative awe.

Despite his argument against the pervasive materialism of modern culture and its inadequacy to account for who we are and for the world in which we find ourselves, Lewis does not want to slight the importance of materiality. As we shall see, modern culture is marked by a curious ambiguity. On the one hand, we tend to credit everything to materiality but, on the other hand, we estrange ourselves from materiality, seeing it as an alien and even threatening "other." If continuity between our sense of what it is to be human and the material nature and context of our lives can be restored, then we may infer that what goes into the construction of the universe and what goes into the construction of us as persons are not unrelated.

I was interested to come across an account by the Soviet cosmonaut Alexei Leonov of his space walk in 1965 that supports Lewis's contention that, rather than cold and forbidding, space is welcoming and supportive. Leonov said, after his space walk of March 18, 1965, "I felt fine, was in excellent spirits and did not want to part with free space. And even after I had received the order to return to the spaceship, I pushed myself away from the hatch once more to check the origin of the angular velocity in the first moment after the push. As to the so-called psychological barrier, which was supposed to be an insurmountable barrier to a man about to meet the voids of space face to face, I must say that I did not feel any barrier at all and even forgot that such a barrier might exist."[3] The cosmonaut's testimony seems to confirm Lewis's fictional proposal of continuity between humans and their material context. Lewis's idealist orientations, then, do not result in disparagement of the material. The material, by being continuous with the ideational, is rescued from the alien and even degraded status and role assigned it by modernity.

I

While we should avoid thinking of the novel as an allegory, it is clear that the two scholars, Ransom and Weston, are representative of differing characteristics of modern, especially academic, culture. Ransom is a philologist and a humanist, while Weston is an astrophysicist and cosmologist. They represent two sides of the university campus, the two separated cultures described by C. P. Snow.[4] This separation is exacerbated by the post-Darwinian move in higher education, especially in the sciences, away from the directives and authority of philosophy and religion. Lewis does not want to accept this separation as either necessary or final. Indeed, it should be lessened, and the consequences of failure to do so are ominous. The separation of science from the humanities not only results in the trivialization of the humanities but in the brutalization of science and its applications. Ameliorating this situation is not a matter of negotiating some kind of peace agreement between hostile parties but of subverting understandings that take this separation to be necessary and even desirable.

The divorce of science and the humanities is not so much a separation between two cultures, as C. P. Snow put it, as the separation of power from the cultural directives as to how power should be exercised. The prestige of science arises not so much from the knowledge of the world it provides as from the power it gives us over that world, including power over other people. The question of how this power should be used is not something that science can itself answer. Answers must be provided by the humanities, especially moral philosophy and understandings of human personhood and relationships.

It is not only that Lewis thinks the sciences and humanities need one another; it is also that they are in fact continuous rather than opposed. It is in the nature of scientific inquiry to study things in isolation, but we as humans are always, in one way or another, related to what we study and use. So it is an error to take things abstracted from their contexts—as is done in the lab—as descriptive of how things actually are. Science can increase not only our knowledge of the world but also our appreciation for it, as Ransom realizes: "You cannot see things till you know roughly what they are" (42). The humanities need that increase of knowledge and appreciation as much as the sciences need the directives that moral philosophy and understandings of personhood and human relations can provide. Lewis seems to make Weston and the sciences more responsible than Ransom and the humanists for the division between the humanities and the sciences. Weston has little interest in the humanities; he says of Ransom, "I don't care two-pence what school he was at nor on what unscientific foolery he is at present wasting money that ought to go to research" (15).[5]

It is important to note, however, that Ransom and Weston are also in some ways similar. While as a physicist Weston is eager to discover the building blocks of the universe, as a philologist Ransom is eager to identify the building blocks of language and consequently of human culture. As he puts it, "And what might one not discover from the speech of a non-human race? The very form of language itself, the principle behind all possible languages, might fall into his hands" (56). It is important also to see that at the outset Weston seems the stronger character. He lacks Ransom's fear, and there is some justice to his accusation that people like Ransom live in an "insufferably narrow and individualistic" world (27). Lewis is critical here of his own academic culture, of the humanities that have withdrawn from the general culture and have allowed scientifically based assumptions to gain the ascendancy. However, although he is also critical of humanists, Lewis stacks the deck against Weston.

First, by joining Weston to Devine, Lewis makes clear that the aims of science have been compromised, if not distorted, by entrepreneurial and imperialistic interests. Devine is a man of lesser character than Weston, a man who has accumulated his wealth in London. (Recall that Lewis has a less than positive view of cities.) Devine is often associated with alcohol (40, 45), a sign of addiction that Lewis weaves into depictions of other characters in his fictions. We are told that Devine is not merely bent but broken, driven by greed (138). He does not share Weston's concern for the future of the species and the meeting of worlds. He wants pleasure, and his imagination is furnished with "ocean-going yachts, expensive women and a big place on the Riviera" (30). This tendency of science to align itself with, if not subject itself to, commercial and political interests contributes to its brutalization and at the same time lends an intellectual veneer to power centers such as business and politics.

Second, Weston's imagination, like Devine's, is what Lewis calls "unbaptized."[6] That is, Weston thinks of the future primarily as an extension of himself and his own interests. He has taken one principle, the survival of the human species, as his only aim. This goal has no moral content. More important, it warrants the use of any means to achieve it. As Weston says to Ransom, "You cannot be so small-minded as to think that the rights or the life of an individual or of a million individuals are of the slightest importance in comparison with this" (29). Weston has no qualms about sacrificing others for the sake of the future he projects and of which he considers himself to be the bearer and custodian. Weston justifies his attitudes by subjecting them to a principle that he elevates to the position of a goddess, namely, "Life." He feels called by her: "she presses forward to that interplanetary leap which will, perhaps, place her forever beyond the reach of death" (135). Like Ransom and unlike Devine, Weston is a believer, oriented to something outside himself and more important than he is. He positions himself on the verge of something great, even immense, and infinite (134).[7] The problem is that his principle, goal, or goddess is an extension and actualization of his own pride and ambitions.

Third, Weston thinks of his beliefs and interests as natural and based on facts, not as expressions of a particular value system or culture. Indeed, he thinks of himself as a person without a culture, oriented solely to facts and the power that knowledge has given him. On Meldilorn he clearly reveals that he views culture as obfuscation. Cultures condition underdeveloped peoples, and he treats his hosts as such, trying to manipulate them first by intimidation and then by bribing them with trinkets.[8]

Ransom represents language and culture. Like other moderns, he has fallen under the sway of popular scientific mythology regarding the world around us, but he not only knows that people in the past thought very differently about the universe but he respects their views. He is prepared to make adjustments when he comes to realize that people in earlier times were not so naïve or mistaken as moderns believe. Indeed, Ransom begins to emerge as a person who can see that scientific and humanistic knowledge can illuminate one another.

More important, Ransom is open to the possibility of having a relationship with the creatures he encounters on Malacandra. If there are conscious beings on other worlds, he assumes there must exist enough continuity between them and himself to allow understanding of their language. While I know of no evidence that Lewis read Ferdinand de Saussure or that he knew what structural linguistics is all about, Ransom exhibits something like a structuralist view of language. All languages, it is held, are affected by a shared structure that can be extrapolated from comparison. Every language bears the traces of shared, though minimal, structural principles. It is not surprising that structuralists are often identified as idealists; the similarity between Lewis and Claude Lévi-Strauss on this matter, while likely not due to direct influence, may be traceable to their similar idealist orientations.

Aided by his interest in, knowledge of, and appreciation for their language, engagements occur between Ransom and his hosts' culture. These engagements bring to Ransom's awareness not only the differences between their culture and his own but also its moral superiority. Ransom is embarrassed, if that is a strong enough word, by his own culture and has a difficult time explaining why things on earth are as he must describe them. When he tries to explain to the Sorns what people on earth are like, Augray replies that this is so because "every one of them wants to be a little Oyarsa himself" (102). The suggestion by Lewis in all of this is that what is awry or evil in human life is not reasonable or even intelligible.

Ransom changes over the course of his adventures. At the beginning he is passive and succumbs easily to fear. Fear, it becomes clear, is often a consequence of self-preoccupation. The more engaged Ransom becomes by his surroundings, especially by the morally superior life of the creatures on Malacandra, the more his fear abates. During the interview with the Oyarsa on Meldilorn, Ransom looks stronger than Weston and Devine, who in contrast look out of place and even comical. During his return from Malacandra, his fear is increasingly "swallowed up in a sense of awe which made his personal fate seem wholly insignificant" (145). By the end of the narrative and under the directives of the

Oyarsa, Ransom is motivated toward action. There is a struggle going on, and he must be engaged by it. His journey to Malacandra empowers him for action.

II

Important as the principal characters are, as much if not more attention must be given to the location, especially to the society that Ransom encounters on Malacandra. It is important to notice how much space Lewis devotes to Ransom's extensive and detailed observations of the natural terrain of the planet. One could easily expect that these matters would be only lightly sketched in, just enough to give a general sense of the location in order to get on with the main business. But Lewis spends a lot of time on the physical characteristics of Malacandra, the arresting variations in landscape, the differing flora, the sensations of rough and smooth and of warm and cold, and the general amazement Ransom feels for what he finds. This attention to physical detail is related to the fact that Ransom is a walker, a fact about him that we learn at the very outset of the novel.

A word here about walking: it is for Lewis a major narrative device. Walking suggests a pace aligned with that of description and reading. Ransom's awareness of and appreciation for his location expands, as does the reader's, through his walking and narrating walking. It is a device that is grounded in Lewis's own experiences and value system. He was an avid walker who never learned to drive a car. He seems to have wanted to retain his identity as a walker, a preference that seems related to his strong sense of place and location. Walking allows a place to reveal itself to the walker, while driving is an attempt to override place and to leave it behind. So on Malacandra Ransom walks or is carried by Augray and thus is alert to new and unexpected vistas. There is a kind of receptivity (a better word than "passivity") that grows as Ransom becomes more familiar with his surroundings. Walking also relates a person physically to the materiality of the wider context. Lewis not only criticizes modern attitudes of separation from and primacy over materiality but reveals in Ransom an open and appreciative attitude, physical and emotional, toward materiality.[9]

Malacandra is an older planet than Thulcandra (earth) and, by reason of its smaller size and lesser density, it has lower gravity. This gives to almost everything a feeling of upward movement. Much of the planet has become uninhabitable, and elaborate engineering projects have gone into creating and securing more habitable areas on the planet. These projects, however, have been executed in such a way as to conceal the transition from natural to constructed formations.

More important, Malacandra is innocent of evil. A reflection of this innocence is the continuity that exists between rational creatures and beings both below and above them. The inhabitants have an appreciation for and understanding of lower creatures and, at the other end, they interact regularly with the angel-like creatures called eldila. This relational structure culminates in the positive relations between all of these creatures and the principal angel of the planet, the Oyarsa of Malacandra.

It is not surprising that there is also continuity or mutuality between the different social groups on the planet. They are by no means alike in physical appearance or in interests and abilities, but they hold each other in mutual regard, although they prefer their own locations and interests to those of their counterparts. They relate to members of the other groups in an affectionate way and respect their abilities. Occasions arise when members of one group defer to the expertise of those of another.

Ransom finds this society difficult to understand. He is culturally conditioned to assume that competition is the principal factor in relations between individuals and groups and that social dynamics are governed by a zero-sum game. He is accustomed to differences between inhabitants producing states or structures of dominance and subservience, and he attempts to understand the society he encounters in terms of a power structure. Although there is a hierarchy on the planet, from lower creatures to the Oyarsa, and among the three groups in the society, hierarchy does not mean domination and subservience. All are under Maleldil the Young who "made and still ruled the world" (69). The hierarchical arrangement is more than offset by the dynamics of continuity, mutuality, and interdependence.

The absence of evil and the strong sense of continuity and appreciation do not erase all competition and conflict. The hunt for the Hnakra is one of the more interesting episodes in the narrative. Creatures on the planet kill and can be killed. The inhabitants are primarily vegetarian, but there is hunting for sport. Killing regulated by appreciation for the encounter and a fair chance for the quarry is legitimate, but killing at a distance, as in the death of Hyoi, is condemned. It is important to see that Lewis's emphasis on continuity, relationships, and reciprocity excludes neither competition and conflict nor distinctions and ranks. Lewis, while he thinks of personal identity as formed primarily in relationships, especially ones that defer to the well-being of others, thinks also of identity affected by difference and rank.

The role of hunting brings up the larger question of death and its relation to evil. The fact that there is no evil on the planet does not mean that there is no death. The inhabitants seem to have a predetermined life span and to know when they will die. This is significant because in the narrative fear, as we see early on in Ransom, is tied to anxiety about one's mortality. Death, like that of the Hnakra, features as an intensifying contrast to life. Death is not feared, because it is seen as a transition to another state. Indeed, the Oyarsa pinpoints fear of death as the principal effect of evil on human life and as responsible for the damaged relations of humans to one another and their world (138–39).

The lack of a fear of death seems to affect other behaviors of these creatures. They are not anxious about possessions and do not acquire or hoard. They have confidence that there is enough for everyone. Also, while they enjoy sex very much, they indulge in it rarely. This is puzzling to Ransom; the answer that he gets seems to be that sex is not something that needs to be repeated often because it is intimately related to, and not abstracted from, other interests. Rather than something that stands out because it is unrelated to other experiences, sex derives its importance from its continuity with much else. Sex arises from and reveals relations, which are secured and enhanced by anticipation of and, even more, the memory of sex. Sex is like an outstanding line in a poem, which, while standing out because of its own excellence, "becomes fully splendid only by means of all the lines after it" (75). The implication is that in our society sex is isolated from our daily existence, which is marked by individuation, alienation, and competition. We need so much sex, Lewis seems to suggest, because its shared intimacy provides an alternative to the isolating brutality of prevailing forms of social interaction in modern society.

A matter of great importance is the positions of the three kinds of creatures, the sorns, the hrossa, and the pfifltriggi, relative to one another. The distinctions between them are clearly drawn, both their dramatic physical dissimilarities and their differing abilities: the intellectual pursuits of the sorns, the skill of the hrossa with language and poetry, and the occupations of the pfifltriggi as miners and artisans.[10]

Despite his high regard for Plato, Lewis does not follow his structuring of an ideal society in *The Republic*. There the intellectuals, the philosophers, are dominant; we read that Ransom initially assumes that the sorns "must be the real rulers, however it is disguised" (70). One would expect Lewis to place the sorns in the highest position in this society because of his admiration of Plato and Platonists in medieval and early modern cultures and also because he is himself an intellectual and a scholar. But Ransom relates first and most fully not to the sorns but to the hrossa, the poets and custodians of language. This conforms, of course, to Ransom's identity as a philologist and to the importance of poetry to Lewis's own identity. But I think more is at stake here. The hrossa do not hold the highest position but rather occupy a middle or mediating position in the society. This kind of position, one is led to conclude, is for Lewis preeminent.[11] The hrossa are located between the pfifltriggi and the sorns and relate them to one another. This suggests a theory of language and culture as mediating a relation between ideas or reason and energies and craft. As we shall see, Lewis has a concept of culture and language as guiding relations between moral and rational principles and their material enactments in society. The relations among these three groups model the relations that should exist but do not among Ransom, Devine, and Weston. Weston is the man of ideas. Ransom is the custodian of language and culture. Devine presides over material power. These three earthly characters represent a society that is incoherent because of the absence of relations between these three kinds of interests, especially because the intellectual and material powers joined in the cooperation between Weston and Devine exclude Ransom and what he represents.

Meldilorn and the Oyarsa are crucial in the setting of the narrative. The island is described as resembling a woman's breast. This is a curious and perhaps objectionable choice on Lewis's part, because it carries male assumptions about what this female feature not only does but should look like. However, it serves Lewis's purpose to tie physical to aesthetic and spiritual desire. The image secures an immediate attachment between Ransom and the location. The island is as it should be, is what one would expect and desire it to be.

The island is a cultural center. There are many carefully crafted artifacts, some religious, others not. This suggests the integration of religious life with the general culture; the highest achievements of the culture find their place in what could be thought of as its religious center. In what is a role not unlike the one that sex plays in the personal lives of these creatures, art epitomizes what is latent in the society and does not stand apart from the rest. There is continuity between the religious and the cultural, the set-aside and the everyday, creaturely creativity and transcendence.

While the inhabitants of the planet show respect and even reverence when they visit Meldilorn, there is no abjection or terror before the Oyarsa. Nor is the Oyarsa zealous to receive what could be thought of as appropriate homage. However, there is no doubt about who is in authority, although it is an authority exercised for the benefit of all. It is left to the Oyarsa to reprimand Ransom, to reveal that he did not arrive on Malacandra by accident but was called, to put Weston and Devine in their places, and to forecast the future.

III

Turning now to the novel's plot, we see that it initiates and traces, as does *The Screwtape Letters*, a pair of contrary processes. The first of these is Ransom's change for the better—what could theologically be called his sanctification. The second, contrary change is Weston's degeneration. Both processes will continue in the second of the science novels, *Perelandra*.

While the plot traces a radical change in his moral character, we should note that Ransom exhibits signs of moral health from the beginning. He can intuit moral imperatives. We read, "It occurred to him that he ought to call on the mysterious professor and ask for the boy to be sent home" (11), although this moral inclination is compromised by the thought that the professor might offer him a night's lodging. Also, he would have turned from his errand if he had not felt "bound by his unfortunate promise to the old woman" (13). Ransom, in other words, is a virtuous man. Also, as a walker, he has a positive orientation toward the physical world. Even before the journey to Malacandra, he is inclined to consider things outside himself to be of value.

These positive characteristics are enhanced by his encounters with the terrain and the inhabitants of Malacandra. He is aware and appreciative of the physical environment as he progresses through it. He becomes aware that the society he encounters is morally superior to his own and recognizes, as he had not done before, the questionable aspects of his own culture and of the attitudes brought with them to the planet by Weston and Devine. He suffers a setback in his moral development when he follows his impulse to hunt the Hnakra with Hyoi rather than obey the summons of the Oyarsa. The consequences include the death of Hyoi and the Oyarsa's reprimand. Ransom becomes more aware and appreciative of the eldila. He is strengthened by the assurance that they will protect him during his journey home and assist him in his future struggles with the likes of Weston and Devine (142). And he is entrusted with special knowledge, particularly that earth may be on the verge of deliverance from at least some of its harmful ideas and distortions. We should note that his principal role in that future possibility is not to bring a religious message but to work on altering the culture. He tells the narrator that what is needed most is not "a body of belief but a body of people familiarized with certain ideas," such as the change of "the conception of Space to the conception of Heaven" (152). For Lewis, a healthy culture is a prerequisite for the right understanding and practice of religion.[12]

As a consequence of his experiences, Ransom now lives in two worlds. On his return he is much taken by the goodness of ordinary, earthly things. And one can imagine that he will return to his work with his customary vigor and engagement. But now he is also aware that there is another reality and other possibilities. He feels attached to his earthly surroundings, but he is also nostalgic for and anticipates something other and more.[13]

While Weston is set on a contrary course, we should recognize that Lewis also gives him a good bit of credit. After all, the whole adventure is due to his knowledge; we are asked to appreciate Weston's ability to determine how they can return to earth despite the difficulty caused by the greater distance between Mars and earth than when they left. His dedication to his work and his remarkable abilities and achievements cannot be gainsaid.

Moreover, Weston employs his gifts for a larger purpose. As even the Oyarsa points out, Weston, unlike Devine, is not interested in accumulating things or in making his own life more comfortable (136). He is a dedicated scientist and explorer, and he shares in the heroism associated with these roles in modern culture. He is intensely interested in the survival and extension of his own species.

It can also be said that Weston serves something that transcends the physical universe, namely, Life. He is a vitalist, and his high regard for humans arises from the fact that they are the highest actualization of the life force, the cutting edge of life's advance. And he thinks of himself as especially burdened or privileged with the task of spearheading that advance. His self-conception is a scientific analogue to Hegel's conception of his own position relative to the advance of the Spirit.

However, Weston's worldview lacks moral content. He is willing to do anything and to injure or eliminate anyone who stands in the way. This puts him in line with the most power-hungry advances of Western culture, the subjection of other places and peoples for the enrichment of the scientifically and technologically empowered societies of the modern West. Life is defined by Weston primarily as power, and the greatest power belongs to those people who have knowledge about the world and can use it to subjugate the world, including other people, for the benefit of their own survival and advancement. Weston's philosophy of Life very much resembles (although in less social and economic terms) the philosophy, if it can be called that, of social Darwinism.

IV

Turning, finally, to the teller of the story, we have at the end his disclosure that he is a friend of Ransom and that the two share an interest in medieval culture. It is worth pointing out that the Bernard Silvestris (of Tours) who is mentioned here is not a fictional character. Lewis took an interest in this twelfth-century Platonist. He included an essay on him in *The Discarded Image* and a description of Bernard's work appears in *The Allegory of Love.* Silvestris's *De mundi universitate* (1147) is a cosmogony, an account of the origins of the constellations and planets. His *Experimentarius* is a treatise on geometry and the Zodiac, and he also wrote a work that deals extensively with moral philosophy. He knew Arabic and drew on Islamic sources as well as on classical texts. In other words, he integrated Christian and non-Christian thought in his own speculations. Lewis was drawn to him because he was more Platonist than Aristotelian.[14] Lewis seems to have been particularly impressed by Bernard's anthropology, which presents the human person as a kind of trinity of head, breast, and loins, and by his affirmation of a hierarchy of beings in which there is a right place for everything, including humans. We can see that these ideas are crucial to the novel, such as in Ransom's new understanding of the heavens, the distinctions between the three kinds of inhabitants of Malacandra, the lack of right relations between Weston, Ransom, and Devine, and the sense of relation and distinction between the society of Malacandra, the creatures below, and the eldila above it. This invocation of Bernard makes clear that the novel is at least a partial vindication of the relevance of medieval thought and culture to the task of remedying the cultural distortions of Western modernity.[15]

7

Perelandra

A Novel (1943)

All four of the languages of narrative are noticeable in this novel, but character stands out among them. The settings clarify the characters' encounters and differing roles, and the plot traces their interactions and the changes that they undergo. The teller also defers to the characters.

The teller is Lewis himself, an Oxford scholar, Ransom's amanuensis, and a person sensitive to the negative aspects of his world. Early on he notes the "apparently deserted industrial buildings on my right" (12); he mentions cold, fog, and war. Later he refers to the bombing of London. The reference to deserted industrial buildings that blight the landscape is not casual. Lewis identified the beginning of the Victorian period, when machines began to dominate, as a defining break in modern culture. Machines are continually subject to improvement, and earlier models become obsolete. For this reason, a machine-oriented culture begins to be oriented to the future and to think of the past as dispensable, something readily discarded. More quickly than other buildings, factories become outmoded and outlive their usefulness.[1] As described by Lewis, the conditions on earth stand in sharp contrast to those on Perelandra. This contrast, we learn, is moral as well as climatological, social-political, and aesthetic. However, there is held out the prospect of an imminent end to the malign conditions that prevail on earth and their replacement by new and more wholesome ones (20, 182).

The opening two chapters of the novel encapsulate the whole, reducing uncertainty regarding the outcome of the main plot. This device adds to the optimistic, one could say comic, quality of the plot, and along with other characteristics of the novel is reminiscent of Dante's *Divine Comedy*.[2] After the opening section, the plot unfolds in three parts: Ransom's travel, arrival, and early adjustment to his new environment, including his meeting the Green Lady; Weston's arrival and repeated attempts to tempt the Green Lady; Ransom's physical struggle with Weston, which ends in Weston's death, followed by Ransom's emergence from the channel into the light and his ascent of the mountain. The extended final scene on the mountaintop echoes the close of the *Purgatorio* and is a fitting conclusion to the complex plot, which comprises Weston's final degeneration, the Green Lady's moral and personal growth, and the advancing sanctification of Ransom.

The planet Perelandra is described in great detail. Even though in *Perelandra* attention is focused on the characters and their interactions, the location is not, as one might expect, sketched thinly. The narrator lingers over the setting, giving it a standing of its own. This adds greatly to the enjoyment of the work, and it conforms to Ransom's growing awareness and appreciation of material places and the surprises and delights they offer. The variety of colors and textures offers a sharp contrast to the bleak earthly terrain that Lewis traversed on his journey to meet Ransom. The undulating islands of Perelandra are an especially engaging invention. Ransom is forced to relearn how to walk, and he becomes somewhat childlike in his delight in these unfamiliar surroundings and in the new behaviors they require him to learn. For Lewis, a childlike receptivity and a sense of wonder and delight are qualities that adults ought to retain and share with children.

I

As in *Out of the Silent Planet*, Weston's objectionable qualities stand out because he is separated from the supporting context of Western modernity. Of the three main characters he alone is clothed, but he is stripped of his cultural context and exposed not only as distasteful but as comic. Weston's arrival is bad news to Ransom. He intrudes on and disrupts what was for Ransom a delightful situation. This heightens Weston's dissonance, his discontinuity with things that are as they ought to be. Seen through Ransom's eyes, Weston's unassailable sense of legitimacy and command is odd. Not only does he believe in his right to be there; he suggests that he should control, if not possess, all that he surveys. As in *Out of the Silent Planet,* his stance underlines the link between scientific advancement, colonialism, and imperialism.

Despite his scientific knowledge and technological skills, Weston reveals himself as obsessive and simplifying. He pursues his fixed ideas, we are told, in a "tense and tedious" way. He later seems more like a precociously intelligent, petulant child than a mature and reasonable adult. Lewis does not mean to caricature science or scientists. He had a high regard for them, particularly physicists, and he himself took an active interest in astronomy. But it is true that science, by virtue of its methods, tends to simplify and reduce things, making them more manageable and measurable. As a consequence, a reductive uniformity is imposed on the world, and for Lewis this was one reason why in ordinary life we should not relate ourselves to the world and to other people by the methods of science.

Weston is pleased to tell Ransom that, since their last meeting, he has amended his understanding of things, moving away from a physical to a biological basis and incorporating a spiritual element into his view of "Life" and its advancement. This allows him to subsume his views under the single, general category of spirit. In his eyes this places Weston above religion because he transcends the differences and conflicts within and between religions and unifies them in a common cause of human advancement, especially triumph over death.[3] Fortified by this newly acquired spirituality, Weston accuses Lewis's Christianity of being anthropocentric in comparison to his own cosmic view. Speaking from an implicit pantheism, he can also accuse Christianity of dualism, dividing the world into good and evil. And, deploying a common modernist critique, he condemns Ransom and his beliefs for being outdated and regressive: "Will you always try to press everything back into the miserable framework of your old jargon about self and self-sacrifice? That is the old accursed dualism in another form. There is no possible distinction in concrete thought between me and the universe" (82). Lewis himself, as we have seen, wants to defend Christianity from the accusation of narrowness and exclusivity. However, as Ransom points out, there is something important to say about particulars. The true nature and consequences of Weston's position are seen in his willingness to destroy the lives of others in order to advance the spiritually warranted scientific and technological program he envisions. The grand end or goal he envisions justifies whatever means may be necessary to achieve it. Weston himself, however, is exempted from the victimization he readily accepts for others because he is at the forefront or, as it is now often put, the "cutting edge" of this advance.

We will consider more fully the important and positive role that pleasure plays in this narrative. While we are attending to Weston, however, we should consider the perverse pleasure he derives from ripping open the froglike creatures. It is not only that he does this for no good reason; for him pleasure comes from the exercise of power over weaker creatures. He directs a conspiratorial smile toward Ransom, inviting him into a "world of its own pleasures, as if all men were at one in those pleasures" (95). Pleasure for Weston dissolves the particularity of those who share it by bringing them down to the level of a shared conspiracy. Finally, this pleasure is tied to repetition; Weston destroys not one but scores of frogs. As we shall see, true pleasure, as it is experienced by Ransom, is something altogether different.

The fragility of Weston's newly acquired worldview is revealed when it fails him in his distress. Surrounded by water, he loses confidence in Life and spirit as the principal realities in the world. In relation to the vast inorganic expanses around him, they seem superficial and vulnerable. The final reality for him becomes not Life but death. Life and spirit, as aspects of our world, must be attributed to and are sustained not only by what lies below them, namely, the physical world of matter and energy, but also by what lies above.

It is important to note that as he is more and more dominated by evil, Weston becomes less himself, less recognizable. His body and voice change. Toward the end he is insectlike. In other words, he loses his identity. As we saw in *The Screwtape Letters*, this is consistent with Lewis's belief that evil has no substance of its own but must feed off what is actually or potentially good. Evil is a great devourer and homogenizer. What is distinctive in Weston is dissolved as he is taken over by what is called the "Un-man."

Ransom's execution of Weston by strangulation, in the name of the divine Trinity, is a highly provocative moment in the novel. It is presented as an act necessary to rid Perelandra of the threat to its well-being posed by Weston. Evil, like the good, takes physical form, and combating evil at times requires not only rational argument and moral persistence but physical struggle. The novel is set in the context of the Second World War, and it is not difficult to see the parallel between the struggle against a nation bent on domination and physical struggle with a person with similar intentions.[4]

Despite his execution of Weston, Ransom pays him a measure of respect. He was "a great physicist after all" (161). Recording his life and death in the soft rock, Ransom dignifies Weston without condoning the actions, goals, and attitudes that led to his death.

II

I see Lewis's creation of the Green Lady as a remarkable achievement. The character of a truly innocent person is difficult to portray and to make interesting. He accomplishes this by depicting the Lady's innocence or purity as incomplete—as needing to mature by means of complication with respect to self-consciousness. Lewis was well aware of the notion, which became prominent in the Romantic period, that evil is related more strongly to creativity than is to goodness. We can see in this novel much not only of Dante but also of Milton. From the Romantic period on, it was common for readers of *Paradise Lost* to find Milton's Satan a more interesting character than his Christ. In his creation of the Green Lady, Lewis shows that goodness is not simple or static, but grows and becomes more complex. Goodness is consistent with maturation, complexity, and creativity.[5] The goodness in which the Green Lady is to progress is not charted for her. She must create her own path, must make her own decisions.

Weston's temptations of the Green Lady occur during the period of her personal development, a process marked by increased self-consciousness, growing awareness of agency, and realization of her own physical beauty.[6] She must negotiate the process of identity formation without succumbing to the self-preoccupation or pride that Weston wants to encourage. The Green Lady encounters options and possibilities among which she must choose. The difficulty lies in distinguishing between a threshold, which should be crossed, and a boundary, which should not. In the temptations that Weston puts before her, the Green Lady has to distinguish between the positive act of adjusting to new circumstances and the error of stepping out into a world from which Maledil is absent.

Her trial is made more difficult by the fact that Weston's temptations contain some truth and are not wholly or obviously wrong. There is always something true in what he says. This is an important point in Lewis: just as evil feeds on the good in order to survive, so falsehoods have some truth in them. Lies are distortions of or partial truths. Weston's words remind Ransom of the tradition in Christianity of the *felix culpa*, the idea that good can be brought out of evil, as the Incarnation of Christ was made necessary by the sin of Adam and Eve. Weston, like the serpent in Genesis and like Screwtape, is subtle.

While the temptations overlap, they are distinguishable. The first is Weston's insistence that "great spirits" or leaders, like himself presumably, must "reach out their hands for the new and unexpected good" (91). Another is the suggestion that Maledil wants her to develop, to "walk by yourself" (99); refusing to defy the fixed-land prohibition is to balk at the opportunity for self-realization. The third temptation is to stand out as a woman, to be a role model for others of her gender. A fourth is that the present is a moment ripe to be seized—when the opportunity to advance, to break out, presents itself it should not be missed. The fifth is the role of the "tragic pioneer," the person willing to put his or her welfare at risk for the sake of others. The sixth is to love oneself, a directive with a biblical warrant but which as presented by Weston is indistinguishable from narcissism. No wonder

Ransom observes that what the Un-man says in these temptations "was always very nearly true" (114). Lewis has done a good job, in my opinion, of including in the temptations a modern case against Christianity and Christian morality, namely, that they are confining and regressive in relation to the creative potentials of persons.

The Green Lady's ability to withstand the temptations of Weston, strengthened as they are by the sponsorship of Western culture, gives her stature. The fact that the fate of Perelandra rests on her responses to Weston's temptations also places her in a very significant position. She does not sacrifice her self-development and does not shrink from following a path of her own making, but she does so within the bounds of Maledil's will, which, it is implied, is supportive of her growth and well-being.

III

Ransom grows, too. This process of "sanctification" leads eventually to his sainthood. It has three, possibly four, stages. The first concerns pleasure. There are two moments in this stage.

When Ransom arrives on Perelandra he immediately confronts pleasure; it was "almost like meeting Pleasure itself" (32). This is no small matter for Lewis. As, by its emphasis on morality and humility, Christianity has gained a reputation of confining or resisting human development and creativity, so also it has gained the reputation of being opposed to pleasure. Physical pleasures in particular seem to be at best disparaged and at worst associated with evil. Lewis wants to free Christianity from this slander. Pleasure is a good thing. When the thirsty Ransom drinks from a gourd, the liquid he imbibes gives him a pleasure that is indescribable, and he muses that for "one draught of this on earth wars would be fought and nations betrayed" (37). Naturally, he is motivated to seek a second experience of this pleasure, but intuitively he thinks better of it. Later he reflects on this episode and on the whole matter of repeating pleasures, this "itch to have things over again" (45). Ransom realizes that this "itch" is the root of evil. His judgment is unusual. As he recognizes, the love of money has traditionally been identified as the root of evil. But money is related to the "itch" because it gives us the power to repeat pleasures, to have them on demand. Ransom understands that repeating a pleasure turns attention away from what brings the pleasure, what comes to us from the outside, and toward our own capacity to experience pleasure. The occasion of pleasure shifts from something we receive to something we possess. That now becomes primary, and it needs endlessly to be confirmed, to be fed. A pursuit of pleasure ensues, a search for that which assures us that the cherished capacity to experience pleasure remains intact. The world then becomes little more than a field of occasions for easing the anxiety that the capacity for pleasure, this great value that one carries within oneself, may be lost.

When Weston shows surprise that Ransom has been associating with a beautiful naked woman without having sexual relations with her, another insight into pleasure is revealed. Ransom replies that their not having had sex does not mean that their relationship is sexless. Rather, the sexual aspects of their relationship have been taken up into something higher, something *more* pleasurable. This brings to mind the earlier occasion on which Ransom responds to McPhee's misunderstanding of the Christian doctrine of the resurrection of the body. Ransom explains that it does not imply that the body is displaced or repressed by spirit but that it is "engulfed" by it. The change is, as Lewis sometimes called it, a transposition. So in the relationship of Ransom and the Green Lady sex is transposed into or engulfed by something else, just as the possible embarrassment or desire they might have experienced because of their nakedness was taken up into the greater delight of having each other's company and being able to communicate.

The second stage in Ransom's development takes the form of his conflict with Weston. From the moment of Weston's arrival, Ransom is aware of the danger he poses, and he becomes more and more concerned as Weston's stay is prolonged. Observing Weston's relentless pursuit of the Green Lady, Ransom asks why Maledil does not intervene. He comes to recognize that he himself is the agent of Maledil, the "miracle on the right side" (120). He realizes that it is no longer enough to combat Weston with words; the combat must move to the physical level, a move Ransom resists. Here is another example of a threshold that must be crossed. He must take the step because it is required by the situation and for the furtherance of his development. Evil, like good, is incarnate in persons and structures, and this calls for physical engagement. Ransom increasingly senses his position as Weston's opponent, but the distance between them remains bridgeable. In the extremities of exposure and combat Weston seems for a moment to welcome a new relation between them, and Ransom responds positively. And, as we have seen, he maintains to the end his respect for Weston's achievements.

His physical struggle with Weston seems to evoke one of the two sources for Ransom's name: the saying of Jesus in the Gospel of Mark that he has come to give his life as a "ransom." The other source is political and national. Ransom is the name of two earls of Chester who championed British royal interests in the twelfth and thirteenth centuries. This association of the religious or spiritual with the political and national seems to attract Lewis, and he employs it again in the last of the three science novels.

The third stage in Ransom's sanctification is his descent into the depths and darkness of the cavern, his passage through the long channel, his rebirth, and his extended recuperation, "a second infancy" (159). In the darkness and uncertainty Ransom is tempted to accept the idea that reality is meaningless. From that crisis a new self is actualized, a process that recalls the understanding of suffering put forward in *The Problem of Pain.* Ransom scales the heights of the holy mountain, takes in the increasing beauty of it as he ascends, and arrives at the valley at the top.

Whether his exposure to the Oyarsas of Perelandra and Malacandra and the arrival of Tor and Tenedril represent a fourth stage or are continuations of the third is a matter of uncertainty, but there is no uncertainty about the inventiveness with which Lewis describes what occurs. The Oyarsas can reveal themselves in many forms but in this case take the form of humans. Ransom witnesses Tor and Tenedril receiving the cultural mandate from the Oyarsas. It is reminiscent of the mandate given by God to Adam and Eve in Genesis. The eschatological scenarios now revealed make the affairs of earth look minor compared to the vast, intergalactic picture. The evil on earth becomes an unfortunate but correctable false start. What is anticipated is not so much an ending as a new beginning. Given the wartime context of the novel, this vision runs counter to the dominant mood. Ransom tells Tor that what he has been talking about is called the Last Things. But the emphasis here is not on ending but on a new beginning and celebration, a Great Dance. Ransom learns the reason for the fixed-land prohibition, and he recognizes Tor and Tenedril as his true parents. The scene culminates in an extended outburst of praise directed toward Maledil.

IV

Three things in the novel deserve more attention. The first concerns self-consciousness. Even before Weston's arrival, the Green Lady is experiencing maturation and development. This is seen in the new sense she has of being able to stand aside from and observe herself, stepping, as she puts it, "out of life into the Alongside and looking at oneself living as if one were not alive" (52). Lewis was intrigued by this moment in human development because it is tied to the ability to make moral decisions and to develop a self-identity. It is also a dangerous moment; it abstracts one from living and can prompt the conclusion that it is by abstraction, self-awareness, and self-construction that one becomes a person. The ability to reflect is also morally consequential, and Tenedril recognizes the risks that lie in abstraction from the immediate and the preoccupation with the future—the danger, for example, of preferring a possible good to one that already exists. We shall see other examples later of Lewis's ambivalence toward self-consciousness, the ambiguous standing in his work of this prominent and even human-defining ability.

The second thing to consider is gender. Although the Oyarsas appear similar, there are important differences. One is more rhythmic and the other more melodic; one more metallic, the other more vegetative; and, most important, one is more masculine and the other more feminine. In the Oyarsas Ransom recognizes "the real meaning of gender" (171). Gender here is a principle more inclusive and extensive than biological sex. This is why, Lewis notes, gender affects languages, as in the gender distinctions among nouns. This recognition is important for Ransom because it reveals that languages are not only cultural constructions but also natural. Finally, this point is important for Lewis because he elevates principle above its various manifestations. Languages have a structural relation to reality, and Lewis traces part of that relation to gender. What is important for him in all of this is that language and culture are not distinct from the physical world but continuous with it. This idea is supported by structuralist linguistic theory, which gives prominence to contraries in the structuring of language. It also is supported by descriptions of sexual intimacy, like those of D. H. Lawrence, that include a kind of impersonal dimension whereby the particularities of personal or cultural identity are absorbed in the impersonality or even anonymity of gender. This treats gender distinctions as rooted in ontology and not determined by cultural constructions, which many will find problematic. For Lewis gender is more inclusive than sex, but gender seems nowhere more fully articulated than in sexual difference. If the difference between men and women is rooted both in physical reality and in language and culture, it becomes hard to imagine any difference greater than this. According to cultural theorists, people are prone to categorize things in twos in order to identify one half of the pair as superior. In Lewis's world men hold positions of greater power and influence than women, and this ontology of gender could well be taken as granting legitimacy and permanence to male superiority. However, it could be argued that the female/male distinction is so important to life and culture, so significant in the ways it plays out, that the distinction should be emphasized, without the imputation of inequality.[7]

The third feature, which appears in other works by Lewis, is the idea of the *felix culpa*, which, as was mentioned, comes up in one of the temptations that Weston puts before the Lady. This is the notion that it was a good thing that evil came into the world, because otherwise we would not have known the great gifts of divine grace (104, 184). Lewis was working on Milton at the time of writing and would have come up against this issue in *Paradise Lost*. Adam, in book 12, responds to Michael's account of things to come with these words: "O goodness infinite, goodness immence! / That all this good of evil shall produce, / And evil turn to good." As a theological question the fortunate Fall asks whether humans would know the grace of God as they do now without having been forgiven by means of that grace. It also raises the question of whether evil can provide a path toward the good. In modernity, this issue comes to the fore in the Romantic period, when creativity is tied closely to transgression. In the Faust tradition, for example, pacts with evil are concluded to enhance discovery and creativity. Morality is tied to conformity and timidity; transgression is related to innovation, risk, breaking out, and the new. Such notions are still endemic in our culture. I am not sure of Lewis's answer to the theological form of this question, although he suggests that had there been no Fall full knowledge of God's grace would somehow have been made available to humans. But on the second form of this question he is unequivocal. It arises from a mistaken notion of what the right and the good are. They are not static and confining; they are enabling, and there can be genuine creativity and full self-actualization only in the realm of the right and the good. The alternative is reduction, homogenization, and dissolution.

The *felix culpa* also has an aesthetic dimension for Lewis. The distortions and evils that human beings devise or fall into can make one aware of their good counterparts. The negatives of Western modernity can make us more appreciative of the value of the good and its potential for sponsoring a world that stands on a more solid moral and aesthetic footing.

8

The Abolition of Man (1944)

This book comprises three lectures that Lewis delivered at the University of Durham in 1943. Their brevity is matched by their complexity, subtlety, and import, which makes them somewhat cryptic. It may be good first to run through the lectures and highlight their principal points.

I

Each lecture has a particular emphasis. The first deals primarily with persons and personhood. The second turns to society. The third deals mainly with nature. However, there are common themes that unify the whole.

The classroom is an important site for personal formation, and the first lecture begins with the school. Lewis takes as his starting point a textbook that for him reveals the failure of schools to teach children how to make value judgments. The book he has chosen considers a passage in which Coleridge describes responses to a waterfall. The book presses the point that, because they convey value judgments, the responses are expressions of personal feelings; they are, in other words, subjective. Lewis contends that this trivializes value judgments. Equating value judgments with subjective feelings makes them matters of preference, and they are thereby shorn of public standing. It thus becomes impossible productively even to discuss value judgments, much less resolve disagreements about them, in an open forum.

For Lewis, this shift undermines one of the cardinal roles of education, which is to teach students both that there are things in their world that they should value highly and how to determine which of them are worthy of high regard and which are not. The skill to recognize the value of something and why an ascription of value is warranted is crucial to the educational process.[1] The future of the culture is at stake, and in schools we can gain some idea of what the society of the future will be like. In this case, it would seem, the schools will produce citizens who think that values are a matter of taste. This is no small thing, since important matters such as ethics, politics, and religion depend on the ability to make defensible value judgments.[2]

Lewis argues that the health of society requires the conviction that objects and events can be seen inherently to deserve the values we ascribe to them. Value judgments are relational; they register that something has a certain value *for us*. But value is objective in that the value of a thing lies within it and is not simply the projection of arbitrary personal preference. We should be able to show that the value we ascribe is merited. We can recognize when someone's value judgments are questionable or even mistaken and when they are defensible and right.

Lewis presses this further. Not only does the health of society depend on an education that makes value judgments a matter of importance, but when education fails to do so students will be less human than they could become. To a large extent, personhood or full human standing can be measured by the ability to make sound and defensible value judgments, to have right relations to things, events, and other persons. If that ability goes undeveloped or its importance is minimized, people are brutalized, because what is left when the process of evaluation evaporates is power. When the content of shared value judgments is excluded from the classroom, students are the unwitting subjects of a process designed to condition them to take their places in society, where they themselves will become the abusers (or victims) of power.

Early education in value judgments is central to human development because it shapes a kind of "second nature." If we think of persons as constituted on the one hand by rationality, with its powers of self-consciousness, analysis, and reflection, and on the other by impulses, with their thoughtless energies and vitalities, no place is provided for developing an ability to make defensible value judgments. The capacity for making value judgments should play a mediating role between rationality and impulse. A useful analogy is the position of the heart relative to the brain and viscera. The "heart," metaphorically speaking, is the evaluating organ, and it needs to be trained, as muscles need to be trained in an athlete. Making sound value judgments eventually becomes a kind of second nature. This does not mean that the capacity becomes fixed. There is always room to question our evaluations or those of others. But this questioning is carried on in a context of previously acquired evaluating skills.

It is worth emphasizing, since the thought is somewhat undeveloped in this lecture, that the problem with the textbook and the educational philosophy it represents is that it withholds from the student the important, even defining, role of the mediating faculty that Lewis refers to as the chest or the heart. This educational philosophy does to individuals what the culture in general, led by scientifically warranted theory and practice, does to the society more generally, namely, reduce it to two contrary elements—mind and matter. A person who is only an amalgam of mind and matter is incomplete because, Lewis contends, "the head rules the belly through the chest" (24). Without trained emotions, which Lewis ascribes to the "chest," "the intellect is powerless against the animal organism" (24). Indeed, it is this "middle element" that defines personhood (25). Lewis presses his point even further; people think that on their own they can rationally manage their desires and drives, but it's more likely that they will become victims of those in power who, driven by their own desires and drives, manipulate the emotions and choices of those less powerful than themselves.

In the second lecture Lewis turns more fully to society. It is in the name of society that value-free education is defended and carried on. Lewis rejects the implicit argument that judgments about value should not be expressed in public because the differing values that are held by people will rend the fabric of society. When personal values are excluded from public discourse, the argument goes, it becomes possible to raise questions about what is good for the society as a whole, good in this case meaning what is useful for or favors society.[3]

Lewis attacks a major defense of the elevation of social over personal values, namely, that it is a human instinct to seek the good of the society. He argues that instincts, while they may be natural, are not always good and deserving to be obeyed. We have many, often conflicting, instincts, and the instinct for self-preservation and personal advancement may well trump the instinct to advance the society. Indeed, the desire to prosecute the welfare of society, not to speak of societies in distant lands or generations in the future, is less instinctive than many people seem to think.

Lewis contends that concern for the well-being of society, like responsibility for future generations and for people in other societies, is not instinctive but must be learned. The public good does not produce nurturing values but rather depends on them. The question of what is good for the society should be addressed in a public arena constituted by people with developed value-assessing abilities who ask what it is good for their society to be, meaning not what is useful or what is power enhancing but what ought to be the case. Concern for the good of society, one is led to conclude, implies responsibility for the well-being of others, including not only fellow citizens but future generations and those in other societies—a sense of responsibility that is not instinctive but has to be learned.

Having argued against the idea that people by nature or instinct want to further the well-being of society, Lewis implies an objection to a norm for social action that has come to be known as rational choice theory. The theory is that we do and should make decisions on a cost-benefit basis, on the basis, that is, of what is good or useful for us. This rational and practical theory of ethics leaves out the question of what is meant by the good or how the norm of "usefulness" is determined (29).

In the third lecture Lewis turns from society to look more closely at nature, and especially the goal, so dominant in modern culture, of using science and technology to subject nature to our control. Power over nature strengthens the notion that we are in a position of self-determination relative to nature. Armed with power, we hold ourselves to be superior to nature. Nature becomes an arena of utility or of material for possession and use. Drained of value, nature is subject to whatever gratifies us. Our dependence on nature as well as its intrinsic value go unrecognized. This attitude toward nature is consistent with the scientific method whereby things are judged shorn of their value and viewed objectively.

It is very important to see that Lewis is not opposed to science or to the scientific method per se. He opposes the extension of the attitudes and methods of abstraction derived from the laboratory to our world and to our relations in and to it. Because we tend to do just that, we begin to think of ourselves as standing above not only natural phenomena but other people as well. We view people, like everything else, as material to be used to satisfy our own interests, needs, and desires. In a society so constituted, science itself changes. Not only does such a society try to subjugate nature to human knowledge and control, it also uses power over nature to give some people control over other people. The result is that a minority gains power and control over the majority, the domination of the less by the more powerful.

The implication is that science itself should be housed within a context of values and value-determining practices. Because scientific endeavors legitimately suspend values, they need to be contained within a value-forming society, and a value-forming society is not possible without individuals who are in the habit of raising questions about what it is good for us as persons, as well as for us as a society, to be.

To put this more starkly, when values and value judgments are removed from any arena, personal or social, what remains is power. This power is not evenly distributed among people, societies, or nations but is concentrated in the hands of some. This means that what is thought to be good or useful will be determined by the relatively few who hold the power. For the main part, what is thought to be good or useful is what enhances and protects the power of those who already hold it.

II

Now that I have surveyed the three lectures to highlight their principal emphases, I can comment more fully and look more closely at what Lewis is after in these lectures and why they are difficult to understand.

The first thing to note is that for Lewis values are embedded in and determining for relations. We tend to think of our position in the world in terms of distinctiveness, contrast, and opposition, especially the split between subjects and objects, between things and what we make of and do with them. Since for Lewis values are relational, his response to the authors of the textbook who locate values in subjectivity is not a simple one. Lewis does not stand on the opposite side of this divide. True, he stresses objectivity, but he does so on the basis that we know that things and events *deserve* to be evaluated. Evaluations are basic to our well-being and that of others, chiefly as answers to the question of what it is good for us to be. This means that, while the value of something resides in it, the value is also a value *for us*. This value of something for us is not limited to its utility.

The second thing to note is that Lewis holds that modern rationality and scientific research proceed according to two primary strategies. The first is to eliminate as far as possible preconceived notions of value or meaning so that what is under scrutiny can be seen in a new or clearer way. The second strategy is to reduce what is studied to its simplest, most basic components. These strategies are fundamental to what we take in the modern West to be the acquisition of knowledge, especially knowledge of which we can have a high degree of certainty. This kind of inquiry is fundamental to learning, and Lewis is not suggesting that it is inappropriate. However, he thinks that these strategies should be limited to certain arenas and occasions. Very likely because of the prestige our culture assigns to rationality, scientific knowledge, and technological control, we tend to elevate these strategies so that they define how we actually are in the world. We place ourselves in the world in a way similar to the way a scientist in a lab is positioned relative to what is under examination. Lewis thinks that education, while it must include rational and scientific inquiries and the knowledge they provide, should be primarily concerned with nurturing the capacity in children to make sound and defensible value judgments.

The third thing to note is that the cultural form of the scientific method creates and reinforces what has come to be called a subject/object or fact/value split. Lewis puts it this way: "On this view, the world of facts, without one trace of value, and the world of feelings, without one trace of truth or falsehood, justice or injustice, confront one another, and no *rapprochement* is possible" (20). In modern culture people think that things and events have no value other than what people decide to give them. This way of being in the world is so pervasive and commonplace that we are unaware that it is a particular worldview; we take it as natural and obvious. In addition, we tend to think, as do scientists as they do their work, that the truth of something resides in what is most simple and basic, which generally means something material—matter or energy. Such things as the value or meaning of something are superficial matters that must be discounted in order to get at what is really going on, is really the case.

The fourth point is that we don't have these attitudes and think of ourselves as being in the world this way because we all want to be scientists or philosophers. Rather, we assume these attitudes because they free us from obligations to others and our world. When we sharply divide our conscious minds from a world shorn of value, we are positioned freely to use the world around us, including other people, in ways that suit our self-interest. Since for Lewis humans are prone to self-preoccupation and pride, humans who construct their world and position themselves in it this way are left to act like children in a candy store or foxes in a chicken coop. The world becomes an arena of self-aggrandizement and self-gratification.[4]

III

In these short lectures, Lewis gives us a shrewd analysis and radical critique of the primary orientations and motivations of modern Western culture, which, he suggests, portend very negative outcomes. Indeed, it may well be that these attitudes are so pervasive in our culture and so attached to power that they cannot be countered or reversed. Does Lewis offer an alternative?

Lewis does not elect to follow the easier road. Often, when people encounter these cultural problems they appeal to a transcendent authority, insisting that we need to reassert the inherent meaning, value, and directives that derive directly from divine sources. While Lewis holds authority and divinity in high regard, he chooses not to go down this road for three reasons.[5]

The first is a practical one. For this option to work, the entire population would have to become believers in an ultimate or divine source of authority. The prospects for such a mass conversion are dim to say the least. If the problems he is addressing are as urgent as he makes them out to be, and I think they are, to wait until everyone accepts value-setting authorities and their divine source would be to postpone a remedy indefinitely. This is one reason, I think, why these lectures are noticeably free of religious appeals.

Second, Lewis does not think of values and morals primarily as handed down from above. Right values, morals, and meanings are not imposed on or alien to us, but rather are consistent with who we fundamentally are and ought to be. Values may seem arbitrary but, like the proper grip on a golf club or the right way to hold the bow of a violin, even if they seem unnatural and arbitrary at first, turn out to be consistent with what is humanly good or beneficial.

Third, to move from subjectivity and relativism to objectivity and absolutism would be to accept the subject/object, fact/value split. It means moving from one side of the divide to the other without questioning the division itself. Any answer, including a religious answer—even a Christian one—that perpetuates and reinforces the notion of this divide is incapable of surmounting the problem in the long run.

What moves are available to Lewis, given the pervasiveness and power of the error and the complex and elusive nature of any remedy for it? The first is an appeal to intuition. Lewis thinks we always already know that some things are actually good and others are not, and we can distinguish between the two even apart from what our society, culture, or self-interest asks us to think. We also can see that other people, other societies, and other cultures are in some respects more right than we are about what it is good for people to be and do. And we can recognize that there are things that are good for us to do, even though doing them may run counter to our desire for comfort or gratification.

We also already know that things and events merit certain value judgments. There are deeds that, no matter where or by whom they are perpetrated, deserve to be condemned. We also know of things that should be lauded wherever and whenever they are enacted. A person who refuses to say that rape is always wrong, or that a courageous act that saves someone's life is always commendable, strikes us as deficient in humanity. Indeed, our humanity is deeply connected to our ability to make and to recognize proper value judgments. The lack of this ability calls one's humanity into question.

Third, when we evaluate other people we are led toward their character and away from their physical attributes, possessions, or social status. It's true that good looks, wealth, skill, and knowledge grant to people powers to attract our attention and admiration, but they lose their appeal in someone whose values and morals are objectionable. We may well admire or emulate people who possess these outward qualities, but we also admire or emulate people whose behavior and attitudes correct or inspire us. We finally define personal excellence not primarily according to outward characteristics but by such qualities as dependability, honesty, kindness, admirable goals, and the like. We think most highly of persons who have, to use what may seem an odd word, an edifying effect on us.

Fourth, Lewis contends that to a remarkable degree cultures agree on what it is good for persons and groups to do. In an appendix to his lectures, Lewis briefly surveys cultures separated by space or time and concludes that on matters such as beneficence, respect for elders, duty to children, justice, truthfulness, and mercy cultures are remarkably similar. Lewis calls his collection of cultural similarities "Tao." By that he means the norms of behavior and relationship that endure and are shared and which, because they are not culturally specific, are revealed as naturally consistent with what it is good for humans to do and to be. Lewis's use of the term "Tao" extends the discussion outside the boundaries of Western culture, in keeping with his point concerning the shared character of human values. Further, Daoism is associated with an emphasis on the natural, on what is basically already there, and this supports what in the first part of this book I identified as one of Lewis's reasonable assumptions.

Lewis's insistence on the similarities between diverse cultures runs counter to a good bit of contemporary cultural theory. In reaction against earlier universalizing attitudes toward other cultures, which came to their fullest expression in Western imperialism toward the so-called third world, cultural theory has emphasized the distinctiveness and autonomy of individual cultures. This was a good thing to do. Under the banner of a universal understanding of human nature, modern Western interests were imposed on indigenous cultures. Lewis shaped the character of Weston, in the first two of his science novels, to reflect this. His attitudes and corresponding actions were violent. However, the violence of a universalizing cultural theory can easily be matched by the violence of the idea that members of other cultures have nothing in common with me. If that is so, I have no real or potential relation to them and need not be concerned about their well-being. Rather than either of these alternatives, Lewis asserts that people and societies are both different from and similar to one another, as he makes clear in *Out of the Silent Planet*. We cannot know beforehand in what or how the differences and similarities will be revealed. Neither can we know in advance how much difference and similarity we will find. We must go into the process of getting to know others, as Ransom does when he encounters the hrossa and faces the similarities and differences as they arise. Our relations not only with people but also with nonhuman creatures and even with the inorganic world are constituted by the play of such similarities and differences.

Finally, Lewis seems confident that when this reality is pointed out to them people will acknowledge it, because it describes the actual position in which they find themselves. The subject/object or value/fact split is an artificial construction, even a distortion. A relational view is true and actual. This is why he can say, "It is not the greatest of modern scientists who feel most sure that the object, stripped of its qualitative properties and reduced to mere quantity, is wholly real. Little scientists, and little unscientific followers of science, may think so. The great minds know very well that the object, so treated, is an artificial abstraction, that something of its reality has been lost" (70–71). This is why Lewis can anticipate a regenerate science, a science that "when it explained it would not explain away. When it spoke of the parts it would remember the whole. While studying the *It* it would not lose what Martin Buber calls the *Thou*-situation" (79).

These bases for believing that the present cultural situation can be effectively opposed and even healed may seem slight, but they are, for Lewis, firm. Indeed, the situation that he exposes and the alternative that he proposes are basic to his entire project.[6] Unless something along the lines of what he is suggesting comes about, talking about religion, including Christianity, will become increasingly pointless because the culture will distort the Christianity that is being advocated.

9

That Hideous Strength

A Modern Fairy-Tale for Grown-Ups (1945)

This novel does not fit neatly with the other two books in the science trilogy. For one thing, the action takes place entirely on this planet. Also, the other books are rather economical, narrating vast journeys, new environments, and strange encounters in relatively few pages. This one is quite lengthy, although it concentrates on a single location in the middle of England. Further, in the two earlier novels Ransom is the protagonist whereas this time he is, while an authoritative figure, somewhat remote from events. In the first two novels Ransom is the center of consciousness; here he occupies an elevated position relative to the reader, the other characters, and the Ransom of the other two books.[1]

However, while noticeably different from the preceding two, this narrative exhibits continuity with them as well. The previous novels referred often to earth and, especially in *Perelandra*, its future. Now we are very much in this world, in England with its particular history, cultural conditions, and future. While the first two novels relate earth to the other two planets visited by the protagonists, this novel, in the visits of the planetary powers to earth, relates the other planets to ours.

Although set in the future, the novel is not apocalyptic, not a narrative of the end of everything. It projects a crisis that readers are asked to take as the logical, historical outcome of attitudes, theories, and practices characteristic of modern Western culture and of the paradigmatic cultural institution, the research university, especially as manifested in the separation of scientific from humanist interests. Ransom's place in the narrative has more to do with the institution over which he presides than with him as an individual. However, by virtue of his accomplishments in the previous books he plays a personal role, as he puts it, of a "bridge" that allows angelic or planetary forces to prevent newly institutionalized powers from taking control not only of English society but, potentially, of global humanity. The events of the book have more in common with the Genesis story of the city and tower of Babel than with New Testament forecasts of the end of time.

The narrative concerns institutions in their competing attempts to affect human society, but it also deals with personal, even intimate, relationships. One of the more inventive devices in the novel is its combination of two very different but related stories, a large story—Belbury's attempts to consolidate power and control society and the transcendent defense against its attempts—and a personal story—a young married couple and their difficulties in adjusting to marriage. This combination of the personal and the institutional, of the particular and the inclusive, is not merely a narrative strategy. Lewis sees the particular and the inclusive as mutually engaged, and difficulties on the macro- and those on the microlevel are closely related.[2] The story of Mark and Jane Studdock's problems, while minor compared to the sweeping changes occurring in the society around them, frames the narrative and, for that reason, strikes us as the more important story of the two. This suggests that for Lewis, in the final analysis, the personal realm is more important than the societal and perhaps even the cosmic. The Studdocks' story begins with estrangement and ends with an impending embrace. Because their story encompasses their involvement in the two opposing institutions, Belbury and St. Anne's, it stands between them and is a part of the larger story of a culture intellectually and morally divided.

The location is fictional. One wonders why Lewis did not pick Oxford as the site, since, as we know, his attitude toward it was not uncritical. Perhaps it suggests that newer English universities are more vulnerable to takeover because they lack the cultural prestige and wealth of Oxford and Cambridge and are given over more fully to the sciences. Perhaps, too, Lewis thought that he had more freedom to include characters who resemble members of the Oxford faculty if he gave the story a fictional location. The decision has its price.[3] The exact location of the University of Edgestow is necessarily left somewhat vague.

The narrator, while for the most part removed from the action, comes on stage several times. He identifies himself as "Oxford-bred and very fond of Cambridge" (15). A guest of Bracton, he anticipates a major episode of the novel by exploring Bragdon Wood. Indeed, he is an authority on the history of the place, able to identify the masonry as "very late British-Roman work, done on the eve of the Anglo-Saxon invasion" (19). This knowledge is crucial to the action, because it provides a clue to the site of Merlin's awakening, which is eagerly sought by both sides in the struggle.

The plot traces the rise of Belbury, its incorporation by and encroachment on much of Bracton College, and its ultimate collapse. Belbury is not destroyed by its opponents at St. Anne's but meets its end by implosion. This end, however, is hastened by transcendent forces to which St. Anne's is hospitable. The role of St. Anne's as a bridge between the imminent and the transcendent explains its rather passive role in the action, even with respect to securing the services of Merlin for the final effort;

Merlin comes to St. Anne's on his own. Belbury, by contrast, is active in advancing its own interests, but it also becomes a site of transcendent powers, in this case malignant, that gradually occupy, control, and corrode it. The contrast between Belbury's assumed autonomy and its actual condition of being possessed is deliberate. As is often the case with plots of destruction, the story takes place in late fall and winter. At the end, signs of spring appear.

While this plot of the ascent and destruction of Belbury and the role played by St. Anne's unifies the narrative, the changes in the characters are equally important, relating the institutional to the personal and the language of plot to the language of character.

I

Mark Studdock is a sociologist just beginning his academic career. He has a fellowship at Bracton, but he is recruited by the National Institute for Coordinated Experiments (N.I.C.E.) to join its staff. Belbury's primary agenda is the reconstitution of society along lines dictated by science. Sociology is important for the institute because it applies scientific methods to the study of human beings. Mark, we read, is initially intrigued by this agenda: "science applied to social problems and backed by the whole force of the state, just as war has been backed by the whole force of the state in the past" (37). Lewis has serious reservations about, if not objections to, the social sciences, and these become obvious in this novel. William Hingest, a physical chemist at Bracton and one of its finest scholars, voices this criticism of the social sciences: "I happen to believe," he says, "that you can't study men; you can only get to know them, which is quite a different thing" (69). The narrator reinforces this when he tells us, "It must be remembered that in Mark's mind hardly one rag of noble thought, either Christian or Pagan, had a secure lodging. His education had been neither scientific nor classical—merely 'Modern'" (182).

As we saw in *The Abolition of Man,* Lewis fears the consequences of the scientific method when it is more broadly applied because it makes facts of things, abstracts them from their relations and from questions of their value and significance, so that they can be studied objectively. One can thus understand his unease with the use of such methods for the study of human beings. Mark is indeed less interested in people than in abstractions that objectify them, such as statistics, and controlling categories like "vocational groups," "classes," and "populations." The dominance of abstractions abets violence; the social programs that Mark helps to develop are applied to actual people. The description of Mark's evaluations of and attachments to abstraction can be taken as deliberately contrasted with the idealist principles or norms that feature so centrally in the novel.

This privileging of abstraction over human actuality also supports Mark's work as a journalist. The narrative draws connections between sociology, journalism, and police work in a provocative way. They all have to do less with the desire to further human well-being than with controlling and even manipulating people. While Mark is at first put off by his journalistic assignments, he warms to them. They give him access to an audience of millions, and he is carried along by the force of his prose. Seduced by the power of journalism, Mark is asked to report on an event that has not as yet taken place, and he becomes aware for the first time that what he is about to do is criminal. He slips into such questionable behavior imperceptibly, "in a chatter of laughter, of that intimate laughter between fellow professionals, which of all earthly powers is strongest to make men do very bad things before they are yet, individually, very bad men" (127).

Mark is also susceptible to the recruitment tactics of N.I.C.E. because he wants to be on the inside and at the cutting edge of things. He longs to be part of the inner circle, a group of academic intimates who view themselves as ahead of or above all the rest. This has far more to do with what is fashionable or new than with what, by traditional academic standards, constitutes excellence. It seems that N.I.C.E does not need to justify its goals, or even explain them. It simply identifies itself with change and critical analysis, which throws everything that is traditionally valued into question as regressive and resistant to the new. Those on the cutting edge are self-conscious about their role and selective as to who is allowed to join them. They view those outside their group with scorn. Mark is drawn to the institute because he does not want to be left out or left behind. He glows with pleasure when he is admitted into the institute's library and feels welcomed by those already there. He "liked to be liked," we are told (215).

When Mark begins to question N.I.C.E., he recognizes himself as "the odious little outsider who wanted to be an insider" and his career as a series of attempts to find acceptance in whatever elite group came into view, even if it required deceiving himself (243). He later learns that his mistake did not lie in his desire to be incorporated within a group; indeed, that is a characteristically human desire. His mistake is to take *this* group as the one able to fulfill his longing for inclusion in something larger and more valuable than himself (358).

Despite the primacy he assigns to abstract categories in his sociological work, Mark is a theoretical materialist (202).[4] That is, he has come to assume that everything that exists or occurs has its source or cause in matter and energy. We are told that Mark believes this despite the fact that he retains belief in his own free will. Free will is not something he has thought about, and, since free will is difficult to establish within a materialist worldview, he would likely be unable to explain or defend it. His materialism puts him in agreement with members of N.I.C.E. who also are materialists but who, unlike Mark, follow materialism to its logical conclusion in determinism. Part of the indoctrination of Mark into the institute is to purge him of vestiges of humanism, to lead him toward a more complete and consistent materialism. This process culminates in the Objective Room, which is designed to have a disorienting effect and to eliminate lingering nonmaterialist assumptions.

It is important to note that for some members materialism, however basic to the institute's self-understanding, proves inadequate for giving an account of their work and goals. Several believe in spiritual supplements to materialism, which is thereby shown to be an inadequate basis for a worldview. Material is what is called in another context a "neutral," something that needs to be housed within a larger, more inclusive theory.[5]

Another thing to note is that with Mark's gradual absorption into the ethos of N.I.C.E. he begins to drink heavily. Lewis often uses alcoholism and addiction to signify individuals succumbing to forces that take over their lives. Of course power is also addictive, and Mark enjoys being within what he takes to be a powerful group. As a metaphor, alcoholism suggests that the pleasure of power derives not from something received from outside but from the gratification of an inward need or desire.

A final characteristic that aligns Mark with N.I.C.E. is that he "had no scruples about vivisection" (100). The institute is willing to carry out experiments on animals without regard to their suffering. This practice is warranted by the assumption, which goes back at least to René Descartes, that because animals are not self-conscious they do not experience pain or suffer. Here it is symptomatic of a lack of respect for any creature that has become the object of study. Indeed, the institute is even willing to subject humans to experimental procedures. It is important for Lewis that when respect for the wider context is lost, that lack of respect can easily be extended from the inorganic to the organic and from animals to humans. Treating all material as matter for control and manipulation severs the relations humans can and do have with animals; treating animals as without feelings leads to treating people in similar ways. Even when it begins with small things, severing a sense of relationship, of responsibility and appreciation, becomes a habit, and the habit becomes "natural."

While Mark is vulnerable to seduction by the lures of Belbury, he does not wholly succumb. One reason for this residue of resistance is his young wife, Jane. He realizes that she would not like many of the people at Belbury with whom he associates or his heavy drinking. He associates Jane with a practical and realistic sense of life, with a genuine interest in ordinary things. Her values are increasingly important for him, so that the idea of the ordinary or the normal becomes urgent in his mind, especially when, in the Objective Room, he is subjected to an environment that is arbitrary and bizarre; "the idea of the Straight or the Normal which had occurred to him during his first visit to this room, grew stronger and more solid in his mind till it had become a kind of mountain" (307). The narrator elaborates on this sense of the normal or straight as a genuine intuition of the real in contrast to the artificial, arbitrary, and abstract qualities of the Objective Room. Lewis would not deny the importance of invention or abstraction, but the ordinary persists as a basis for sound evaluations. The Objective Room has no relation to the ordinary, and its abstraction and arbitrariness awaken in Mark a new appreciation for its opposite, the quotidian—another instance in Lewis of the fortunate fall.

II

Like Mark, Jane is not a religious person, but that does not stand in the novel as her basic fault. More important is that she wants to be self-sufficient, her own independent person. She sees the institution of marriage as a threat to that desired goal. Unlike Mark, who wants to be included in a group, part of something larger, Jane wants to be separate. She prizes her individuality and resists being drawn in.

Despite her desire to be independent, she is taken outside herself by vivid dreams that foreshadow actual events. Like the materialism associated with Mark, Jane's visionary gift is another "neutral," a potential that can be used by differing interests for different purposes. As Camilla Denniston says to Jane, "don't you see... that you can't be neutral? If you don't give yourself to us, the enemy will use you" (113). Jane, like Merlin, is sought by both Belbury and St. Anne's. It may be useful to note in passing that for Lewis to ascribe visionary powers to Jane is not so outré as it may appear to today's reader, because such powers had a role in some psychological theories at the time, especially those of Carl Jung. Visionary experiences seem important for Lewis because of their potential to bridge the separation that modernity has introduced between spiritual internality and the external, material world.

When she enters St. Anne's, Jane learns that her "power of dreaming realities" (63) is hereditary. She is surprised by the interest that Grace Ironwood takes in her and surprised to learn that, because she is a Tudor, she is "a more important person than she realizes that she is" (63). Rather than being flattered or intrigued by this revelation, Jane is put off by it because she wants to ground her identity on her individuality. For similar reasons, she resents Mark and "love itself" (71): "this fear of being invaded and entangled was the deepest ground of her determination not to have a child—or not for a long time yet. One had one's own life to live" (71).

Jane's individualism is a point of interest during her interview with the director of St. Anne's. Ransom exudes an aura of authority and power that, rather than arousing Jane's resistance, leaves her vulnerable—"without protection" (141). Ransom uses the language of obedience to open to her the possibility of being herself not by retaining or protecting herself but by giving herself. He calls "humility" an "erotic necessity" (146). Jane's interview with Ransom contrasts sharply with her interview with Fairy Hardcastle at Belbury. That interview has erotic overtones as well, but in a sinister, sadomasochistic way. The contrast between Ransom's authority and that of the institute propels Jane back to St. Anne's to make her home there, even though she is not yet fully convinced about Ransom and his principles of vulnerability and obedience. Jane's sense of and desire for personal autonomy are doubly beset by her visionary capacities and by the persuasive effects of St. Anne's.

Life at St. Anne's draws Jane in because she is attracted to its feminine qualities. She admires Camilla Denniston's beauty, and she is dealt with firmly but graciously by the physician Grace Ironwood. She is disarmed by the warmth of Margaret Dimble, and she shares with Mrs. Maggs her feeling of separation from her husband. This complex of feminine experiences, understandings, and abilities, while underdeveloped in the narrative, stands as a complement to the very masculine force and appeal of the director. The femininity at St. Anne's is also contrasted with the expressions of femininity in Belbury, the exaggeratedly masculine Fairy Hardcastle on the one hand and on the other the Woman's Auxiliary Institutional Police, the WAIPs, who flit about in a display of girlishness carried "to the point of imbecility" (94). Jane is responsive to the complex but unified feminine culture of St. Anne's rather than to the homoerotic gestures of Fairy Hardcastle. It should be said, too, that homoerotic qualities are recognizable in the relationship between Frost and Wither, so that the tie between homosexuality and the designs of Belbury becomes clear. While this linkage likely reflects an implicit—and objectionable, I would add—equation of homosexuality with evil, it may also suggest the subjection of difference and particularity to the principle of the Same.

As Jane's self-understanding as an autonomous individual is challenged, so also is her understanding of religious feeling as neutral and vague. She begins to see that the religious and spiritual require firmness and clarity. Religious language is the antithesis to that of N.I.C.E., which, despite its scientific aura, employs a language of vagueness, abstraction, and imprecision. It is impossible for Mark to get a clear answer about anything. Because the language of N.I.C.E. is abstracted from reality, Mark can fictionalize events in his journalistic reports. Fog is the image used for the world as overrun by Belbury; getting above the fog indicates the world of St. Anne's. This recognition alters Jane's goal of self-actualization. She can be a more fully realized person by making her roles and positions more, rather than less, defined. She had thought it was by means of dissociation and abstraction that she would become her "true self" and "soar upwards and expand in some freer and purer world" (315). But the true path to self-actualization is through involvement, through particular embodiment and relationships.

This is confirmed by her life-changing vision in the garden. She encounters a presence that makes her aware that to be fully herself she must try not to possess but to give herself to something or someone outside herself worthy of that gift. She comes into her own when she leads the expedition to find Merlin. This attempt turns out to be unnecessary, because Merlin comes to St. Anne's voluntarily, but it reveals Jane's courage and her leadership abilities. This does not compromise but rather ultimately enriches the enactment of her role as a wife and potential mother.

III

On either side of Mark and Jane stand the two institutions. In terms of the plot, the primary institution is N.I.C.E., because the book depicts its rise and fall, while St. Anne's provides a mediating site for the powers that contribute to the undoing of N.I.C.E.

It is important to notice, I think, that the narrative creates a strong continuity between Belbury and the University of Edgestow. Belbury's connections to the state do not detract from its close relation to the university; the state, which is the source of grants for the development of what will enhance the state's power, is very much a part of academic life. Nor does the fact that Belbury is a bureaucracy distance it from the university. It can be said that while Belbury is something other than the university, even an intrusion, it is also an outgrowth or a logical extension of ideas and practices pervasive in and promulgated by the university. The novel exposes the direction in which modern academia is headed. There is no doubt that Lewis has transferred his intimate knowledge of Oxford to Edgestow, and in this novel he works out his critique of the university, of which he seems never to have felt fully a part. Indeed, the characters may well resemble some of Lewis's Oxford colleagues. Finally, Belbury, like St. Anne's, mediates power that comes from another source, in this case the state. Unlike St. Anne's, Belbury, standing between and dependent on the university and the state, exploits its mediating position and attempts to absorb their roles into itself, to control, if not to supplant, both. This assumption by N.I.C.E. that it is in control when actually it is controlled by powers outside itself is continuous with its mistaken belief that it has real or potential cosmic and spiritual control when, in reality, it has no substance of its own, collapses internally, and is subjected to the vengeful powers of reality.

The continuities between Belbury and the university are substantial. When Frost expounds his quite extreme vision of what N.I.C.E. should pursue, Mark "recognized it at once as the logical conclusion of thoughts which he had always hitherto accepted and which at this moment he found himself irrevocably rejecting" (293). It is possible, without causing alarm, to propound views that when taken to their logical conclusion are violent and inhumane because these views originally arise from legitimate methods of investigation designed for specific uses. When detached from their specific sites and occasions and deployed broadly to subjugate and manipulate people, these methods become violent and grotesque.

No agreed-upon goals or directions define N.I.C.E. except the desire to combine the expertise of the university and the power of the state in order to control people and reorder society. The question of why these goals are improvements is not raised or addressed within the institute.[6] What presides is the assumption that the knowledge and power acquired by it should be used first of all to increase and secure its own position at the expense of society. The vagueness on the question of what kind of society the institute plans to create suggests not so much a failure to reflect as a certainty that the process is self-evidently justified by the needs it addresses and the means by which it intends to produce change. This overriding though largely tacit assumption is not threatened when individual participants in the institute have differing ideas of what the future should be like and what is the best way to get there.

Lord Feverstone, Devine from *Out of the Silent Planet*, wants science to take over society and recondition people first psychologically and then biochemically. His goal is clarity, which he sets in opposition to obscurantism. He is a member of Parliament and his close association with London suggests involvement with economic interests as well as politics. He advocates experimentation on human subjects, especially criminals, in order to extend control over human minds.

Filostrato, the physiologist, has great faith in N.I.C.E. as the only hope for the survival of the human race. His ultimate goal is to sever human life from its organic base and develop an artificial human, epitomized by the "Head" of the institute, which will be free from dependence on a body and therefore immune to death. While Feverstone wants clarity, Filostrato wants cleanliness. He thinks of nature as messy. Metal plants should replace organic trees. He is dedicated to separating the human mind, which he thinks of as the seat of personal identity, from physicality.[7]

Frost's goal is to achieve thoroughgoing individuality. He wants N.I.C.E. to develop "a hard unchangeable core of individuals really devoted to the same cause as ourselves" (240). In this he is the opposite of the deputy director, Wither, who wants unity. Several times Wither uses the term "family" to refer to the personnel at N.I.C.E. He expresses his desire for unity in a particularly vivid way: "I would welcome an interpenetration of personalities so close, so irrevocable, that it almost transcends individuality" (240). This difference between Frost and Wither reflects the narrative's strong interest in the relation of particulars to wholes and individuals to groups, as seen in Mark wanting to be part of a group and Jane wanting to be her own individual person. Wither takes his desire for unity to the extreme when he goes on to say, "You need not doubt that I would open my arms to receive—to absorb—to assimilate this young man" (240).[8]

Frost is a determinist, a materialist who holds that all human emotions and actions have chemical causes (252). Motives and intentions are not to be explained in terms of will; he tells Mark, "When you have attained real objectivity you will recognize, not *some* motives, but *all* motives as merely animal, subjective epiphenomena" (293). As such, they should be discounted or eliminated. Frost brings Mark to the Objective Room in order to rid him of human emotions. His determinism is thoroughgoing. He "theoretically believed that all which appears in the mind as motive or intention is merely a by-product of what the body is doing" (354). In fact Frost concludes that there is no good reason to believe in mind at all, leaving "the body and its movements" as the only reality: "the self which seemed to watch the body... was a nonentity" (355). Consciousness he thinks is an illusion, although it screams for attention, and the body, severed from consciousness, can do nothing to silence these screams. One has to admire the rigor and consistency of Frost's materialism, which, by denying not only will and intention but the mind itself, undermines personal identity and what is significant about being a human person.

Frost is a determinist in a second sense. He believes in what he calls "macrobes." Just as there exist microbes that we do not see but which can radically affect our lives, so there are also unseen transcendent or spiritual beings that affect us. Frost thinks that the head of Alcasan, which has been mounted on a tripod and artificially kept alive, is being used by these macrobes as a medium by which to communicate with humans (254), a parody of the relation of Ransom and St. Anne's to angelic powers. To communicate with them, one must, for Frost, go "outside the whole world of our subjective emotions" (255). It is important to note that Frost's denial of human subjectivity and agency, of feelings and free will, leads him to believe in an objective domain of spirits. He denies personal identity and will and transposes them to transcendent, immaterial substances. Mark is an apt target for Frost's campaign because, while also a materialist, Mark inconsistently retains belief in free will (266). Mark represents what Lewis in *The Abolition of Man* takes to be the pervasive self-understanding of modern people: we live in a world that we account for materialistically but at the same time we affirm our autonomy, our ability to exert our will over that world. By working past this inconsistency to a clearer, albeit bizarre, conclusion, Frost represents the future.

In contrast to Frost, Wither takes his free will and inner life as the only reality. We are told, "his inmost self was free to pursue its own life. That detachment of the spirit, not only from the senses, but even from the reason, which has been the goal of some mystics, was now his" (248). This detachment or abstraction renders the person undefined and therefore capable of the kind of merger that Wither seeks.

Surprisingly, the deployment of scientific methods to alter human society finds its fullest articulation in Straik, the priest and theologian. He thinks society as now constituted is "an organization of ordered sin" and a "body of Death" (76–77). It obscures the genuine message of Jesus, which, Straik thinks, requires the establishment of God's Kingdom on earth. Science is the instrument by which this will be accomplished. Science, like a kind of messiah, comes both to judge and to destroy, to tear down and to rebuild: "I knew that He was coming in power. And therefore, where we see power, we see the sign of His coming. And that is why I find myself joining with communists and materialists and anyone else who is really ready to expedite the coming" (77). This radical but recognizably Christian theological view is an extreme extension of an actual theological reaction to the evils of modernity, which advocates an alliance with materialist and Marxist interests against that culture. Straik seems to follow this line to its logical conclusion, to the emergence of a "Son of Man" who will be humanity itself, "full grown," with the power "to distribute life without end and punishment without end" (125). Straik has so turned against the culture as to side indiscriminately with any attempt to dismantle and replace it. He represents an extreme form of the radicalization of Christian theology after the First World War that repudiated not only modern culture but human culture itself, a position for which Lewis had no sympathy.

It makes sense that Lewis does not make any of these visions dominant in Belbury, since there is no way of adjudicating between them. Like the language of journalism that Mark adopts, language here is deployed in the service of opinions and theories without relation to, not to speak of deference toward, anything real. Opinions and theories gain position not by merit but by power. The scientific method, which seeks knowledge that is verifiable and on which there can be wide agreement, when applied in these totalizing ways, deprives culture of its contact with reality because facts stripped of value and meaning become the norm for knowledge. As the narrator puts it, "The physical sciences, good and innocent in themselves, had already, even in Ransom's own time, begun to be warped, had been subtly maneuvered in a certain direction. Despair of objective truth had been increasingly insinuated into the scientists; indifference to it, and a concentration upon mere power, had been the result" (200). There is no appeal to truth regarding what is good when the culture is determined solely by power, and power creates addiction.

This loss of connection between language and reality sets up the confusion that ensues when Jules's speech at the banquet becomes more and more incomprehensible. In a context in which language is not held to account and where opinions can be tossed about freely, language spins out of control and mayhem results.

IV

Although it is not clear what kind of institution St. Anne's is, it clearly is not a church, although its name may well refer to the mother of the Virgin Mary and the patron saint of mothers.[9] This raises the question of whether its not being a church makes St. Anne's more or less important in Lewis's eyes. People seem drawn to it as a refuge but also because they long to be fulfilled, to know a kind of acceptance or inclusion that is not available in the society. In some respects it resembles Belbury. Its standing and purposes are not all that clear, and, like Belbury, it is hierarchical. Like Belbury, too, it is intellectual. Ransom, Dimble, Denniston, Grace Ironwood, and MacPhee are all highly intelligent and well educated. Indeed, we are told that at St. Anne's there is unprecedented knowledge of the Arthurian period and materials that is unlikely to be equaled (197).[10]

St. Anne's seems to represent what has been neglected at Edgestow University—the traditional cultural riches of England, marked by the relation of the material to the spiritual, and of power to the direction of human life toward worthy goals. While there is analysis and abstraction at St. Anne's, especially as represented by MacPhee, they are balanced by inclusiveness and edification. Deference to what lies above allows what lies below to be more fully actualized. This is clear in the life of the animals at St. Anne's. They are treated as potential partners, and they flourish, unlike their counterparts at Belbury who are caged and await their fate as objects of experiments.[11] From the gardens to the animals and from the least sophisticated, such as Ivy Maggs, to the most exalted, Ransom, all are incorporated within a structure dedicated not to its own interests or those of the individuals within it but to the purposes of something that lies above it and them. Group identity, like personal identity, is not self-generated; it develops as a consequence of deferring to something more important.

Under these conditions language also thrives. There are precision, weight, and economy that culminate in the return to an original language, in which conversations with Merlin are held. When Dimble speaks the Great Tongue, "great syllables of words that sounded like castles come out of his mouth" (225). Here language and truthfulness are inseparable. Things, events, ideas, and the language by which they are conveyed and summoned are bound together. Language, like persons, derives its character from deferring to something else and something more.

St. Anne's does not itself do battle with Belbury. Rather, it becomes the site for a descent of forces that usually maintain their distance from earth, the great eldila of the planets. Nor is the ruination of Belbury a final battle; it is only a particular, although major, episode in a long history of this struggle, of Logres being forgotten for the sake of power, and of the necessity for Logres to reemerge, to return history to a saner course. When distortion occurs, the need for rectitude and normality becomes felt, the need to rejoin meaning and goals to action and power, and the need to recognize that personal and group identity are not self-generated or self-contained. Personal identity and the identity of groups, institutions, and societies are dependent on mutuality, interaction between the needs and potentials of persons and others. In every age there remains, however neglected, a Logres that can provide "the tiny shove or the almost imperceptible pull, to prod England out of the drunken sleep or to draw her back from the final outrage into which Britain tempted her" (367).[12] This potential corrective is not only to be found in England. "Every people," Dimble points out, "has its own haunter. . . . The whole work of healing Tellus depends on nursing that little spark, on incarnating that ghost, which is still alive in every real people, and different in each" (368, 369).

Many principles basic to Lewis's work are operative in this novel. One of them deserves special emphasis. It has to do with "neutrals." These are resources, potentials, and powers that end up being appropriated by one or the other of the two camps by which the story is structured. One of them is materiality. Mark is a materialist, although he has not thought through the implications of this position when used as an explanatory account of all things. The problem is that materialism cannot satisfactorily play that role. It cannot take into account what is, for Lewis, of key importance for personal and group identity: that we are aware of ourselves as persons, are able to think, and are able (as Mark thinks he is) to perform acts freely. Materialism is not wrong when used to account for things in terms of their material causes and sources, what is sometimes these days called "physicalism," but it goes wrong when it is used to explain everything and when anything that it cannot account for is discounted or dismissed. Some members of Belbury devise various theories to augment the materialism that seems otherwise to unite them, seemingly because they recognize the limitations of materialism as totally explanatory.

Merlin and the magic powers associated with him offer another example of a "neutral." Merlin is related to magical powers that are inherently neither good nor evil, with sources in the very distant past. Lewis thought that such powers were available to humans, although most of the time humans do not know what they are getting into by trying to make contact with and to employ them. Merlin, while he has power, is also a medium pointing to powers beyond himself, and such mediation calls out to be incorporated in an institution or culture that gives it a role and a direction.

Jane, with her intuitive and visionary powers, offers another example of a "neutral," and like Merlin she is sought by both institutions. Lewis apparently thought that such gifts of clairvoyance were real and must be taken seriously. It's important that they be housed within a larger set of values, directions, and goals.

One more example should be mentioned, namely, the character of Lord Feverstone. Some of his characteristics are continuous with those of Devine in *Out of the Silent Planet*. But Devine in the earlier novel is more closely associated with money and entrepreneurial interests, and he is depicted as a more objectionable character than Weston, because he is broken while Weston is only bent. The economic and political interests he now represents, although compromised by his desire for science to control society, seem more complex and less objectionable than his interests in *Out of the Silent Planet*. That may be because Lewis sees economic and political powers as "neutrals," as neither good nor evil in themselves but needing to be housed within a set of directives that condition the uses to which they are put. This is consistent with the broader implications of the novel as seen, for example, in the roles of Britain, suggestive of power, and Logres, suggestive of moral and spiritual directives, in relation to the well-being of England. Each requires the other. Left to themselves, "neutrals" will likely be subjected to human pride, the desire for power, and the goal of self-exaltation.

Lewis's interest in "neutrals" relates to the very important point, exposed by the changing attitudes of Jane Studdock, that individuals are not persons in themselves but only in relation to an incorporating complex of duties, responsibilities, and opportunities. Individuals become persons by being so incorporated. All of these neutrals require such housing or context. Left to themselves, they easily become captives of destructive interests and directions.

Finally, it is important to note the exemplary role Lewis gives to Jane at the end of the novel. When she and Mark are reunited, they are so as a married couple. Jane goes to meet Mark with the imprint of Ransom's kiss and with the possibility of conception on her mind. I do not think that this should be taken to suggest that Lewis believes a young woman should invariably find her fulfillment in marrying and bearing children rather than writing a dissertation on John Donne.[13] This interpretation could be warranted by the way in which Lewis associates the repellent Fairy Hardcastle with participation in social movements for the advancement of women's rights. Lewis did not share the high regard in which Donne was held by his contemporaries such as

T. S. Eliot, but it seems unnecessary to speculate that he interrupts Jane's work for that reason. Rather, he is using this scene, complete with the kiss of Ransom, as suggestive of the *heiros gamos*, of Ransom's mediating role, and of the Virgin's acquiescence to the angel's announcement. It represents for him at the conclusion of the novel the paradigmatic act of allowing oneself to become related to something higher and more valuable. Indeed, the child conceived by the union may well be the new Pendragon. It is a sharp—perhaps so sharp as to verge on caricature—example of what is involved, for Lewis, in the process of receiving identity by letting go.

10

Some Cultural Critiques

The texts treated in this part draw attention to a second constituent of Lewis's project, his critique of modernity. The critique of modernity expressed in these texts is sharply focused, well informed, consistent, and both theoretically and practically defended. The science trilogy leads the reader to the implosion and destruction of N.I.C.E., an institution that is the inevitable outcome of radically mistaken assumptions that Lewis takes to be embedded in late modernity, and which underlie the scientific project epitomized by Weston in the first two novels.[1] As critiques of Western modernity, the novels can be read alongside Lewis's more explicit and extended treatment in *The Abolition of Man*. In all four texts, Lewis's critique is both diagnostic and remedial in intent.

Unlike many of his literary and religious contemporaries, Lewis did not, after the First World War, totally turn against modern Western culture. Nor did he give himself over to nostalgia for a lost Paradise, flight into an imagined utopian future, or retreat into a culturally separated church. The culture misconstrues, distorts, and even perverts, but it is not, as is Weston in *Perelandra*, placed by Lewis under total judgment.

I

Lewis's first and perhaps most basic critique of modernity is that the culture is radically affected by the dissociation of human interests, potentials, and identities from their relations to their wider contexts. Several things should be said about his view of this dissociation.

First, unlike many others, Lewis does not trace the source of this dissociation to René Descartes. While Descartes hovers in the background, Lewis seems reluctant to accord to him the cultural authority necessary to affect modern culture so widely and deeply. Rather than blaming modern philosophical questions that arise from the separation of mind from materiality Lewis points to something more concrete, prevalent, and contemporary, namely, science and its methods. The sciences, particularly the natural sciences, occupy a position of enormous prestige in modern Western culture. Science and its methods are taught in schools, and students develop skills and attitudes in a setting more attuned to the authority and prestige of science than to the influence of modern philosophical rationalism.

It is important to emphasize that Lewis, by identifying science and its methods as the principal source of modernity's erroneous assumptions, does not condemn or dismiss science per se. Scientific methods, especially the reduction of whatever is under observation to its basic and constitutive components and its dissociation from preconceived opinions, create what we take as "facts." Lewis recognizes these methods as legitimate and productive. The problem is that they have broken out of their specialized and artificial locations and, by virtue of science's authority and prestige, have spread throughout the culture as ways of relating to things in general. People treat what they daily encounter in ways similar to how scientists treat what they study in their labs, and they think that their relation to what is outside them is similar to a scientist's position above what is under investigation. A highly specialized, artificial, and tactical approach to things has been absorbed by the culture and is now the way in which people think they stand in relation to what lies around them.

The application of this highly specific and artificial approach is not limited to physical matter but is extended to living creatures and even to other human beings. This allows and even encourages people to behave as if the methods used by physicists to understand the nature and behavior of elementary particles can appropriately be applied to our ordinary relations with our natural and social contexts. The authority and prestige of science warrant the practice of viewing even other people as though they were facts, data, or raw material. These culturally embedded assumptions and habits marginalize other forms of understanding and relationship, making them optional and, relative to the authoritative realm of factual knowledge, trivial. This relegation of all else, including values, to the margins of culture or to personal taste is abetted by the increasing anonymity of the culture, brought on in the nineteenth century by urbanization and industrialization.

Modernity's separation of mind and intellect from their contexts leads people to form their identities mentally. This too is sponsored by the modern philosophical tradition from Descartes and John Locke on, but Lewis also attributes this to the influence of science. The notion that we should be identified primarily as individual minds dissociated from and standing above our contexts has important consequences, Lewis believes. It separates and even alienates us from our contexts, our bodies, other people, and the wider organic and inorganic world. Our bodies become things we use to enhance our identity, but they also threaten our identity by their vulnerability to harm and illness, aging, and death. This alienates us even further from our bodies; we become minds not at home in or at peace with physicality.

This is also true of our relations to other people. We encounter other people not first of all as other minds but as other bodies, and so we tend to think of them as objects that we can use or as obstacles to our intentions and needs. Our contacts with other people thus intensify our sense of identity as individuated, internalized, and isolated. Finally, identifying ourselves primarily as minds separates us from the wider context of the organic and inorganic world in which we find ourselves. This at first seems liberating. Standing apart from and even above our context allows us to make of it what we will. Our world extends before us as potential for our own interests in knowing, using, or owning it in order to bolster and protect personal identity. But this view of things also has a contrary and darker consequence. There is so much that is external to us, such vast expanses of what is other than ourselves and which precedes us and will continue long after we are gone, that we feel fragile and insignificant by comparison.

Lewis personifies these cultural habits of mind in the physicist and cosmologist Weston and in the leaders of the National Institute for Coordinated Experiments. He does this not to condemn science but to narrate how and with what consequences scientific methods and attitudes are absorbed by the culture and applied far beyond their original and legitimate purview. In the first two novels he takes these cultural assumptions and practices and their consequences out of the modern Western context where they have been normalized and naturalized and places them in altogether alien contexts. The effect is to denaturalize or denormalize them. As embodied by Devine and even more by Weston, they appear odd, arbitrary, and even comic. In the final novel he portrays the institutionalization and social-political empowerment of these assumptions and behaviors, the resulting social havoc caused by them, and the inevitable implosion and destruction of the institution.

II

Lewis's second major critique of modernity is its endemic materialism. This he attributes again not so much to philosophical materialism as to scientific methods and criteria. The sciences emphasize what can be observed, and what can be observed is first of all matter and energy. Indeed, the authority of facts and their identification with truth is based on materiality and its observability. The assumption is that objects and events freed from value and interpretation are what we have in common, that facts are the currency that unifies humans and offer the only method of preventing or resolving cultural conflicts.

Given that moderns tend to identify their personhood with mind, Lewis finds the materialism in modernity paradoxical. At one time he pressed the argument that the theory of materialism is inherently incoherent because it depends on the mind that produces it, despite the fact that the theory gives no real place to mind. In the science trilogy Lewis shows that those oriented to materialist accounts of their world are always supplementing those accounts with matters not encompassed by or compatible with materialism, like Weston's interest in Life and spirit, Mark's persistent belief that he has free will, and the various idealist or spiritualist notions that pop up among the members of N.I.C.E.

What bothers Lewis is not so much that materialism is an inadequate basis for an account of what exists and occurs; there have been theoretical materialists around for a very long time. But in modern culture materialism is closely associated with power. In the third section of *The Abolition of Man* he asserts that the scientific project to understand nature is motivated by the desire to have power over nature and to use nature to exert power over other people, a point embedded in *That Hideous Strength*. Associated as they are with power, scientific pursuits are attractive to other forms of power, especially political and economic. This is why Weston appears not alone but in the company of Devine, who has economic and, as we see in the third novel, political ambitions. Science, the quest for financial strength, and the extension of political power, including colonialism and imperialism, are, despite their differences, ready bedfellows. The marginalization and trivialization of values in academic culture turn learning primarily toward the generation and accumulation of power. The supremacy of the sciences, especially the versions of the scientific method extended into academic culture, and the consignment of the humanities to decorative, optional, and even obscurantist roles, makes power and its acquisition the name of the cultural and academic game.

Aggravating this situation is the fact that, for Lewis, power is addictive. One can never have enough of it. Greed, self-enhancement, and obsession with the accumulation of wealth are causally related to the increase of power. Gaining social and political power becomes a primary goal. The desire for power shapes culture, since those who have power can shape the culture to conform to their own interests, needs, and desires.

One more thing that worries Lewis about the pervasive materialism of modern culture: it has a constricting effect on human development and awareness. When learning is primarily geared to the acquisition of power, the skills of mastery and manipulation determine the agenda and define what equips a person to take a place in society deserving of respect. But materialism measures achievement according to something less than what we are, something we can acquire and control. The truth is that, while we may admire and even envy someone who amasses financial, social, or political power, admiration will wane and envy turn to scorn if that power is deployed foolishly or in ways insensitive or hurtful to others. In other words, our admiration for others and our recognition of other persons as worthy of emulation are not finally based on power but on what it is that persons think of as worthy, what they value.

III

Lewis's third major critique of modern culture concerns its orientation toward the future. The future of modernity is determined primarily by technological advances, particularly the development of new and increasingly efficient tools. Lewis traces this shift in orientation, from looking at the past and present to looking to the future, to the beginning of the Victorian era when machines began to play an increasingly important role. New machines consign those they replace to the junkyard or museum. The principle that tools are made irrelevant by those that supersede them is easily extended. New theories and practices supplant old and outmoded ones. Advancement, improvement, progress, and maturation are associated with the future, a movement away from where we are into something new and greater that lies ahead. This assumption is basic to N.I.C.E.

In academic culture this widens the divide between the sciences and the humanities. Science and technology are, arrowlike, pointed toward the future, toward what still can be discovered or designed. The humanities are oriented mostly to the past, to tradition, history, and texts. This division between the sciences and humanities becomes a matter of competition. It is easy for science and technology, in their need for ever greater funding, to disparage whatever identifies itself with the past or is superseded. But the situation is even worse than that. Moral and spiritual interests, the wisdom of tradition, and enduring values, which the humanities need to preserve and reapply, are what, in scientific methods, should be set aside if progress is to continue.

The past is viewed not only as outmoded but as retarding and restricting, as needing to be put aside.

This orientation creates fertile ground for the spreading of the Faust principle, the idea that creativity, inventiveness, and advance in knowledge are related to, if not dependent on, breaking rules and defying tradition and authority. The role of the hero is transferred from the social and political onto scientific and technological locations. The past gains whatever value it may have from its contribution to the pursuit of future accomplishments. If the humanities are to relate to this culture the burden rests on their defenders to make the case, which likely cannot be made, that the past is relevant to the quest for advancement and mastery.

One more thing must be said about this modern Western orientation to the future and the new. Scientifically identified persons and groups place themselves at the forefront of advance. Weston and the leaders of N.I.C.E. see themselves as representing the cutting edge of innovation, discovery, and the future. This allows powerful people to consider themselves more advanced than the culture at large, and it allows all of us to see ourselves as superior to other cultures and as representing the future of humanity. The figure of Weston standing as though in a position of superiority before the Oyarsa of Malacandra, arms akimbo, epitomizes these assumptions, which legitimized colonialism and imperialism because they empowered moderns to stand above other cultures deemed captives of wishful thinking, obscurantism, and custom.

IV

Finally, two lesser but still important critiques contribute to this component of Lewis's project. The first is the elevation of self-consciousness above daily practice and relationships in our understanding of human life and personal identity. This too has philosophical sources, especially in Descartes, but Lewis sees it more as the inevitable consequence of the idea that self-awareness is the basis of personal identity. We are already engaged in a mental act when we raise the question of who we are; we become aware of ourselves and set in motion a process that offers the content of that awareness as an answer to the question of who we are.

Lewis was not an enemy of self-consciousness. Indeed, he assigned important moral roles to it. When we reflect on who we are, we can become aware that we are not who we want or ought to be. By acts of reflection we may become aware that things we have said or done or our attitudes and feelings toward other people are objectionable. Many other important mental acts—invention, comparison, and critique, for example—depend on abstraction and on self-consciousness. But it is also the case that we are more ourselves and reveal more about ourselves when we are un-self-consciously going about our daily lives. Indeed, we are uneasy in the presence of people who are constantly self-conscious. Their words and actions seem insincere and artificial rather than personal and natural.

This is why Lewis so strongly emphasized morality as a set of attitudes and behaviors that are not so much consciously chosen as constitutive of a person's identity. They become second nature, like the practiced movements of an athlete or musician. By the metaphors of heart or chest Lewis affirms those learned but eventually embedded inclinations that affect and even direct our minds and impulses. While he also recognizes will or agency as central to personal identity, the practice of the moral life leads to the gradual naturalization of moral behavior, to the formation of character. It is also why Lewis gives an important place to intuition. Self-consciousness is a form of control; intuition is passive and receives.

This is also why Lewis ties personal identity to relationships. We become persons as a result of a process by which we are open to what stands outside ourselves and receive things that are given to us. We are already always in relationships, especially with other people, and it is by means of those relationships that our personal identities are formed.

Lewis also critiques the assumption that our relations in the world are necessarily competitive and oppositional. Social and political philosophies, economic theories, and assumptions about personal identity often make difference, opposition, and even conflict basic. Continuity, mutuality, a sense of commonality, and the feeling of being at home in society are temporary and epiphenomenal for modernity when compared to the actual, constant, basic conditions of difference and opposition. Hobbes, Hume, and Herbert Spencer come to mind as sponsors of widely accepted ideas that reinforce our feelings of isolation, our fear of others, and our preoccupation with empowerment and survival.

Lewis was not an enemy of competition and its role in establishing differences between people. Competition is productive of excellence, and people differ from one another in ways that elevate some above others. Equality and democratization were for Lewis political principles and not anthropological or ontological ones. But difference, competition, and opposition must be housed within or undergirded by human continuity and interrelatedness.

Lewis wrote the texts treated in this part during the stirrings of war and its subsequent horrors. He lived through both world wars and was well acquainted with conflict. But unlike so many of the most influential of his artistic, intellectual, and religious peers, he did not take war as revealing of our true nature and condition as human beings. Competition, opposition, and even conflict occur, but they are and must be viewed as secondary and conditional.

V

Although Lewis's critiques of modern Western culture are far ranging and radical, we should keep in mind three things. First, Lewis did not reject modernity entirely. Despite the way he depicted scientists, he admired them, especially physicists. He believed that modernity had potential for genuine advancements, and he admired modern cultural achievements and creativity. His critiques were diagnostic and remedial in intention. They did not arise from or warrant pessimism, despair, or escapism.

Second, Lewis believes in the coincidence of opposites and in manifestations of the principle of the *felix culpa*. He thought—and this is very clear in the third of the science novels—that distortions, deprivations, and deceptions create a hunger for rectitude, actuality, and reliability. Human beings and human cultures have the capacity for self-correction, for becoming aware that something is very wrong or that something is missing. And that something can be valued even more highly in its absence.

Finally, Lewis thought that resources for better ways of being in the world were always available. While marginalized or forced underground, they continue, like Logres, to be part of the culture, and they can spring into action when needed with a freshness and relevance that causes cultural change. This is why the ending of the science trilogy is not apocalyptic. While some people, groups, and institutions decay or become distorted beyond repair, their inevitable demise can make room for their replacement by more worthy forms of human identity, relationships, and constructions.

PART THREE

11

The Lion, the Witch and the Wardrobe (1950) and *Prince Caspian* (1951)

Texts treated in this part reveal Lewis engaged in the construction of the human world by applying Christian principles and fleshing out their consequences. Principles and their applications are both necessary and require one another.[1] While applying of principles appears in texts already considered, it now comes into clearer view.

The Narnia Chronicles have received so much attention that it may appear gratuitous to comment on them further. It should be noted, however, that by writing fiction for children Lewis was able in a free and elementary way to construct a world that was both readily accessible and structurally sound. It is said that introductory college courses are difficult to teach because it is necessary to make very basic things accessible without compromising them. That is equally true for writing children's stories, especially ones that can also be read with profit by adults. I have selected four of the Chronicles as examples of Lewis engaged in this task.

I call attention to a principle that is crucial to his understanding of how we should view and relate to the world, to other beings, to other humans, and to God. We are, Lewis believes, relationally situated in our world; having relationships and constructing a world according to Christian principles are closely linked. The application of principles is not done once and for all; it must be done by persons in various locations and in response to differing situations. These texts are performances, illustrative of rather than norms for this task.

Lewis didn't want the Narnia Chronicles to be categorized as allegories because this would make their impact and significance depend on their relation to something outside themselves. No, he wanted the stories and the world available in them to stand on their own. True, there are many similarities to the Christian gospels in these books, but this can be said of many stories. Many modern writers give their narratives suggestive resemblances to the life and person of Jesus Christ. Lewis's tales should be read as applications of principles, some recognizably Christian, to the task of constructing a world. It is because of shared principles that events and actions call to mind various biblical and Christian parallels or antecedents.

I

Lewis wrote *The Lion, the Witch and the Wardrobe* first, and after all seven were completed he seems to have preferred that this one be read first. This could be because this narrative recounts the sacrifice and resurrection of Aslan, which might suggest that Lewis wants to introduce the Christian doctrine of atonement as a principle basic to the Chronicles as a whole. I tend to disagree with this interpretation. It is not clear which of two major Christian doctrines, atonement or creation, is the more important for Lewis. I think that this narrative is the first in the series because Lewis's imagination is more spatial than temporal. If he had designed the Chronicles to be read beginning with *The Magician's Nephew*, temporality would dominate and structure the Narnian world. However, it is neither its origin nor its demise that is primary but Narnia itself as a world constructed in relation to principles.[2]

The spatial character of Lewis's imagination is evident in the role played by houses in the Chronicles, especially in *The Lion, the Witch and the Wardrobe*. The four Pevensie children are evacuated from London because of the German air raids. (Lewis himself took in children from London at the Kilns during the Second World War.) The children are delighted by the countryside and the house into which they have moved. We are given the impression of a large house with endless "unexpected places" (4), levels, nooks, and hiding places, and one that has a cultural and historical reputation, since it is an object of pilgrimage or at least of curiosity for many visitors. Indeed, it is to get away from visitors who are being conducted through the house that the children first enter the wardrobe that leads to Narnia. Most London houses are not like this, which may be a hindrance to the development of the imagination in children who live there. Animals too can capture the imagination of children, and their scarcity is another drawback of growing up in London. The children's interest in animals, even the fur coats in the wardrobe that Lucy likes so much, is carried over into Narnia, where interactions with animals are an important part of their experience.

The interest in houses continues. The dwellings of Tumnus and of the Beavers receive close attention and are described in almost loving detail. Tumnus is revealed as having intellectual interests; on one wall of his house is a shelf full of books. The Beavers, as we might expect of such diligent workers, adorn their house with tools. Children often identify with the living places of animals, their nests and beds. A child knows well the security and centrality provided by its own place of rest and can therefore identify with animals, which are also often strongly attached to their resting places.

The old house that shelters the children is maintained by four women, but it is presided over by the elderly male professor. In *The Magician's Nephew* we learn more of this professor and of the origins of the wardrobe that is so crucial to the narrative. It is good to know that the professor, although elderly, has not lost his sense of other worlds and unexpected possibilities. He comments briefly but pointedly on a number of matters. He shows concern about the nature and quality of the education the children are receiving. He gives instruction in virtue ethics by noting that if Lucy has been known to be truthful in the past it is right to expect that she is truthful in this instance, too. He makes a point on natural philosophy when he discredits absolute time and observes that if other worlds exist they very likely would have different time systems. And toward the end he stresses that it is not possible to attain entrance to Narnia by one's own efforts; entrance is provided, is a gift.

In terms of its physical characteristics, Narnia resembles our own world. The children are surprised by and unprepared for the winter weather, but it is something with which they are well acquainted. And the terrain, although somewhat difficult, is very much like that of a sparsely inhabited earthly countryside. The children have been prepared by their reading for creatures like those they encounter in Narnia, including fauns and talking animals. Continuity between the past and new experiences is created by personal experiences and textual traditions. What is most striking about Narnia is that the natural world and its creatures suffer under the rule of the White Witch. The conditions of her reign are gradually revealed to the children. Narnia is not under attack, like the world that the children have left behind. It is under control, and the nature of that control and what is required to end it are the principal revelations for the children.

Jadis is nonhuman, a descendent of Lilith and the giants, a controller, and the cause of constant winter and Christmas never coming to Narnia. Her intolerance for joy is dramatically demonstrated when she turns into stone the celebrants at the meal the squirrels have sponsored. At her palace she also turns her captives into stone. The objectification of these creatures shows her lack of interest in their internality. Her domination of them obliterates their particularities. Her actions are consistent with the modern disenchantment, objectification, and leveling of the world; she elevates herself above her world and imposes her will on it. Her secret police are reminiscent of the Nazi Gestapo. Their raid on Tumnus's home, after it has been so lovingly described and enjoyed so much by Lucy, certainly shocks the young reader. Narnia is in need of liberation; its inhabitants and natural conditions are suffering under Jadis's rule.

Narnia's need for emancipation is related to the need for Edmund to be redeemed. Some of Edmund's preexisting characteristics make him easy prey for the wiles of Jadis. We learn that he had begun to go wrong during his first term at the "horrid school" (197). Peter says that Edmund always liked being beastly toward anyone smaller than himself, which means that he is enticed by power. Lewis makes this tendency credible in Edmund. As the third child and second boy in the family, he alone lacks a distinctive place. His position in the family also puts him under his older brother, Peter, whom, we are told, he has come to hate (99). In addition, we learn that Edmund is bad tempered and spiteful. While Lewis did not think that mood and temperament are entirely matters of choice, he did think that they could be consciously modulated or curtailed. Edmund jeers at Lucy's report of her early experience in Narnia, displaying the sarcastic and dismissive attitude toward others that, as we have seen, Lewis found so troubling first in his schoolmates and later in academic circles. When Jadis tells Edmund about his prospective elevation, he reacts by not wanting to share power with his siblings. He is distrustful of the Robin, the children's guide in Narnia, and when he hears the name of Aslan for the first time he experiences a sensation of horror. A final indication of Edmund's vulnerability to the blandishments of Jadis is that he uses his imagination to project himself into positions of power and gratification, rather than to anticipate situations that would remedy present wrongs and lacks. He wants, we are told, his own sort of palace, a private cinema, and many cars, and he entertains schemes to keep Peter in his place (98). In other words, Edmund's imagination is what Lewis at times called "unbaptized," an imagination in the service of self, detached from relations, and unmindful of the well-being of others and the surrounding world.

Edmund is depicted as somewhat nasty, a liar and betrayer, but we should keep in mind that later Edmund emerges as very strong. Even here we have glimpses of another side of him. He recognizes early on that Jadis is "bad and cruel" (97), and we read that when she turns the celebrants at the dinner into stone Edmund, for the first time, feels sorry for someone other than himself (128). While the change in Edmund is caused in part by his disappointment at his treatment by Jadis, he never completely loses his attachment to his siblings. So grounds for his reinstatement are already there within Edmund before the decisive act of liberation that is so crucial for the story as a whole.

The children are not so much the agents of Narnia's liberation as they are the occasion for and witnesses of it. Their presence is tacitly secured by the saying of Jesus that unless we become like children we do not have a place in the Kingdom of God. I suspect that Lewis understands this to mean not that we must become dependent but that we need to have imagination, to be able to entertain possibilities, to see the world differently, and to apply principles in various contexts. Children learn morality in a way similar to how they learn to speak a language. Both linguistic and moral principles are learned by experience, imitation, and practice. Our ability to imagine alternative worlds and our ability to be better persons are strengthened by reading narratives such as this one. We see where the lack of principles leads and we see at what cost the consequences are rectified.

Lucy stands out among the children as morally admirable. She is consistently the most susceptible of the four, and she displays appreciation for others and sensitivity to suffering and need. She has an open attitude toward encounters; she is delighted to make Tumnus's acquaintance. This susceptibility is a principle often affirmed by Lewis. He thought it was important for us to be open and receptive toward others, the new, and the possible.[3] A suspicious, resistant, or self-preoccupied attitude seals a person off from the world, and such confinement diminishes one's humanity. Unfortunately, today we live in a society in which, perhaps more than in Lewis's time, many people cannot be trusted. Lucy's willingness to talk with a stranger and even to go to his house for tea must strike the contemporary reader as a kind of susceptibility and trust that should not be encouraged in children, especially little girls. It is a serious problem for readers of Lewis who affirm, as I do, the principle of an open and receptive attitude toward our world and toward other people, that we must these days also be wary and on our guard.

The children are intuitive, which seems for Lewis to be a valuable trait more likely to be found in children than in adults, who can fall into the habit of repressing their intuitions regarding moral principles. We saw that intuition keeps Edmund from falling completely under Jadis's spell; he recognizes deep down that something is wrong with her. Lucy and Peter intuit a moral imperative when they recognize that they must save Tumnus from the castle, especially because he had saved Lucy's life. Above all, their immediate recognition of what Aslan is like upon hearing his name suggests their capacity to intuit the truth. When the Beavers tell them that Aslan is both good and terrible, they understand at once what that means. It is important to note, however, that Aslan affects the children differently. Edmund experiences horror; Peter is made brave and adventurous; Susan has an aesthetic reaction of delicious smells and delightful music; and Lucy is as excited as a child at the start of a holiday. The principle is constant while its applications are partial and various.

Aslan is the primary agent in the story. Why a lion? He is, as Mr. Beaver reminds us, King of the Beasts, but there also is biblical warrant, in the book of Revelation (5:5). Why the name? It is Turkish for lion, and this perhaps counterbalances the negative role played by Turkish delight, which the witch uses to tempt and corrupt Edmund. But I also think that the name suggests aspiration, breath. By breathing on them Aslan revives the creatures that have been turned to stone, an action that has a Gospel warrant in Jesus breathing on his disciples (John 20:22). Aslan is strong and sensitive, wise and dignified, and also able to enjoy a good time.

Lewis vividly depicts the range of emotions that Aslan exhibits. In a moving scene we watch Aslan walk to his death asking Susan and Lucy for their reassuring touch. His sadness is palpable. By making Aslan a lion Lewis avoids any awkwardness in his physical contact with the girls: children are naturally drawn to affectionate contact with animals. It is important that it is the girls, like the women in the Gospels, who are most attentive to the suffering of Aslan, as they are also witnesses to his resurrection. The depiction of Aslan's suffering duplicates the slow pace, detail, and brutality of the passion narratives in the Gospels; Aslan is bound, shaved, mocked, muzzled, and killed.

Lewis does a good job of making insult rather than pain the most shocking aspect of Aslan's trial. The reader is struck by the contrast between the nobility of Aslan and the nastiness and degradation to which he is subjected. I do not think this choice is wholly motivated by Lewis's desire to protect the young reader from descriptions of physical pain. I think it is an attempt to evoke the shock to our moral sense caused by the stark contrast of how things that happen can counter how things should be. Indeed, for Lewis the disconnection between moral principles and what actually occurs may be more painful than physical suffering, as we saw in *The Problem of Pain*.

I have commented in an earlier chapter on Lewis's interest in theories of the atonement, including Origen's ransom to Satan theory, St. Anselm's substitution theory, and moral influence theories such as Abelard's. Lewis does not confine himself to Anselm's theory, which holds a dominant position in Christian theology down to the present day. The Emperor over the Sea, whose position seems parallel to that of God the Father, plays little role in the narrative. Anselm relates the meaning of the passion to the justice of God, but here it serves to cancel Jadis's claim on Edmund. This is closer to Origen's ransom to the devil theory. Moral influence is also present, however; the example of Aslan's willingness to undergo this torment for the sake of Edmund and of Narnia is powerful and morally effective.[4]

The resurrection of Aslan is witnessed by the girls, and they participate in it, removing his muzzle. Aslan's joyful reaction to the renewal of his life forms a sharp contrast to his earlier sadness. We see not anger or resentment in response to his treatment but, rather, the romp, the great roar, and the exuberant ride that he gives the girls. Aslan is exhilarated, and his delight is inspiring.

Two further things should be mentioned here. One is Susan's decision that Edmund should not be told of the sacrifice that Aslan made at least partly on his behalf. It would be too "awful" for him to know. This is an interesting detail. Lewis believes that humans have hope because of the sacrifice of Christ, but he seems not to want Christians to be preoccupied with Christ's suffering and sacrifice. In order to illustrate this point for my students I use the example of the sacrifices at least some of their parents make to enable them to attend college. A student could well respond to that sacrifice by sitting in her room mourning the fact that her parents must forgo vacations, repairs to the house, or a better car because they are using their money to send her to school. But if her parents were to hear that she spends her time bemoaning their sacrifice, they will quickly tell her that she should instead show her gratitude by participating fully in college life, singing in the choir, going to programs on campus, taking valuable courses, making good friends, and the like. Lewis seems to imply something similar about the sacrifice of Aslan and the Christian doctrine of the atonement. The best way to show understanding and gratitude is to live the lives that they have made possible, lives of gratitude, caring, and joy.

The second point is that Aslan tells the girls that the law invoked by the White Witch is temporally bound but that the deeper law, namely grace, is eternal. Another way of saying this is that grace is more spatial, or at least more capacious, than law.[5]

II

Prince Caspian follows closely on its predecessor. It was written next, and the same four children are central to it. It tells of conditions in Narnia in the years when belief in the events recorded in the preceding story has faded. Consequently, this narrative closely resembles the cultural situation of its readers, which is marked by a decreasing confidence that what was recorded in the Gospels many centuries ago actually happened or still is relevant to the present world.

The narrative is constructed of four roughly equal parts. The first three chapters present the transport of the children and their arrival in Narnia. The second part, chapters 4 through 7, gives us the story about Caspian that Trumpkin relates to the children. The third part, which runs from chapter 8 through chapter 11, recounts the children's long and difficult journey to Aslan's How. The final four chapters, 12 through 15, describe the conflict with Miraz and its aftermath. This structure is productive for the reader's engagement, since it provides four smaller narratives within the inclusive one. It may not be too much to say that the narrative as a whole is framed by the figure of a threshold. At the beginning the children are at a threshold or in a position of transition as they await the train to take them back to school. Toward the end, Aslan provides a door, a threshold, for the Telmarines who want to return to the place from which they came—a passage that also enables the children to return to England. Thresholds and points of transition are traditionally uncertain places. As people move from one place or world to another, they are in a doubtful or vulnerable state. It is not merely for decoration that the thresholds of sacred places such as cathedrals are often watched over by images of saints and spiritual beings. The time in which they are living, between the departure and return of Christ, is also transitional for Christians, just as is the time in this narrative during which the children are in Narnia.

The action of the story arises from the division that has arisen in Narnia between those who deny Aslan and do not believe the stories told about him and Old Narnia itself, and those who continue to believe. This distinction, as we shall see, also enters the community of the four children, though to a lesser degree. We should look at some of the unbelieving characters first.

Chief of the deniers is Miraz. He tells his nephew Caspian, "There never were those Kings and Queens. How could there be two Kings at the same time? And there's no such person as Aslan. And there are no such things as lions. And there never was a time when animals could talk." All of that, he insists, belongs to personal and cultural infancy: "Only fit for babies, do you hear? You're getting too old for that sort of stuff" (43). The unbelief of Miraz is particularly important in the story, given his position, but the association he makes between unbelief and maturation is equally common in the culture of the reader. The general waning of belief over which Miraz presides has had far-reaching negative effects. The Telmarines have cut down trees and spoiled the water. None of their animals talk; animals that can talk have fled and are in hiding. In addition, the horizons of their world have shrunk. People fear the sea because it is associated with Aslan, and they have allowed the woods to grow up between them and the sea. Now they fear the woods as well. The reader is led to believe that those conditioned by unbelief are vulnerable to fear and to disregard for the well-being of their world.[6]

Nickabrik, one of the "black" Dwarfs, is not a denier like Miraz but a skeptic. "All said and done," he mutters, "none of us knows the truth about the ancient days in Narnia.... Either Aslan is dead, or he is not on our side. And anyway, he was in Narnia only once that I ever heard of, and he didn't stay long.... He just fades out of the story. How do you explain that, if he really came to life? Isn't it much more likely that he didn't, and that the stories say nothing more about him because there was nothing more to say?" (177, 178, 179). The consequences of Nickabrik's doubt are apparent in his disposition to do harmful things, such as killing Caspian and Doctor Cornelius. He is unable to enjoy himself; when the fauns dance, he does not join them. His lack of belief has two other important consequences. First, it leaves him with confidence only in power, even if that power is associated with evil. He even advocates invoking the aid of the White Witch. Second, for him difference means antagonism. He distrusts humans and is antagonistic to Doctor Cornelius because he is only half Dwarf. When belief evaporates as it seems to have for Nickabrik, power becomes the chief thing left, and the social world contracts to a concern for oneself and one's own interests. After Nickabrik dies, Caspian says that he "had gone sour inside from long suffering and hating" (184).

Trumpkin, although given a mediating role in the narrative, is also resistant to belief. He will not believe things he cannot see. The opposite of this position, that believing is basic to seeing, is important for the narrative. When people are disposed to believe, Lewis suggests, they are able to see things that others do not.

The Pevensie family is also touched by a falling off of belief. Susan shows signs of becoming a doubter. She holds back from exploring the castle when they first arrive in Narnia (22). She has become, we are told, a "wet blanket" (125), and she nags Peter (130). When Lucy claims to have seen Aslan, Susan says that Lucy *thinks* that she has seen him, and when Lucy awakens Susan to tell her of Aslan, Susan tells her she is dreaming. We are told that "Susan was the worst" (157) during the journey, and, when Aslan finally appears, Susan is the last of the four children to see him. Aslan says to her, "You have listened to fears, child" (162). Despite these signs of weakening, Susan has strengths. She is athletic—a prize-winning swimmer and excellent archer. She also has practical wisdom; she advises the group to save some of the sandwiches until later and to keep track of their shoes. We are also told that she is tenderhearted; she is not strongly competitive (112) and "hated killing things" (127).

There are many forms and many degrees of unbelief. It may arise from self-interest, since it allows a person like Miraz to do as he pleases. He has done many evil things to preserve and advance his self-interest, including killing Caspian's father and plotting to kill Caspian as well when his own son is born. Unbelief can also arise from disappointment and discouragement. It can take the form of placing demands on belief that, when not met, give a person a reason, however inadequate, for rejecting belief. Finally, it can take the form of a gradual falling away from participation in the life of faith, as with Susan.

On the other side of the ledger are the figures of faith. The nurse and Doctor Cornelius are crucial to the plot because they keep alive the stories about Aslan and the Narnia of long ago and pass them on to Caspian. Lewis may well have had in mind caregivers and teachers who in our own world and time continue to introduce the stories of faith to children despite the skepticism and unbelief so prevalent within the broader culture. These two quite ordinary people display the courage of genuine heroes.

There are also a considerable number of talking animals who have kept alive the hope for deliverance and continue to await a new day. Trufflehunter the Badger stands out among the faithful and loyal. He continues to believe in the kings and in Aslan, and he will be true to Caspian because Caspian, though a Telmarine, is true to Old Narnia.

The outstanding person of faith is Lucy. She is sensitive to the consequences of evil that can be seen in the trees and in animal life, and she sees the suffering of the world around her. At first she lacks the courage of her faith, but finally she does follow her intuitions. In her nighttime vision she has a feeling that the trees want to talk, and she hears Aslan's voice when her name is called. When Aslan begins to lead, Lucy is willing to follow even when the others are not.

When Lucy sees Aslan she comments on how much bigger he is than when she last saw him. This, she is told, is due to the fact that she is older. Lewis may be suggesting that in our own world some people who find religious belief unacceptable are acting out of understandings they developed as children and which failed to grow in scope and complexity as they themselves matured.

When Lucy meets Aslan, she hugs and kisses him. In addition to the physicality allowed by the child-animal relationship, what is notable is that Lucy's relation to this extraordinary figure is direct and immediate. In the world of Narnia, Aslan is an authoritative, one could say sacred, figure. Usually relations to such a figure are mediated. Among Christians there is a range of thinking on the need for mediation between believers and the object of faith. In Catholicism the church itself and, especially, its sacraments provide the principal means by which people encounter Christ. At the other end of the scale, Baptists emphasize a more unmediated, direct relation between the believer and Christ. Calvin and Reformed Christians, with whom Lewis often seems to be in sympathy, fall somewhere between these two positions. For Calvin Christ is mediated to the believer by the sacraments and, even more, by direct experience of Scripture. Calvin was uneasy with both Roman mediation and the more Anabaptist emphasis on immediacy, fearing the imposition of the institution on the one side and, on the other, a relationship so immediate as to risk becoming a personal fancy. It is difficult to say if Lewis had in mind any position on this range of options concerning immediacy and mediation when he presents this joyful and direct encounter of Lucy with Aslan.[7]

Finally, it is interesting to note that Edmund is the second of the children to see Aslan. Edmund is also the one most inclined to believe Lucy when she reports having seen Aslan, and he repeatedly comes to her defense (134, 156). Edmund, who was the betrayer in the previous story and a cause of Aslan's suffering, is now restored, and he seems to be a person of stronger faith and sounder intuitions than his older siblings. Indeed, because Aslan had breathed on him, we are told, Edmund had about him "a kind of greatness" (191). This is another application in Lewis of the "fortunate fall" principle.

Aslan returns to Narnia on a mission of deliverance. He restores the Ford of Beruna, destroys the schools of Beruna and Beaversdam, liberates farm animals, and heals Caspian's former nurse. Vitality is released, and the world begins to awaken. The past is vindicated. As Cornelius had said to Caspian, "I know that you also, Telmarine though you are, love the Old Things" (220). It is not possible to turn back the Narnian clock, or to restore the Old Narnia. There is something new now, particularly the reign of the Telmarines, and what is needed is to apply the principles that shaped the old world and to configure the new in relation to them. The past and present are not incompatible, but they also are not fully continuous.

A major event in this part of the narrative is the duel between Peter and Miraz. The course of this "most horrible and most magnificent" (207) conflict is detailed, as is the result. But it should be pointed out that the ensuing celebration is also described in detail. Indeed, we are given the full menu (225). Surprisingly, perhaps, Lewis includes not only Bacchus and Silenus in the celebration but also the Maenads, who might be called girls "gone wild." The question is whether this elaborate and exuberant occasion is a victory celebration. I do not think that it is, strictly speaking. For one thing, there are other celebrations that precede the story's final festival. More important, victory celebrations depend on someone's defeat. No, there is something more here. For Lewis, celebration is latent and always wanting to break out. However, the potential for celebration is regularly repressed by forces of self-interest and control, by the killjoy of confinement and reduction. When evils are removed, celebrations break out.

A major tenet of modern social and political theory, usually attributed to Thomas Hobbes, is that societies are always in a state of conflict, both externally and internally. This view is buttressed by social Darwinism, according to which people are pitted in competition against one another in a zero-sum game. Life is primarily a matter of conflict. Peace is occasional and fleeting, and celebration is at the expense of an enemy or a competitor overcome.

Lewis contests this notion. Life is not necessarily in conflict with itself. True, conflicts occur and often are warranted, and they feature as recurring scenes in his fiction. But their role is necessary to remove an evil power and its deadening effects or to alter an unfortunate situation. Conflict is occasional; celebration is always at least potentially there. I would say that a major principle for Lewis, which he applies in this narrative, is that we, our worlds, and our relations to one another carry within them the urge for celebration and that the restraint or repression of celebration is due to evil, is evil's major consequence. This alignment of Christianity with dancing, exuberance, and enjoyment and evil with confinement, repression, and control is among his more provocative and distinctive themes, one that puts him somewhat at odds with his culture generally and with many of his Christian devotees as well.

The final point that seems worth making about this narrative is its emphasis on crucial sites, Lantern Waste, Aslan's How, and Cair Paravel (100). The three seem to correspond to three offices of the Christian life as traditionally framed, the prophetic, the priestly, and the kingly. Lantern Waste suggests the prophetic office because it is a point of access to another world. Toward the end of the story Aslan comments on such places, saying to the Telmarines, "There were many chinks and chasms between worlds in old times, but they have grown rarer" (232). Aslan's How, with its crypts, vaults, carvings, and status as the place of Aslan's sacrifice, suggests the priestly function. And Cair Paravel obviously suggests the kingly office. It is clear that Lewis applied principles not only in structuring the sequence of events but also in structuring the narrative's space, its geography. The most meaningful sites are those that, by virtue of these principles, structure the world and the believer's life.

12

The Four Loves (1960)

For Lewis personal identity—a topic that is prominent in his work—arises from or is established through personal relationships.[1] Relationships are always taking us outside ourselves. In small ways they testify to the fact that in losing ourselves we gain personhood. Identity and character rest on the willingness to respond and relate to what lies outside us, especially other people. This runs contrary to what we generally think of as answering the question of who we are. We think identity is primarily, if not exclusively, an individual possession. But for Lewis individuality, especially in the aggravated form of self-possession, is an illusion. We are always in relations, either negatively in order to possess, diminish, or dominate others or positively in order to appreciate and care for them. Ultimately we are in a relation either to the great devourer or the great caregiver and releaser.

In these essays Lewis discusses three kinds of natural human relationships. These relationships are goods in themselves and structure human interactions. They can easily go awry and often do. Lewis uses a typology and arranges the three types from less to more important. Although these types often overlap, Lewis distinguishes them for the sake of clarity. The value of his treatment is enhanced by the fact that the types of relationships he has chosen have behind them a history of philosophical and literary treatment.[2]

By way of introduction, Lewis reminds us that some Christians think of the life of faith as affirming our natural relationships and others think of the Christian life as needing to diminish the importance of those relationships. Christians in the first group believe that our relations with things and people point beyond ourselves; they lead to, support, or coincide with our relation to God. Those in the second group believe that our relations with things and people compromise, deflect from, and even block our relation to God.[3] Lewis himself inclines toward the positive way. He is aware, however, that natural relationships can go sour and have a deleterious effect on our moral and religious lives.

Lewis takes up a second distinction, what he calls "need-love" and "gift-love." Some theologians see these two as at odds with one another; a highly developed example of that position can be found in Anders Nygren's book on the distinction between charity and desire, *Agape and Eros* (1930–35), which was read by Lewis and many others.[4] Given how important it is for Lewis that persons get out of themselves, we might expect him to agree with this argument, because need seems to arise from self-interest and charity from concern for others. Indeed, Lewis admits that at one time he did think this way. However, here he argues that not all human needs and desires are selfish or detrimental to our relationships with others and with God. In the Bible, people are often addressed in terms of their needs: "Ho, everyone who thirsts" and "Come unto me all you who are weary and heavy laden." However, a relationship is positive only if it is determined not only by one's own needs and desires but by the inherent value of the other. In relationships we begin to see that our own strengths and potentials are awakened and strengthened by our relationships with others.

Lewis seems less concerned about the dangers in our time of the positive than of the negative way, particularly the danger of mistaking a misanthropic attitude for an otherworldly orientation. While other cultures, such as the tradition of courtly love in the medieval period, may have erred by overly stressing love for other people, our culture, due to the emphasis on individuality, competition, and opposition, makes loving others as much as we should difficult. Indeed, "inordinate loves are less contrary to God's will than a self-invited and self-protective lovelessness" (122). Otherworldly fervor can become a substitute for the task here and now of loving other people and of understanding ourselves as related to them in various and complex ways.

Lewis complicates his introductory discussion still more by relating love to pleasure. He distinguishes two kinds of pleasures, need pleasure and appreciation pleasure. Need pleasure is related to need-love and appreciation pleasure is related to gift-love. He seems to elevate appreciation pleasure, the delight taken in something or someone because of the quality of that thing or person, to the highest form of love. It takes on some of the characteristics of what earlier he called "joy." When applied to one's relation to God it takes the form of praise and glorification. So love of God can be need-love, which cries out to God from poverty, gift-love, which is a willingness to serve God, or appreciation-love, which delights in God and wants to give God glory.

I

It is interesting that Lewis begins his study of human relations not with relations to other persons but to things, which he sorts into two categories, nature and nation. I think that he does this for two reasons. First, he wants to see our relations to other people and God as continuous with and contextualized by our relation to other things. How we relate to trees and our government, how we relate to persons, and how we relate to God have something to do with one another. Our relations, although distinguishable, are not separate or compartmentalized. Second, I think that he wants to deal head on with the fact that orientations to nature and to nation are the principal substitutes for religion in modern Western culture. Personal identity is frequently thought to be rooted in the relations people have to nature and to nation, particularly their bodies and their ethnicity, culture, or nationality. It is an interesting sign of this turn to nature and nation as objects of authority and reverence that subjects of paintings shifted, with the rise of modernity, from religious figures and events to natural and political figures, scenes, and events. Art not only records the high regard in which moderns hold these two interests but elevates them to levels that make them worthy of that regard.

Given that nature and nation have become objects of reverence and sources of identity formation, often replacing Christianity, one would expect Lewis to come out swinging against them. But he does not. Indeed, he is himself very much oriented both to Ireland and England and to the English countryside. Our relations to nature and nation are vulnerable to distortion and excess, however, and Lewis's own experience seems to tell him why and how this occurs. We see that in this discussion he sets up a pattern that continues throughout the book: he identifies and describes the positive forms of a relationship and then points out how it can and often does go awry.

An important initial step is Lewis's emphasis, against many nature advocates, that a relation to nature is not something immediate or that we intrinsically possess. Our relations to nature are learned and mediated. This has a postmodern sound, in that nature is seen as a kind of text that we have been taught to read in a certain way. Rather than expressing skepticism concerning our ability to relate to and to know the natural world, however,

Lewis is very likely retrieving a medieval and Reformation idea of nature as a second scripture, as a book in which one can read what God is like. Moreover, learning to read something and encountering what actually is there are not for Lewis necessarily different. His discussion of the sublime, of our sense of something vast, magnificent, and terrifying in nature, offers an example. By asserting that experiences of this kind are universal, as in the opening section of *The Problem of Pain*, Lewis wants to see them as "raw," as immediate and unlearned responses to nature. But we also learn to interpret nature and to cultivate a relationship with it. Our relation to nature can produce a beneficial deference toward something outside ourselves that is vast, unpredictable, and captivating—experiences of awe and wonder. In its highest form this enables us to develop an idea of what it means to be related to God, because nature can be frightening as well as welcoming.

Lewis makes experiences of awe, particularly as evoked by nature, the basis for religion, as seen in his introductory comments to *The Problem of Pain*. However, he does not put forward one's relation to nature as a basis for Christian faith and thought. Christianity affirms regard for nature, but it is neither dependent on nor simply an extension of that regard. This may seem like an easy point to make, but it is somewhat tricky. Lewis tries to occupy the middle ground between two positions that, if nothing else, have the virtue of clarity. On the one hand it could be argued that Christianity clarifies, directs, and perhaps corrects what already is present in human awareness and relations so that one begins with a reliable base in the natural state of things. On the other hand, it can be held that Christianity reveals a whole new ball game that requires a radical reorientation distinct from the natural state of things. Lewis wants to harmonize these contrary options, which continue to define the spectrum of Christian thought today. As in his dual affirmation of discontinuity and continuity in his discussion of the relation of loving other people and things to loving God, he wants to incorporate these contrasting orientations into a complex understanding of our relation to nature.

As he resembles the Romantics in his high regard for nature, Lewis is supported by idealists from Hegel to Arnold in his high regard for the state. Increased national self-consciousness and identity are primary characteristics of modernity. For many people in Lewis's day and in ours, national and religious identities are closely related, and religion and politics are found together in various forms of tension and convergence.

Given this history, Lewis could have been justified in divorcing national from religious identity and even in seeing the two as inimical. He does not, because he sees national identity as an expression of place attachment, of the relations of value we have with places, especially those where we grew up or now live. This attachment carries content. We remember events that happened in these places, and memories give us an understanding of how things have come to be as they are. This enables us to make connections and comparisons between places and their histories.

National identity also relates us to ideals concerning human needs, potentials, and aspirations that extend beyond our individual reach. Like nature, nationality includes us in something larger than ourselves to which we also make a contribution, however small. And national identity speaks to our desire for unity with others, for a sense of common history, a shared enterprise, and shared concerns and goals. Nation thus stands in a complementary relation to nature. It elevates us by relating us to something more than human, while nature reminds us of our continuity with physical reality and nonhuman forms of life.

National and religious identities are easily intertwined in England because Christianity has the status of an established religion. Little contradiction or separation exists between being English and being Christian. In very recent decades this unity has seen attenuation, alterations, and complications. But in England it still is easier than in America to identify national with Christian interests. Lewis is alert to this tendency. Like nature, nation should not be the object of religious devotion, and Christianity should not be subsumed under it. A nation is defined not only by its goals and ideals, which can easily be associated with religious warrants, but also by power and control. Religion must therefore be as much a critic as a support of political life. Moreover, we should be able to recognize when another nation is morally superior to our own and to see why ours falls short. Patriotism should not become, as it is for many people, an alternative religion or primary source of identity. However, Lewis does not, in the name of Christianity, condemn or even question power and national identity per se. The question for him is what power is used for and what form patriotism assumes.

Lewis takes this discussion in an interesting direction when he goes on to identify relationships with organizations as susceptible to excesses similar to those that appear in relations to nation. He could well have pointed to the fanaticism of sports fans both in England and in the United States. Had Lewis addressed this form of excess I think he would have pointed out that sports fans are not only loyal to their teams but intensely hostile to opposing teams. Identities that are significantly derived from nation, institution, or sports are potentially oppositional. This is, for Lewis, a faulty and sometimes destructive way of being related to the world.

Lewis even questions excessive devotion to the church. It seems to me that Catholic readers would have a difficult time understanding how one could be too devoted to the church, because for them it is very closely related to the presence of Christ in the world. It is clear Lewis holds to a Protestant ecclesiology, which subjects the church to critique and the constant need to reform. He says, for example, "If ever the book which I am not going to write is written it must be the full confession by Christendom of Christendom's specific contribution to the sum of human cruelty and treachery" (30). He speaks here of Christendom rather than the church, but the church is implicated. It is provocative that Lewis includes one's relation to the church in his discussion of subhuman loves, of devotion to organizations, and of the fact that our personal identities can be positively affected by many attachments, of which church is only one.

II

In his treatment of positive human relations, Lewis begins with the most general and, in his eyes, the least significant; in the sequence he works toward specificity and importance. *Storge*, or affection, with which he begins, encompasses our relationships with other people that are most natural or even animal-like.

Relationships of this kind develop slowly and largely unconsciously, principally within the home. When extended beyond the home they call for a kind of trust and confidence that one ideally and most fully associates with family. *Storge* depends on a high degree of acceptance.

Lewis wants to establish why this kind of relationship is valuable and contributes to identity. He argues that affections can have a broadening effect, can allow a person to view a wide range of people positively. It is not a relationship that takes social status or attractiveness into account. We can feel affection toward people very different from ourselves. Lewis sees some continuity between this kind of relationship and those we can have with animals. It is not marked by discrimination or self-consciousness, and it carries traces of physicality.

If Lewis were discussing this matter today, I think he would question the common use of *comfortable* or *uncomfortable*, terms suggested by this kind of love, as ethical norms. Moral reservations are verbalized as "not being comfortable" with doing something or other. Our normative use of comfort may suggest the importance of easy and warm relationships in a society as marked as ours is by competition and "snark." But for Lewis comfort is not an ethical norm.

As with all natural human relationships, *storge* can easily go awry. People, especially family members, may think that they have it coming as a kind of right. Affection is neither a right nor a duty. There are people with whom I will never feel at home, and, I am sure, there are people who will always be uncomfortable with me. Also, affectionate relationships can create the notion that we can say or do anything we please. "If I can't say what I think at home (or with you), where (or with whom) can I?" The answer, of course, is nowhere and with nobody. One is never free to disregard the sensitivities and well-being of others. I think Lewis would have made his point more clearly if he had included the role of respect. There cannot be positive relationships of any kind that do not include an element of respect.

With Mrs. Fidget, Lewis suggests the role of affection in parental relationships. Parents are in a difficult position. They are called on to provide for their children, but they must do so in ways that keep their children from staying dependent on them. However, in the desire to nurture independence, parents must avoid making children feel that they are being rejected. It is not easy to provide without creating dependence or to release without rejecting.

Finally, because affection carries with it the benefits of security and ease, it resists significant change. It values the status quo. It is not always easy to forgo the familiar in order to accept development or change. Affection's inertia can result in stagnation and homogeneity because changes and differences are disruptive. Affection, then, cannot get on well by itself. It needs to be augmented. However, despite its potential for abuse, affection ought not to be neglected. It enables us to have a broadly positive attitude toward other people, to be affirmative, supportive, accepting, and encouraging. It is basic to everyday interactions with people, both those very close and those more casually encountered. And, while other kinds of human relationships do not require *storge*, affection can have a place within all of them. Indeed, it seems possible to say that the other forms of love are enriched when some degree of *storge* is part of them.

III

To an extent, Lewis casts friendship as contrary to affection. Affection easily suggests the warmth of physicality, and friendship is the least physical of human relationships. Friendship is the most deliberate and intellectual relationship, and affection is the least. Friendships have content and are formed, Lewis stresses, by mutual interests, especially cultural and intellectual ones. Friendship is important for Lewis. For one thing, it was highly regarded in the ancient world because it was dissociated from bodily factors. Friendships were also important to him personally. It is interesting to note that Lewis had close friends who disagreed with him about significant things. My own friendships tend to be formed on the basis of agreement not only because I and my friends have certain interests in common but also because we tend to agree in our opinions. Perhaps our friendships these days tend to contain more of what Lewis calls affection, and we look to friends for the comfort and reassurance that agreement on important matters can furnish.

Lewis not only wants to distinguish friendship from affection, he also wants to distinguish it from erotic relationships. This is why he is uneasy with the possibility of friendships between men and women, which carry the potential for physical desire. He also wants to avoid the idea of latent physical attraction in friendships between people of the same gender. This is typical of Lewis. He resists the modernist tendency to relate human behaviors causally to the physical and sexual. Friendships, strictly speaking, are not to be complicated by physicality.

Because friendships are formed in relation to shared interests, Lewis points to the workplace as a likely locus of friendships. He may have in mind the kinds of relationships that can be formed in the Senior Common Rooms of Oxford and Cambridge colleges—exclusively male environments in his time, we should note. In our own time and culture this may seem less possible not only because of the increased gender mixing in most places of employment but also because the workplace has become, has even been designed to be, competitive. I would have thought that Lewis, with his strong interest in bureaucracy, would qualify his point here with his awareness that modern workplaces foment nontrusting, nonsharing, and self-serving relationships. The increased effects of bureaucratic paradigms on university life, for example, threaten to infuse the relations of faculty with such ingredients.[5]

Friendships go awry because they are, by nature, exclusive. A shared interest inevitably forms a condition for inclusion. Pleasure can be derived from the dynamics of inclusion and exclusion; such pleasure can become a sustaining element for a group of friends. This easily gives rise to pride, a feeling of superiority that becomes part of the spirit of the group. It can easily occur that the group becomes closed to, if not hostile toward, points of view and interests at variance with its own. Finally, groups divert attention away from the needs and potentials of their wider context, and loyalty to the group excludes other important loyalties. This can even happen in churches, where a group formed around some common interest may become more important for its members than the well-being of the church as a whole. And it is very much a part of university life that faculty members form cliques, often political in nature, that are more important to their members than relationships with other colleagues, even in their own disciplines, and more important than their relation to the university as a whole. In an environment marked by individuality and competition, it seems inevitable that associations are formed less because of shared interests than for the sake of the group as such and as a power center to advance particular interests.

Friendship has its difficulties in our culture, and friendships and the groups they foster can easily go awry. Nevertheless, friendship contributes to our identity by offering us relationships that are particular and have content because of shared interests and even enthusiasms for something outside ourselves. It shows our desire and capacity to be drawn into association because of something highly valued that has an external standing.

IV

Eros, limited for Lewis to love between a man and a woman, combines and outstrips characteristics of both affection and friendship. It takes up some of the physicality of affection, its nonintentional nature, and the conscious and meaningful qualities of friendship. But eros is something more because it turns the attention of those who experience it toward one another.

Eros is often misunderstood as limited to the physical aspects of the love relation. Lewis calls the purely physical attraction "Venus." While it always is a part of eros, it is not the most important part. Eros is the interest that a person takes in the entirety of the other. Venus, by contrast, has behind it a desire to possess the other or to gratify oneself. In a relationship of eros, we also value and have regard for the interests and needs of the other.

I think Lewis could have sharpened his points on the question of the relation of eros to romantic love. The feeling of being in love can be very intense and delightful, and the ability to experience this feeling can become more important than the person by whom it is aroused. Perhaps he could have suggested that the pleasure of being in love, like the pleasure of "Venus," can itself become the object of desire, can become addictive. It could be argued that in our culture popular romances play a role analogous to that of pornography. The two feed the addictions of different audiences. These two distortions of eros are damaging, and when ardor of either sort begins to cool the need to rekindle desire for the carnal or the romantic can prompt a search for a new object of physical or romantic delights.

Lewis makes the point that in our culture, carnal desire is not only overemphasized but taken too solemnly. In contemporary America we see a curious combination of carnal freedom and judgmental responses to the sexual behaviors of other people. The sixties and early seventies witnessed what some students of American culture call a third disestablishment: the separation of sexual behavior from religiously sponsored directives. However, while many people conduct their sexual lives without regard for former restraints and inhibitions, American culture does not have the degree of tolerance for, or even lack of interest in, this area of behavior seen in many European cultures. Sexual behaviors in our culture are treated as casual or personal but also as fascinating and socially consequential.

For Lewis, the primary value of erotic love relationships derives from the high regard in which lovers hold one another and the experience of being brought out of themselves by the emotion and power of the relationship. It is not surprising that this experience can be used as an analogy for the intensity of religious experience. Mystics often employ erotic language to evoke their relationship with the divine. This does not mean, in Lewis's view, that religious experiences are really erotic feelings that have been suppressed or misidentified. Rather, our capacity for consuming relationships is taken up into religious feeling. Eros thus plays an important role in the formation of human identity. For Plato its intensity is evidence of the possibility of the close association between two souls. For vitalists in Lewis's own day, like D. H. Lawrence and G. B. Shaw, it suggests a life force that is fundamental and creative in the world.

However, because eros is extravagant, it can cloud judgment and take over a person's life. In addition, because it is so highly valued in the culture, we may expect too much from this kind of love. Lewis points out that in much nineteenth-century fiction meeting the right person, falling in love, and marrying take on the role of eschatological fulfillment, representing the highest level that human life can attain.[6] Such high expectations are treacherous. The fickleness of love is well known. Something more is required if a love relationship is to have permanence. That something more is the will to love, the decision to love. It is for good reason that in Christian wedding ceremonies the partners are not asked whether they love one another but whether they *will* love one another. That is, they are asked whether they will act in love toward each other. Love is an intention and deliberate act as much as, or even more than, a feeling or state of being. The basis of marriage is promise rather than emotion.

V

Charity is set apart from the first three kinds of love. This is because it is the only kind of love that can be associated with God. When we say that God is love it is this kind of love that is meant. It also stands in a class by itself because the other three kinds of love, if they are not conditioned by charity, will almost inevitably go awry. Charity is orientation to the well-being of the other, and this quality keeps human relationships from being distorted by selfish designs.

It is not clear whether Lewis thinks of charity as having a separate status or as requiring any or all of the other three. This touches on a recurring question, namely, whether Lewis thinks that Christian principles clarify, correct, and fulfill things inherent to human life and the creation more generally or that Christian principles have an existence of their own and take a person out of the shared and natural. Does Lewis think that the other three loves and our love of nature and nation will inevitably go wrong if we do not acknowledge the special, even divine, status of charity in explicitly Christian terms? I think he believes that when the lesser loves do not go awry it is because charity is present, even if not recognized for what it is. When charity and its primacy are recognized, we can achieve a fuller realization of what our human relationships should be like, why they are important, and how they allow us to become persons.

How it is possible to have a love of this kind for God? Charity suggests care for the well-being of others, and God, one would think, is not in need of our care. But two ingredients in charity do apply to the relation we can have with God. One is the delight we take in, the appreciation we can have for, another person. Charity in relation to God does not serve the self. We have a relationship with God not finally because we get something out of it, such as a heavenly reward, but because God creates in us a desire that expresses itself in doxology or praise.[7]

Love of this kind is a gift. There is, in our culture, a good bit of skepticism about gift giving. It is commonly thought that gifts are really forms of transaction; you give me a gift, and I give you one in return. To put it more crassly, I give a gift because I feel obliged to or because I want to get something in return. In such a context, it is difficult to understand what, if anything, it means to say that love is a gift. Is it possible to think of love as expressed in attitudes and acts that are not self-serving?

Charity designates qualities and acts in our relationships that are not self-serving. But a charitable relation to others gives us something important in return. Acts and attitudes of charity give us ourselves. Charity also does not mean that our relationships require total self-denial. We always have a sense of who we are and, more important, a sense of what it is good for us to be. So there is a degree of self-awareness that need not be destructive of our concern for others. Indeed, it is ourselves that we give to others, in our attention, regard, and concern for them. But in the process of caring we also become persons, because the most important aspect of caring is regard for the other, of losing our self-awareness in the relationship. Gift, then, designates that quality in our relations to others that is not self-concerned. Charity means being taken up by or into something else, an event that requires genuine interest and a certain kind of vulnerability that may be rebuffed or misunderstood. Lewis emphasizes the risk of vulnerability in relationships when he says, "Love anything, and your heart will certainly be wrung and possibly be broken" (121). Charity carries the risk of pain; love of this kind is as difficult as it is essential.

It is important to add that charity is an example of what I am calling Lewis's applied principles. Charity as a principle is the primal and divine love that human loves require if they are not to go awry. The application of this principle in our relations to the world is analogous to the Incarnation; by means of it natural loves can be taken up into the inexorable, primary, and immutable principle that Lewis calls "the Divine energy" (121). A corollary of this point is that the Divine energy or principle of charity evokes, even needs, human or natural loves and relationships in order to be actualized.

13

The Magician's Nephew (1955) and *The Last Battle* (1956)

Like the first two Narnia Chronicles, the last two form a set. They are concerned with the origin and the end of Narnia and the roles played therein by nature and morality. Lewis does not see good and evil as simply cultural phenomena. For him, morality and the natural world are distinct but related. Although origins and endings certainly are important and even determinative in relation to the events of the other narratives in the series, I think that for Lewis they are secondary. By leaving these events for last, Lewis downplays the role of chronology in the Narnia narratives. The narrative sequence as written leads us to read not from the beginning of Narnia to its end but from the center to the edges.

I

In *The Magician's Nephew,* Lewis creates a sharp contrast between Narnia and London. The city is pejoratively described. Digory, who ordinarily lives in the country, thinks London is a "beastly Hole." This view of the city is later echoed by the cabbie, who is also originally from the countryside and is not at home in London. Strawberry, his horse, thinks of the city as a "hard, cruel country," because it has far more stones than grass. Charn, the vast, dead city that Digory and Polly discover, seems to be the ultimate depiction of London. This negative view of urban life is a constant in Lewis. It raises the question of whether, given that the majority of the world's population now lives in cities, this view is becoming increasingly irrelevant.[1]

Added to the unhappy condition of the world in which the narrative begins is the fact that Digory's mother is terminally ill and his father, for unexplained reasons, is away in India. Digory and his mother are living with his uncle and aunt, whose relationship is fraught with difficulties. And as if that weren't enough, the weather is inhospitable. It is a cold, wet summer, and Digory and Polly are driven by the weather to indoor explorations.

The site of their explorations is an extensive attic that joins several houses below it. It is not perverse to see, as Michael Ward does, an erotic undercurrent in these youthful explorations in an isolated place. Ward, who has identified each of the Narnia Chronicles as related to one or another of the seven planets, sees Venus and erotic love as thematically unifying elements in this novel.[2] The attic seems to attract the children for additional reasons. The neatness and symmetry of the rafters allow the children to calculate their position, and they suggest the rudimentary geometry of the carpenter. The measurable order is a subtle nod to the prestige enjoyed by reason and mathematics in modernity. By joining several houses, the attic occupies a role somewhat similar to that later played by the wood between the worlds; both offer positions of elevation from which descent into specific locations is possible. Finally, the attic is a retreat and a locus of personal identity. Polly keeps her cashbox there, which holds personal treasures, a story she has written, and some food.

The children move from the attic into the seductive space of Uncle Andrew's secret room. Uncle Andrew welcomes the children because he may be able to use them. Like Jadis, he is interested in things and people only to the extent that they may be of use to him. This attitude is reflected in his use of animals for cruel experiments, as it is in Jadis's statement later in the book that she was justified in causing the deaths of so many because they were her people: "What else were they there for but to do my will" (71)?

We are given further evidence of Uncle Andrew's questionable character. He did not keep his promise to his godmother; he thinks that keeping promises does not apply to him but only to children, women, and other people he thinks of as ordinary. He is also, we learn, a closet drinker. This prepares the way for his comical treatment by the animals of Narnia, who name him "Brandy" because he calls for it. We are told that he is vain. His desire for exploration is motivated by his pride and hunger for recognition. As the story progresses it becomes clear that Uncle Andrew knows little about other worlds. Like most magicians, according to Lewis, he is dealing with matters about which he has little knowledge. Magic and his use of it confine him. This becomes clear during the creation scene, when he first refuses to hear the singing of Aslan and finally is unable to hear it. While the children are introduced to other and larger worlds, Uncle Andrew's world becomes smaller and more confining. His condition is unmistakable when he thinks of Narnia in terms of its commercial possibilities and wants to shoot Aslan.

It is not surprising that Uncle Andrew finds Jadis enormously attractive. She focuses and epitomizes his desires. Like him, she treats others, including Uncle Andrew himself, as her slaves. She is interested in other worlds because she wants to reign in them. Also, like Uncle Andrew, she thinks that moral obligations and directives do not apply to her because she stands above other people. Her major accomplishment is destruction. She brings down Charn by uttering the Deplorable Word, although she blames her sister for making her do it. The narcissism of this act—taking the world down with her—is clear. Her antagonism to Aslan is obvious, as she throws a piece of lamppost at him. In the garden she plays the role of temptress to Digory, urging him to eat the fruit and suggesting that by so doing he will advance himself, help his mother, and avoid being Aslan's slave. In saying that helping his mother is more important than serving Aslan, Jadis inserts a degree of truth in her deception. Here she plays a role similar to that of Weston in *Perelandra* and, of course, Screwtape.

If Lewis had made Digory and Polly unqualified opposites to these figures of evil the narrative would be simpler but less engaging. While Digory ends up well, he is vulnerable to temptation and impulse, as is evident when he is "enchanted" by the writing under the bell in Charn. It is important to notice the roles played by vulnerability and enchantment for Lewis. The disposition toward being taken in or enchanted is important in his eyes, since we can live in a larger world only by openness to new persons and new places. It is not easy to discern in Lewis how to distinguish between the good and the undesirable forms of such susceptibility. In Digory, we can trace the undesirable form to his self-concern. For example, in order to protect himself from disappointment, he tends not to hope for much (100). And when called on to explain his role in allowing evil to come into Narnia, his first impulse is to blame his uncle.

However, Digory also has, from the outset, good qualities. He allows his uncle to send him into another world so that he can rescue Polly. He undertakes the trial of the journey to the garden, and he resists the temptations of Jadis. Finally, he confesses to Aslan his role in the entrance of evil into Narnia.

Polly has a stronger moral character. She is adventurous but when necessary also cautious, as the events in Charn show. In the creation scene she is observant of the relation between kinds of singing and the emergence of the particular creatures. And she has courage, a virtue that Lewis particularly admired.

But of all the characters, the cabbie is the most morally admirable. He is kind and brave, and when things get difficult he leads the others in singing a hymn. When the occasion to do so arises, he is reluctant to reign. This rejection of power and leadership is warranted by tradition and is in vivid contrast to the attitude toward power epitomized by Uncle Andrew and Jadis. It should be noted that, with the cabbie, Lewis deposits virtues in a person of humble social position, perhaps suggesting that those with less enfranchisement in a questionable culture are less affected by its negative characteristics and influences.[3] Performing a useful service, having a good marriage, and maintaining a positive attitude toward his world and an appreciative relation with his horse are signs of his moral strength.

The creation of Narnia is the principal event of the story. A number of things should be said about how it is narrated. The first thing to note is the role of music and singing. This puts the reader in mind less of the two creation narratives in Genesis than of the brief description of creation in Job 38, in which the stars of the morning sing with joy. Many cosmogonic myths posit conflict as basic to the creative act, and traces of conflict may be present in the first chapter of Genesis. The waters, dark and without form, over which the spirit of God hovers, suggest an element of adversity and difference. But in Job the waters are not dark, alien, and menacing but rather something to which God is already related. He affirms them and clothes them as a parent does a newborn infant. I think Lewis's avoidance of dissonance in his creation story is consequential. He rejects the notion that difference and opposition are basic to creativity. Instead, positive relations are basic to and productive of order and of life.

An important aspect of Lewis's thought becomes clearer here: his understanding of Christianity as offering principles that in various circumstances must be applied or fleshed out. The Christian doctrine of creation offers a good example of this. The two creation stories in Genesis, despite attempts in the history of interpretation to combine them, are quite distinct from one another, and the brief account in Job 38 is yet another. Fiction allows Lewis maximum latitude to exercise what I think is a constant in his project, namely, showing principles, both moral and doctrinal, as needing to be applied in ways relevant to various, complex, and changing situations. Both imagination and intellect are involved in such acts of application.[4]

The narrative makes an implicit connection between divine and human creativity. The wood between the worlds and the London attic are alike; they suggest a position of elevation and possibility above decisions, actions, and embodiments. Humans are able to stand above and consider possible applications, although they are, it would seem, more fully themselves in acting or actualizing than in contemplating possibilities and alternatives.

Lewis was ambivalent toward consciousness. Since John Locke it has been designated as the site of personal identity. In the philosophical tradition, we are generally taken to be most ourselves when we are conscious of ourselves, when we think about who we are, have been, and are becoming. Lewis, on the other hand, seems to find our identity primarily in our daily lives, especially when we act according to those virtues that have become, by repetition, a kind of second nature to us. However, he did not want to disparage consciousness as alienated from the obligations and resources of ordinary interactions. Jadis is uncomfortable and depleted in the wood between the worlds. This seems related to Lewis's point in *The Screwtape Letters* that it is advantageous to the designs of hell that people be unconscious of what they are doing when they are going to do something evil. I think his ambivalence toward consciousness and abstraction is captured very well in the images of the attic and the wood between the worlds.

It should be noted that by Aslan's creation of talking animals Lewis suggests substantial continuity between humans and animals. Distinctions between kinds of creatures and distinctions of abilities within kinds are clearly a part of the unified whole of creation. The unequal levels of ability create responsibility to care for and to enhance those who are less able and to avoid, by maturation and right relationships, regressing to a lower level.

The final question to ask concerning this story is this: which is for Lewis the more important principle, creation or atonement? This may seem like an unimportant matter, but it is not. The answer to this question affects the shape of one's theology, and conflict over this question has troubled the Christian tradition repeatedly, as in the Pelagian/Augustinian, Arminian/Calvinist, and Jansenist/Jesuit controversies.

At stake is what kind of problem exists in the human world to which the atonement is a response. How ruinous to the human world are the effects of sin? If we emphasize the creation, we will tend to think that the human world, while gravely affected by sin, retains a potential that divine grace can employ. If we emphasize the atonement, any such potential in the world will be reduced or denied. When atonement is dominant, divine grace has to make a completely new beginning. People often seem to think of the first of these options as characteristic of liberal theologies and the second as associated with conservative ones, but this is an oversimplification.

Lewis stakes out a position between these options, as he tends to do when faced with sharply defined alternatives. He takes a position that, in the Pelagian/Augustinian version of the conflict, is somewhat but not fully Pelagian, as reflected in his stress on free will, on the general accessibility of human virtues, and on the importance of human culture for creating attitudes conducive to the Christian message. Lewis thinks the effects of sin on us, on Western culture, and on the natural world are grievous but not ruinous. Lewis has a stout doctrine of creation, and he believes there is goodness in the world around him. He affirms and actualizes this doctrine by giving music and harmony central and causal roles in his own creation narrative.[5] However, he believes that modernity poses an unprecedented threat to the health of our cultural, and therefore also our natural, environment. Aslan's warning to Polly about the potential for evil in the Deplorable Word makes this clear.

II

There are so many Christian versions of the ending of all things (which theologians call eschatology) that Lewis can have free rein in his imaginative application of this Christian principle. In *The Last Battle* Lewis uses this freedom to avoid, it seems to me, clear support for any one choice from the repertoire of theological variations. I do not think that we should infer a firm eschatology from this narrative, although I do think Lewis's application of the Christian principle of the end here is expressive of his views. We should keep in mind that Lewis considered the ultimate questions of origins and conclusions to be less important than questions raised by the here and now.

As we saw with Charn, for Lewis the ending of a world is both the result of an inevitable process and an event hastened by evil and its ripening. In this narrative the evil in question is Shift's usurpation of Aslan's position. This is a clear reference to the brief apocalypse in Mark 13, where Jesus warns that at the end there will be many who claim his identity. It also carries forward Lewis's point that there is a grain of truth in the most pernicious lies, because it is true that Christians are directed to "put on" Christ. Shift exploits another basic truth when he defends his destructive policies by insisting that Aslan is not tame. However, while these lies hasten the end, they do not initiate it. Narnia has for some time been in a state of decline; Shift's program serves to worsen and hasten this decline.

Shift's self-serving project envisions the extension of "cities, schools and offices"—another barb directed at some of the manifestations of modernity and urbanization that Lewis questioned. Shift's program also includes the enslavement of people, a perversion of yet another valid principle, namely, that we should not pursue autonomy but should be servants. The multiplying lies and growing perfidy coincide with the decline of the natural world, showing the relation between moral and natural processes and culminating in the reversal of Creation, the fall of heavenly bodies, darkness, and the return of the waters.

The responses of the characters to the ripening of evil and natural degeneration and dismemberment are as important to the story as the events that inspire them. The Dwarfs suffer from what could be called belief fatigue. They have been fooled before and cannot muster belief in Aslan, the stories about him, or the existence of other worlds. Nevertheless they are, however minimally, included in the world that continues. Lewis suggests that in the end some, without intending to be, will be included, although not all are included to the same degree. The Dwarfs may reflect people known to Lewis who, in the confusion of many beliefs and the dashing of many hopes, have lost the capacity to believe and to hope. The Dwarfs are distinguished from Ginger, who also lacks belief but is not included. Ginger's denials are self-serving, motivated by the desire to gain power.

The response of Emeth, whose name is the Hebrew word for truth, has been controversial.[6] His place on the spectrum of belief and unbelief is provocatively crafted by Lewis. Although he is a follower of the god Tash, who turns out to be a demon, Emeth is nonetheless included. The reason for this is that Emeth directed his life toward a good outside himself that he believed to be worthy of his service. His desire is to do right, even though the object of his devotion proves unworthy. As we have seen, Lewis does not want to pit Christianity against other religions: other religions carry truth. Religious views of life and the world are more satisfactory than their principal modern competitor, materialism. Because his good intentions and actions were unknowingly directed to Aslan, Emeth is not condemned. As Aslan puts it, "all the service thou hast done to Tash I count as service done to me" and "no service which is vile can be done to me, and none which is not vile can be done to him [Tash]" (205). Lewis is alluding to the notion of the "anonymous Christian," the idea that there are people who, without benefit of the Christian faith, live lives of faithful service in the context of their own religions. Until the end religions must be viewed favorably; they direct their believers outward to a good that they take to be higher and more important than themselves. What counts as truth in a religion is that which directs believers' desires and intentions toward what lies above and beyond them and inspires genuine concern for the well-being of others. Lewis seems to characterize religions by their ability to direct adherents to a way of being in the world that is fully actualized in Christianity. Implicit in this construction is that, as there is truth and goodness in other religions, not all that we find in the existing forms of Christianity is truthful and good. Finally, it implies that we should not expect or try to enact in and to our present situation the eschatological principle that in the end true and false and divine and demonic are clearly distinguished and unrelated.

A concluding element in the narrative is Lewis's deployment of an idealist view of worlds as manifestations of possibilities or principles. This is consistent with the distinction, pervasive in his work, between principles and their actualizations. It also gives him the freedom to combine two biblical principles, the end as destruction and the end as replacement by a new heaven and a new earth. The inevitable passing of the present order, dragged down by the weight of its age and precipitated by the effects of moral evil, coincides with the rise of a newly minted world, the actualization of a possibility more real and lasting than the one it replaces. This intriguing conceptualization, however, raises questions about the Creation itself, particularly the traditional principle of Creation as ex nihilo, because Lewis's version seems to show the new Creation as one of a series.

Amid all the loss and destruction, the ending is also a summation. While there is a sorting, it is carried out rather calmly, and there is less stress on judgment and ruination than on replacement and inclusion. This may suggest something of Lewis's eschatology, but it also fits with the role of the ending as the culmination not only of this narrative but of all seven. Lewis effectively incorporates much of what appeared in the earlier chronicles at the end of this one. The process of degeneration and destruction defers to the dominant process of fulfillment. The ending of the old coincides with a new Narnia, and all Narnias are versions of the real thing. The real continues.

The unicorn sums up the nature of the real Narnia when he says that this feels like home as nothing else ever has (213). The sense of reception, what in the tradition is called "assumption," is vividly evoked (222). Reepicheep, Tirian's father, Tumnus, and many others are there to receive the new arrivals. As one would expect, given Lewis's critiques of urban life, we find a garden rather than a city (as in Revelation) as the ultimate location. There King Frank and Queen Helen reprise the roles of Adam and Eve. The garden is a microcosm that implies the whole. Interestingly, the new Narnia is not static but vital. It has temporality. The story, although completed, also continues.

Lewis reveals a good bit here about the relation between principles and their applications and between doctrine and imagination. It could be argued that his depiction should strive for closer resemblance to biblical accounts of the end. But that would be difficult because, even more than the various accounts of the Creation, the biblical references to the end are not only various but also sketchy and to some degree in tension with one another. I think Lewis sees biblical uncertainty or complexity about the form of the end as a further warrant for the distinction between doctrines or principles, which should not be slighted, and their necessary applications or embodiments. The principles associated with ending include the primacy of Aslan, the ruinous effects of evil, the ultimate separation between good and evil, and the distinction at the end between those who are included and those who are not. While retaining principles that he takes as axiomatic, Lewis lets his imagination play with the repertoire made available to him in biblical, creedal, and theological sources. His playfulness in dealing with grave matters is not irresponsible. Imagination and principles or doctrines are not opposed to the world but rather reconstruct or complete it. Nor are applications final or complete.[7] Imagination provides the sense of a whole in which particular principles are applied to various and changing circumstances. Imagination, including what we think about the ending of things, is not arbitrary. All of us have some sense of where we are relative to it and where we ought to be headed. We relate to people and events here and now accordingly. Recalling his application of the principle of creation to the origins of Narnia, Lewis's depiction of Narnia's ending, despite the presence of evil and destruction, emphasizes the positive. The harmonies of the creation turn dissonant, but they are replaced by a new wholeness. The repeated observation that everything gets bigger the further up and the further in one goes, and that the inside is larger than the outside, suggests that in the re-creation an advance and not simply a replacement is made.[8]

It would be nice to end, as Lewis does, on this positive note, but we must look at two problems that remain. The less serious of them concerns Susan. Peter reports that Susan "is no longer a friend of Narnia," and Eustace adds that she has come to think of Narnia as a game they used to play as children. Jill is more specific: "She's interested in nothing nowadays except nylons and lipstick and invitations. She always was a jolly sight too keen on being grown-up" (169). This moment in the narrative has been seized on as epitomizing Lewis's disparaging attitude toward what should be viewed as normal and healthy, namely, the maturation of female sexuality. It has been taken as Lewis's judgment on the socialization of girls into young adulthood and therefore hostile to freedom for women.

Polly's commentary somewhat clarifies Lewis's intention. Polly says that it is not a matter simply of Susan's growing up. Rather, she has wasted "all her school time wanting to be the age she is now, and she'll waste all the rest of her life trying to stay that age" (169). Lewis often turns to the hazards of late adolescence. While it should be a transition from innocence or a first naiveté to a growing wisdom and a second naiveté, adolescence can become a trap, a turning point at which increased self-awareness becomes self-preoccupation, exchanging development for arrestment. In addition, nylons and lipstick, commodities that at the time were either new or newly displayed publicly, portend the commercialization of femininity and the absorption of sexuality by self-awareness and the desire to attract attention. All this to one side, however, it is undeniable that the inclusion of this moment in the general sorting out at the end carries connotations that compromise whatever valid points Lewis may have wanted to make by including it.

The second problem, one that appears from time to time in Lewis's work, is more serious. We find it here in his creation of the agents of destruction, the Calamorenes. In contrast to the "white" Narnians, they are dark-skinned, and they come from that great cruel country across the desert and to the south. They use scimitars, wear turbans, and smell of garlic and onions. And during the battle there seems to be no end to their number. This bundle of characteristics reproduces the prejudice in English culture toward peoples to the south, and the Arab, Persian, and Turkish elements pinpoint those being demonized. There is no squirming out of this awkward, indeed, objectionable aspect of the narrative, especially in a narrative written for children! It will not do to say that this sort of thing is part of English culture dating back at least to the sixteenth century. Lewis should have had the insight to recognize caricature and prejudice and the harm it can do, especially after the Second World War and the role played in it by genocidal hatred.

It should also be noted that this instance of racial caricature and "othering" is not unique in the Lewis corpus. In *The Pilgrim's Regress*, for example, John is tempted to abandon his quest by what Lewis calls the Brown girls, who are naked and personify carnality. To make matters perfectly clear, we are told: "And John rose and caught her, all in a haste, and committed fornication with her in the wood" (17).

One can cite other instances of bias. In several places, as in *That Hideous Strength* and *The Four Loves*, Lewis takes gratuitous swipes at homosexual people, despite withholding judgment on the homosexual behaviors of boys in the schools he attended. Although Lewis gives more prominent positions to women and girls in his narratives than would be warranted by the state of women in his society at the time of writing, he views them somewhat positively because of their marginal positions in the general society that he questions. The problem is that his relational view of personal identity formation is not matched by a critical assessment of the way in which, especially for homosexual and female persons, identities are constructed and imposed by society. It cannot simply be affirmed, consequently, that a woman is to find her identity at least in part by her relation to a man without taking into consideration the fact that men hold privileged positions in the society and impose on women expectations as to what they should be like and how they should behave.

It is possible to view the whole of Lewis's work in the light of his sexual politics. Indeed, it is legitimate to stress the importance of political and social advantage and the way in which it attracts principles that warrant and sustain it. It could be argued that Lewis's fiction, philosophy, and theology are really efforts of this kind, legitimations of a world in which he, as a white, heterosexual male, holds a privileged position. In fact, despite his many, often radical, critiques of the culture, his quite positive view of the world could be seen as implying that, politically and socially, things should basically stay the way they are.

Another response would be to say that Lewis cannot be expected wholly to extricate himself from his culture. He generally advances girls and women in his fiction and seems largely tolerant of diversity in beliefs and identities. That he is less sensitive than we are to some matters is due to cultural differences and should be overlooked. He takes up and accomplishes so many more important things that making much of these lapses is to make central what is incidental.

I endorse neither of these positions. There is much in Lewis that raises questions. It is not possible, it seems to me, to transport the house he constructed to these shores and times and to move into it. In addition to the things already mentioned, there is his disdain for cities. Now that a majority of the world's populations live in urban settings, it is necessary today to take cities and urban life more fully and positively into account.

Despite these failings, however, as I emphasize in my conclusion, there is much in Lewis that should be taken seriously. For every devotee of Lewis, and there are many, especially in the United States, there may well be an equally adamant critic. I join neither side, noting that divided opinion marks the reception of many influential and accomplished thinkers and writers. Lewis is surely one of them.

14

Some Principles Applied

While considering the Narnia Chronicles as a set, it is good to mention Michael Ward's *Planet Narnia*. Ward's argument is that the seven separate tales hang together primarily by participation in a unifying planetary idea, each of the seven oriented to one of the planets. Ward's argument serves to support the third element in Lewis's project that should be taken into account. That element is the act of applying and recognizing enduring and universal principles in particular, complex, and changing circumstances. This third element places intentionality in a crucial position; it implies that such applications are constantly necessary and that they require all of a person's imaginative and rational capacities. The task is never completed because conditions vary and because every application is partial in both senses of that term, that is, incomplete and slanted.

There are two kinds of principles that in various ways and in ever-changing circumstances need to be recognized and applied. The first kind is doctrinal, and such principles determine how Lewis sees his world organized and furnished. These principles establish what is possible, what kinds of accounts of things and events can be taken as adequate, and how the person's own position in the world is to be evaluated. Because doctrinal principles have to do with very large matters, their embodiments or applications tend often to be taken for granted or accepted as fixed. Most people assume that they have no need to alter how they understand and relate to things and events. Lewis sees world construction as an ongoing task; being aware of principles and their structural applications is an ongoing process that requires an admixture of certainty or fixity and openness and change.

The second, related kind of principles is moral.[1] The question of what is a right and what is a wrong way of acting in specific situations is not as easily answered as one may think.[2] This is so for at least two reasons. First, while moral principles may be clear and relatively simple, circumstances are complex and always changing.[3] Second, it is sometimes difficult to distinguish between the good and the evil forms of something. Because we live in an imperfect world, nothing we encounter is wholly good. At the same time, because evil has no being of its own but is parasitically attached to something good, nothing we encounter is wholly evil. Distinguishing a good from an evil form of something, especially when the consequences have as yet not fully revealed themselves, is a difficult but necessary task.

The application of principles, then, is the continuous, somewhat tentative, and always partial act that employs imagination, discernment, and rationality in the task of fleshing out doctrinal and moral principles in complex and changing situations. It is important to keep in mind that for Lewis this act is not like relating order to chaos or intelligibility to meaninglessness. Principles and situations are not contraries. Both doctrinal and moral principles are also already implied and warranted by actualities; things and events evoke, warrant, and confirm principles. So while the task of relating principles and situations to one another requires attention and effort, sometimes it is a matter of recognizing a principle that is implicit in the situation.

This suggests three things. First, Lewis did not distinguish principles from conditions as though the first is good and the second evil. Both have value and are continuous or compatible with one another. Second, we can encounter principles as already embodied in our daily lives. Not everything needs entirely to be changed. And third, Lewis, while he wants to distinguish between principles and the conditions in which they are applied or embedded, is more interested in emphasizing the continuities between principles and conditions than in the differences between them.

I

It is possible (if somewhat inaccurate) to call doctrinal principles as Lewis uses them ontological. The term is appropriate because Lewis uses religion generally and Christian doctrines specifically as doing some of the ontological work that traditionally has been done by philosophy and science.

Lewis's interest in religion and his conversion to Christianity were driven by the inadequacy of philosophical materialism to account for the world as we experience it. From adolescence to young adulthood Lewis himself was a materialist, but he seems never to have been wholly satisfied with it. Earlier in this study some reasons for this dissatisfaction were given. Of primary importance were the many texts, from ancient to modern, oriented to the spiritual or supernatural and his fascination with such matters, even during his materialist period. Another contributing factor was the recurring role of idealism in the philosophical tradition. In the account of his conversion, Lewis reveals how he initially turned to idealism, particularly a form of Hegelianism.

But absolute idealism failed to warrant the role of principles and spirit. Idealism generally and Platonism specifically had been useful to theologians in the past, but they were less useful in validating religious accounts of things, rather needing themselves to be validated by religion. Lewis understood his cultural location in late modernity as determined primarily by opposition between materialism and idealism, and idealism had the more difficult case to make. Such principles as moral axioms and spiritual realities needed to be validated by appeals to religion. It is for this reason that Lewis did not pit Christianity against other religions but instead saw religious people, despite their differences and conflicts, as making common cause against materialism.

The knowledge that the ideational and spiritual precede, give rise to, and are traceable within materiality is a crucial principle to apply in constructing our world.[4] Cosmogonic myths across history and cultures bear witness to this, as do the biblical accounts of the Creation. By saying that for Lewis the doctrine of creation is a principle that secures the primacy of idea and spirit I suggest that for him the differing biblical accounts of the Creation are applications of that principle. Consequently, Lewis was not adverse to modern evolutionary theories, and he was not hesitant to give his own account of creation in *The Magician's Nephew*, an account that more closely resembles Job 38 than the accounts in Genesis.[5] What is important in the principle of creation and its application is how we should understand the world in which we find ourselves, a world that does not confront us as raw materiality but that engages us by also being like us. That is, it was made and therefore presents an admixture of materiality and intention. One application of the principle of creation seems to stand out, namely, that there is always a right way of understanding and doing things, a right way of being in the world in which we find ourselves and relate to it. As we saw in "Some Reasonable Assumptions," Lewis held that things, events, creatures, and people retain reliability and a potential for truth and goodness because they bear the consequences of having been created.

A second ontological principle follows closely on the first, and is equally important for Lewis, namely, that humans are primarily to be understood in terms of their rational, moral, and spiritual capacities. Lewis saw a major deficiency of materialism in its inability to take adequately into account our ability to think, to act intentionally, to intuit, to imagine, and to create. He could not be content with an account of things that failed to do justice to what is most important to us as persons and enables us to view, evaluate, and give an account of our world in the first place. Persons, while continuous with all else that exists in the world, are different from all else as well, and Lewis liked to be blunt about that; in one of his sermons he noted that while it could be said with certainty that the hallowed halls of Oxford would someday cease to exist the same could not be said of the person in the next pew.

These two ontological principles threaten to form a dualism of materiality and mind. A third principle must be invoked to keep that from happening. That principle is the relatedness of everything to everything else. Only by deliberate acts of separation and abstraction, or by false assumptions, are material and mental separated from one another. This is not to say that everything is rightly related. Indeed, many relations can and should be altered and improved. But the truth is that we are always already in relations to things, events, and, especially, other people. We have our place in the world through our relations to the whole of it and to its particulars. More than that, we are persons by virtue of these relations. And of course, because the world we find ourselves in, with its continuities and differences, has its qualities because of the first principle, creation, we are persons most fully in and through our relation to the Creator.

Certainly there are more doctrinal principles in Lewis's project, but these are relevant to understanding his account of the world and of our place in it. This focus on the authority of principles frees Lewis to apply them in suggestive, corrective, and reconstructive ways, as he does in his fiction and in such theoretical works as *The Four Loves*.

II

Turning now to moral principles, we should first see how they are clearly related to the principles already cited. Morality, for Lewis, has a natural standing. Much that exists is also as it ought to be. We naturally possess a potential for recognizing what is right or how things ought to be. This natural morality finds its way into human culture. This is not only due to the presence of principles in things but also to experiences that teach us that certain ways of relating to things and other people, certain attitudes and behaviors, promote life and well-being while others have the contrary effect. The first moral principle is that there is already continuity between who we are and who we ought to be. Lewis goes further. We have a desire to be who we ought to be. Distortions, confusions, falsifications, and evils are impositions, intrusions, and warps. If it is true that to a degree we already know what it is good for us to do and to be, one would think that we would develop and reflect this in our relations to others and our world. A second principle explains the apparently anomalous fact that, despite our knowledge of what is good for us to do and to be, we do not behave accordingly.

This second moral principle is related to the second ontological principle. All the resources that lie within us, our capacity to understand, to act intentionally, and to imagine and create, are our own. I become aware of this fact in late adolescence, as I become aware of my own particularity or individuality, distinguishing between myself and others. I identify myself with the first person pronoun in the singular. Lewis thought of this stage in human development as crucial but hazardous. While it includes something natural, necessary, and good, that is, my becoming a person distinguishable from others and responsible for my life and its direction, it easily can and usually does go awry. A person becomes not only self-conscious but also self-preoccupied, not just distinguishing the self from others but relating to the self as primary. This is a rehearsal on the individual level of the process of human development that is embodied for Lewis in the narrative of the Fall. Indeed, there is no clearer instance of Lewis's distinction between a principle and the versions of the principle that can exist than his provocative displacement of the biblical account of the Fall in Genesis by his own evolutionary account of human development.

This event in our development does not completely erase the awareness that a self-centered way of relating to the world is erroneous and unnatural. I am never fully at ease when I construe my identity in terms of what I possess or want for myself. I may persist in this direction, but I will likely not be fully convinced that it is the right one or that it supports my well-being. Unfortunately, in order to appease this haunting doubt, I do not question the path that I have taken but instead follow it more intently, bringing more of my world into my own domain. This program of self-enlargement is helped if I think of my world, things and events, other creatures, and even other people as being, unlike myself, objects to be treated as my needs and desires dictate. My uncertainty about this program does not go away easily, so acts of accumulation, possession, and domination become obsessive and my interest in things that I think will secure my identity becomes addictive. Because the path itself is wrong and as the pursuit of it becomes increasingly concentrated, I begin to be not more but less myself. I gradually become strange to myself and to other people. I become increasingly inconsiderate and even rapacious toward my world and its particulars. So while I begin with a sense of attachment to my own capacities for thinking, willing, imagining, and creating, I end by allowing things in my world to dominate and absorb my identity.

A third moral principle is the process by which this falsification and distortion in the formation of personal identity can be avoided or rectified. Not surprisingly, it is encapsulated by the Gospel principle that whoever tries to save his life will lose it and whoever gives his life will find it, the paradox that one becomes a person by losing the self.

For many Christians the soteriological process, being brought from a destructive and distorted way of living into a vital and true way, directs attention solely to the person and work of Christ. Lewis has a high Christology, as we see in the figure of Aslan, but his Christology and soteriology are not as dominant as many think it is. This evokes an earlier point concerning the distance between Lewis and some of his Evangelical admirers, namely, that Lewis has a less negative view than they of what he finds in the world around him.

The first step in the process is recognition that there are things in the world that are valuable and important, indeed more than we are. This does not refer to those things that one wants to possess or consume. Rather, it is a matter of deferring to something outside oneself as having intrinsic value. One of the major functions of culture, for Lewis, is the inculcation of this recognition. This principle also appears in his theory of reading; in *An Experiment in Criticism*, Lewis relates reading to the Gospel text concerning losing and finding oneself. But reading is only one example of this kind of attention.[6] Like reading, encounters with nature, other people, or events require a shift in the center of attention. This does not mean that we must consider every other person, thing, or event as more important than ourselves. But the shift in attention, in priority, is crucial, and a text, thing, event, creature, or person also draws its value and significance from its place as part of a larger world that is itself significant and valuable, as experiences of joy bear witness. We find ourselves in a world that deserves our appreciation and trust. We can and should be open to it, especially to other people, and we become persons through what happens to us as a result of this engagement. Vulnerability is a precondition for anything of this kind to occur.

The counterforce of self-direction, however, is so strong and engrained that occasions of deferring are most often taken as exceptional or eccentric. We are captives of the need to affirm, reinforce, and protect ourselves.[7] Our actions driven by this need become naturalized and allow the things by which we think the self is served to become objects of obsession. It is not only difficult but painful to alter this way of being in the world. People cannot be expected to recognize on their own that deferring is necessary to become who they can or ought to be. The anthropological principle requires Christology.

I am not certain which, among the options offered by the tradition concerning the relation of Christ to redemption, is primary for Lewis. Given what I already have said, however, it seems that a moral influence theory is prominent. Jesus gives himself over to his world, even to institutions that represent what is distorted and self-aggrandizing. His life and death were not acts of self-development or self-enhancement but of giving. As Paul writes in his letter to the Philippians, by humbling himself he is exalted, that is, brought into his own. A moral influence theory of atonement is, though not theologically dominant, widely influential, and Lewis seemed to recognize it in the value he places on self-giving.

A moral influence theory does not seem adequate to the severity of the problem, however. Lewis uses the metaphor of addiction to suggest our condition as we go down the mistaken path of trying to be persons by self-preoccupation and acquisition.

The world of the addict becomes increasingly constricted and determined by the object of obsession. This suggests the relevance of a second theory of atonement, Origen's ransom to the devil. That appears clearly in the Narnian sacrifice of Aslan to release Edmund, and it is suggested by the name of his principal character, Ransom, in the science trilogy. Somehow the power by which one is possessed can be countered or broken, as the Patient escapes the power from below in *The Screwtape Letters* or, as in *The Lion, the Witch and the Wardrobe*, Edmund's captive state is reversed.

Lewis goes further. Atonement imparts to humans the power to be released from what absorbs and devours them, the ability to see a truthful way of being in the world and to follow it, that is, to take on or imitate Christ. This process, because it is hidden, cannot be narrated, but its embodiments can be seen. We recognize moments when we are drawn out of self-preoccupation and acquisition into a world and a life that is primary to and more abundant than our own.

III

The final thing to point out about principles and their applications in Lewis is that acts of applying principles take several forms. Four stand out. The first is the productive imagination. Lewis was undoubtedly aware of the technical use of this term, especially in Kant. I mean by it only the capacity we have for relating to things in ways that exceed or even counter how they present themselves to us. We do this most commonly in our relations to people. We confront them immediately as physical objects; but we encounter them more fully as thinking and intending persons. Similarly, when we pass a building we take it to be more than a façade and as containing rooms where we imagine people are living or working. This capacity Lewis quite noticeably extends to our relations with animals. Often in our society they are treated simply as physical objects, as when they are cruelly used for medical experiments, but animals can and should be attended to as actually or potentially more than that. This is why, in Lewis's imagination, animals can talk. This is also true of our larger material context. Lewis shows the productive imagination as widespread in human cultures; it is surprising that modern Westerners tend to reduce what they encounter rather than imagine it to be more extensive, resonant, and significant than appearances suggest. This reductive habit may well be due, Lewis implies, to our desire to control and even consume what we encounter rather than be attentive to what it is and what of value it suggests.

A second form of application is reason. We must be careful here because the use of reason does not impart to things an intelligibility that they formerly lacked. Reason is an act by which our ideas and what we experience are brought into alignment with one another. This is possible because what exists or occurs already has within it that which contributes to its intelligibility. True, we do not understand everything; some things simply baffle us, and *The Problem of Pain* addresses some of these. But ordinarily we engage things we encounter as open to rational clarification, and we press on with this assumption even when at first there is a disjunction between our ideas and what we experience. A good instance of rationality so displayed is Peter's insistence, at the outset of *Prince Caspian*, that some reconciliation must be possible between the ruins where the children find themselves and the fact that they look very much like Cair Paravel—a rational reconciliation, that is, between the time lapse suggested by the ruins and the children's awareness that they have only been away from Narnia for a year.

The third form of application is intuition. I am not interested in the roles played by this concept in ancient philosophy or in moderns like Kant, Bergson, and Jung. But I want to add it to

Lewis's repertoire because it differs from the productive imagination and rationality. First of all, relative to intuition a person is largely passive. Lewis emphasized the moral and spiritual roles of intuition. Human beings somehow know that some things are wrong and other things right, although they may not have adequate grounds to defend this crucial distinction. Lewis had such a high view of intuition and its role in providing moral axioms that he thought, for example, that someone who thinks that oppression, treachery, or disregard for the weak and the young are permissible has been self-exempted from full humanity. While intuition is more passive than rationality and the productive imagination, it resembles them in that it arises from an alignment between our capacity to receive and what in a particular situation intuition conveys. This is because the world around us is devoid neither of rationality nor of morality. Lewis does not defend the place he gives to intuition, but he grants it the ability, first, to foresee things, as Jane Studdock does; second, to recognize things that others do not, as Lucy recognizes Aslan; third, to know, as the children in Narnia know, that some unusual things, like the ambiguous nature of Aslan, are nevertheless true; and, fourth, to know that one thing is morally necessary and another morally unacceptable.

The final component of the task I am calling application is discernment. While it is related to the productive imagination, rationality, and intuition, it has qualities of its own. It is rich, having biblical and traditional standing, is directed especially to spiritual and moral matters, and implies sagacity and wisdom. Discernment is a kind of insight, an ability to recognize and weigh the value or truthfulness of something. Discerning the spirit is the ability, as well, to distinguish a bad from a good form of something, to have an awareness of something's source or goal. It has a passive, receptive side—being patient, letting something appear, and not jumping to conclusions—but it also has an active side, distinguishing, interpreting, and seeing the implications and consequences of something. While discernment is refined over time and suggests experience and even sophistication, discernment is also childlike. Children seem able immediately to detect insincerity or deception when they encounter it. This immediacy accounts for the relation of discernment to intuition. Working through uncertainty and finding a basis for making a distinction between alternatives or a judgment of something's value accounts for its relation to rationality. And seeing what is at stake even when it is only implied or even hidden relates discernment to the productive or constructive imagination. It is also similar to aesthetic discrimination, which for Lewis is very close to value judgment. The Narnia Chronicles provide many applications of discernment, especially distinguishing between right and wrong ways of acting.

The task of applying or relating principles to and in complex situations and to and in a changing world is not only difficult and taxing; it is also edifying because it unifies, reinforces, and enlarges one's world, one's view of and relation to it, one's *Weltanshauung*. In addition to that, it gives a person, however indirectly, an identity or personhood not secured by him- or herself but given to a person as the fruit or consequence of right relationships, a reciprocity between oneself and other persons, moral and spiritual realities, and, by such means as these, God.[8]

Conclusion

While my treatment of Lewis's work is, as I hope is clear, appreciative, I am not fully at ease with him. One reason for this uneasiness, as already mentioned, is the appearance in his work of racist, sexist, and homophobic attitudes that counter his otherwise strong emphasis on openness and care relative to our world and, especially, to other people. A second reason is his acceptance, although perhaps by default, of a certain construction or adoption of him. Because of his emphasis on retaining moral and doctrinal principles even if or when they are difficult to understand and apply, he was sharply critical of Christians who, when those principles become difficult to apply, modify them. This reaction opens him to conscription by readers who deploy the principles even when unable to apply them to present conditions or mistake particular applications of the principles for the principles themselves. Identifying with one side far more than with the other, that is, with the retainers more than with the appliers or reinterpreters of principles, while a defensible tack, easily aligns him with religious rigidity, exclusiveness, and obscurantism, as often occurs in the views of him by both devotees and detractors.

This placement of him is underserved, and I hope that my readings suggest well enough why I think so. Along with much more that could be said in defense of this opinion, of primary importance is the fact that he himself modified or reshaped traditional theological views in his application of principles to current understandings and conditions. Prominent among these are his account of the Fall as a moment in the development both of the species and of persons, his own account of creation along with his positive attitude toward evolutionary theories, and his quite peculiar eschatology. The problem arises because, while Lewis was explicit and even emphatic about retaining principles even when they become difficult to apply or to understand, he was not equally explicit or emphatic about the need and warrants for the rational and imaginative departures, variations, and recasts in applying them to current understandings and conditions that his own work reveals.

His failure to clarify the need and warrants for rational and imaginative reformulations of traditional theological views made my offering a course on Lewis for the last several years more difficult than it otherwise would have been. To a degree, the negative response of some of my colleagues was understandable, given the conflation of Lewis with the dominant portion of his American readers. My appreciation of him, therefore, rests on a view of his work rather different from that of many others, both devotees and detractors.

Some of my colleagues also seemed to view Lewis unfavorably simply because of his popularity. I disagree with this assessment of him and view his popularity with appreciation. I began teaching a course on him because a group of students asked me to do so and because I found their interest in him worth examining and complicating. Rarely does one find a writer and thinker as learned and creative as Lewis who is read by such a large portion of the American public, including college students. It is difficult to imagine a course offering in religion devoted to another recent or contemporary writer and scholar who is both so widely admired and so inventive and learned as Lewis.

My appreciation of the combination in Lewis of popularity and stature was sustained because, as I became more acquainted with his work, I began to realize that he was deserving of recognition for additional and, perhaps, more substantial reasons than many of his devotees seemed to recognize. Consequently, I was goaded by an urge to understand and assess him in broader terms. Parts or aspects of his work have been treated well by others, perhaps more adequately than I have here, but I wanted to look at his project more extensively. I found it to be a project that commends itself by virtue of its complexity, consistency, and involvement with the dynamics of late modernity. While I am not in full agreement with all of it, I think it is a project that deserves to be taken seriously even by those who disagree with it, a project that any attentive reader should treat with respect.

While I have tried in the course of this book to make his larger project more accessible and appreciated, there are some specific points that I would like to emphasize in conclusion. One of them is his attention to a major component of late modern culture, namely, the troubled and often contrary relations of idealism and materialism to one another. While it may be that the conflict between idealism and materialism does not describe our culture as fully as it did his, the conflict continues to have place and force in academic culture. One finds in the academy a culture grounded by a theoretical and methodological materialism that found its way from the natural sciences to the social sciences and has become, in many places, dominant in the humanities.

This materialism is countered by separatist forms of Christianity. One of these, present for example in student groups on campus, withdraws into and dwells on personal interiority and feelings. Another is a theological position that separates Christianity or the church from its cultural context and construes Christianity, the church, and their tradition as self-contained and centripetally oriented. These two responses to materialism, while in other ways very different from one another, are alike in abstracting Christianity from its cultural-historical context and placing it apart from or above that context as a separate discourse, as housed by a specific tradition or institution, or as sequestered in personal internality. Lewis's estimation of this kind of theological stance is unmistakable. Writing to his brother, he describes his encounter with advocates of what became known as neo-orthodoxy:

> They've all been reading a dreadful man called Karl Barth, who seems the right opposite number to Karl Marx. "Under judgment" is their great expression.... [T]hey don't think human reason or human conscience of any value at all; they maintain as stoutly as Calvin, that there's no reason why God's dealings should appear just (let alone merciful) to us: and they maintain that *all* our righteousness is filthy rags with a fierceness and sincerity which is like a blow in the face.[1]

Of particular interest in this comment is Lewis's placement of Marx and Barth as opposites, which I take him to mean the opposite positions of a materialist and an idealist. This would be, I think, his assessment of a position that continues as a major force in American theology today, a position that readily attaches itself to popular forms of Evangelicalism. Another way of putting this is that the kind of Christian theology with which Lewis cannot be closely associated is a kind in which the doctrine of creation is dwarfed by the doctrine of atonement, in which history is overwritten by eschatology, and in which Christianity draws people away from the natural world and human history and culture into a separated interiority, language, or institution.[2] While Lewis is critical of modernity, particularly of a materialism that has established itself as culturally naturalized, he would insist that moving from modernity into a religiously cordoned contrary reinforces a separation and potential conflict between materialism and idealism that can and should be avoided and healed. His project is directed toward undercutting the contrary relations not only of theories based on materiality and on spirituality but also the contrary relations that are assumed by both sides to exist between the material and the spiritual themselves.

I appreciate not only Lewis's attention to the problem of disconnection between materialism and idealism, including idealism in its Christian forms, but also the way he goes about addressing it. First, he argues that materialism provides a demonstrably inadequate account of us as persons, of our world, and of our relations, especially to other people. The point that materialism provides at best a partial account of our world allows Lewis to make his second move. Rather than participate in a game in which materialism determines what is real and reliable and in which religion or the spiritual is an intruder that needs to explain and defend itself, Lewis challenges the conditions that materialism sets. Not to do this is from the outset to assign the religious or spiritual a place out of bounds, a place that the forms of Christianity mentioned above seem ready to accept. Implied by Lewis's challenge is his refusal to accept his opponent's claim that the conditions set by materialism provide a neutral space. To define a position as neutral concerning religion, like a position defined as nonreligious or atheistic, is only to say what it is not, what it excludes. It avoids or conceals the question of what the proposal or the game actually is or implies. The answer, Lewis contends, is some form of materialism. While there must be neutral arenas so that the interests and needs of both religious and nonreligious people can be established, managed, and discussed, those arenas are limited and secondary. They cannot be taken as providing answers to questions as to who we are as persons and what it is good for us to be. Materialism is unable to address these matters. For example, it is unable to take human agency into account because materialism has a difficult time dissociating itself from determinism. It then becomes possible to conclude by saying that materialism sets up a game that treats as secondary and dubious what for us as human persons is primary, urgent, and real.

At first Lewis tried to augment or offset materialism with a form of philosophical idealism, particularly based on Hegel. But he found this inadequate, too vague, or unable to stand by itself. Consequently, he turned to religion or theism as pointing to and warranting the reality of the spiritual. This move, while crucial, also was unsatisfying, and he turned to Christianity because it gave him not only a way of affirming the spiritual but also a way to take seriously the aspects of personhood that were so urgent a matter for him. In addition, Christianity provided a way of undercutting or overcoming the separation between the material and spiritual. It enabled him not only to retain his strong interests in materiality, in nature and the natural sciences, but also to argue that Christianity could deepen and enlarge appreciation for materiality. Indeed, he liked to suggest that people who lived in a world defined solely by materiality ended not with a larger but with a more limited and more questionable view of nature and the material. At the same time, Christianity gave weight and specificity to the spiritual, so that the spiritual, rather than vague, made the kind of urgent claims and presented challenges and attractions of equal force and complexity for humans as those posed by their material context. Finally, Christianity held the material and spiritual together without making clear in what ways the undergirding unity was to be understood.

As I mentioned earlier in this book, I think that Lewis reiterates the division that the anthropologist E. B. Tylor so long ago laid out, namely, between two ways of being in or understanding one's world, either a materialist or a religious way. Lewis turned from materialism to philosophical idealism, from idealism to religion, and finally to Christianity as providing a worldview that holds contraries together in ways that continually need to be recognized, fathomed, and understood. I do not think that the case he makes for religion generally and for Christianity in particular is necessarily convincing, but the challenge he presents the non- or antireligious alternative is to come up with a more adequate worldview than materialism in its present forms provides. As he was aware and pointed out, religion generally and Christianity particularly have their problems, but so does materialism, and those who hold to or promulgate it should also acknowledge its deficiencies and distortions. I think that Lewis was primarily intent on and quite successful in making the case that a religious worldview is as, even more, capacious, inclusive, and productive of human well-being as its nonreligious, that is, materialist, alternative.

Another basic and recurring interest of Lewis's that I appreciate and think is relevant to our present cultural situation is the persistent question of personal identity. While Lewis inherited an interest in this problem from his training in philosophy, it also focused for him one of the major inadequacies of materialist views. Materialism struck him as slighting or ignoring something of huge importance for us, namely, the sense we have of ourselves, a sense that is not exhausted by reference to our bodies. While not a rationalist, Lewis must be seen, I think, as agreeing with an orientation that places self-awareness as a primary item in any adequate account of our lived world. Of particular interest to him is not self-consciousness but reason and creativity, and they imply agency or, as his friend Austin Farrer put it in the title of one of his books, *The Freedom of the Will*. Lewis did not like determinism. This is why he is uneasy with Calvin and does not, as far as I know, talk of him without caricature. He likely thought

Calvin to be, in a theological way, also a determinist. Whether it was in philosophical or theological forms, Lewis resisted determinism. I think that intensifying this dislike are such factors as his Romantic fascination with human internality and originality, his fascination with myth and the imagination of writers attentive to the spiritual, his own identity as a creative writer, and his emphasis on the necessary and ongoing rational and imaginative task of applying principles to changing circumstances. He saw human imagination and rationality not in isolation from or as exceptions to either the natural and quotidian context or enduring principles but in reciprocal relations to them. Another way of putting this is to say that Lewis did not answer the personal identity question by grounding it on human self-awareness. Rather, he locates it in the responsive-creative relations that a person has with his or her world, especially, but by no means only, other people. He took his complex encounters with his world and its particulars as primary, and theories about or accounts of that world were for him secondary and derivative. I think that he viewed Christianity as so valuable because, among other things, it provided or allowed for inclusiveness and unity, an affirmative and celebratory attitude that encouraged positive encounters and relationships with one's world and, especially, other people. Lewis did not take theory, philosophical or theological, as a substitute for or as superior to the rich, mysterious, but also often painful interactive relationships with the world around him but thought of theory as needing to secure its warrants in and to do justice to the realities of those encounters and relationships. Personal identity is for him not something we establish or already have but something that is given to us as a consequence of our interrelations.[3]

I appreciate, then, Lewis's advocacy of the primacy for human well-being of relating as generously, receptively, and creatively as possible to the world in which we find ourselves and to particulars in it, especially other people. Lewis did not posit this basic orientation for human well-being because he was himself a gregarious and outgoing person. Indeed, he seems in disposition to have been quite the contrary; it was not as though he advocated something that was natural or second nature to him. Encounter, open and interested, became primary for him, and I think that in our own narcissistic and oppositional culture we need to see and do things more his way. Political convictions, social positions, theoretical certainty, and religious exclusiveness, including Christian, should not become ways of delimiting or determining our encounters with others. Surely such things affect our encounters, but their influence should be secondary to and affected by encounter. Encounters not only confirm but also challenge and even alter our accounts, evaluations, and explanations of our world. Certainty, while a necessity rather than an evil, needs to be less determining than openness.

Another way of saying this is that Lewis had a rich and traditional sense of what it means to read.[4] In his *An Experiment in Criticism* he makes this very clear. Reading requires an openness and vulnerability that coming at reading with theories and expectations would jeopardize. It is a theory of reading that he extends, particularly in his emphasis on walking as both an act and as a metaphor for encountering one's world, to encounters with the world beyond texts or that turn the world and its particulars into texts that can, in this sense of the word, be read.[5] Reading C. S. Lewis, therefore, is to engage a guide who has a firm proposal as to how to relate to and move about in the world. It is also to follow a guide who, with an encouraging smile and nudge, urges the reader to begin reading and walking in ways and directions that are his or her own.

NOTES

Introduction

1. There may well have been for Lewis also a distinction to be made between Irish and English religious identities. Harry Blamires says, "the spectacle of unbelievers who seem unable to get Christianity out of their systems is an Irish spectacle, whereas the spectacle of supposed believers, especially theologians, who seem incapable of getting Christianity into their systems is plainly an English spectacle." Harry Blamires, "Teaching the Universal Truth: C. S. Lewis Among the Intellectuals," in *The Pilgrim's Guide: C. S. Lewis and the Art of Witness*, ed. David Mills (Grand Rapids, MI: William B. Eerdmans, 1998), p. 20.

2. Corbin Carnell's point regarding the interest of Lewis and other modernists in myth is worth taking: "Lewis' use of myth is indeed the opposite of the use made by James Joyce and other modern writers who seize on myth to give some kind of form to the chaos of experience. Lewis believes, instead, that in its imaginative appeal the myth conveys meaning that cannot be conveyed in any other way." Corbin Scott Carnell, *Bright Shadow of Reality: C. S. Lewis and the Feeling Intellect* (Grand Rapids, MI: William B. Eerdmans, 1974), p. 108.

3. A friend of Lewis's in Cambridge says, "neither in conversation nor in his works did he show much interest in organized religion. He was orthodox in belief but seemed to have little sense of the Church." Richard W. Ladborough, "In Cambridge," in *C. S. Lewis at the Breakfast Table and Other Reminiscences*, ed. James T. Como (New York: Macmillan 1979), p. 103.

4. Terry Eagleton, *Literary Theory: An Introduction* (Oxford: Blackwell, 1983), p. 31.

5. Ibid., p. 32.

6. A point about the relation of Lewis to this reconstitution of a moral English culture after the Great War should be stressed. Lewis joins his nonreligious contemporaries in an affirmation of an enduring and sharable cultural morality. He differs from them in his conclusion that the only way by which culture and morality can be sustained is by their deference to something beyond them. As Walter Hooper puts it, "One great difference between them [Lewis and Leavis] was their respective attitudes towards 'cultures.' As Leavis made clear in his *Education and the University* he wanted to see Culture made the basis of a humane society, but without it being based on any objective standard, and certainly not Christianity." Walter Hooper, *C. S. Lewis: A Companion and Guide* (London: HarperCollins, 1996), p. 74.

7. For a description of the role of the "productive imagination" in Lewis, see Franklin Arthur Pyles, "The Influence of British Neo-Hegelians on the Christian Apology of C. S. Lewis" (diss., Northwestern University, 1978), p. 55.

8. Indeed, Lewis seems almost to take a page from Tom Paine's undermining of the Bible's authority when he says, "The human qualities [of biblical writers] show through. Naivety, error, contradictions, even (as in the cursing Psalms) wickedness are not removed." C. S. Lewis, *Reflections on the Psalms* (London: Geoffrey Bles, 1958), p. 111.

Chapter 1

1. Alister McGrath tells us that Lewis stopped keeping a diary in March 1924. See his *C. S. Lewis—A Life: Eccentric Genius, Reluctant Prophet* (Carol Springs, IL: Tyndale House, 2013), p. 140.

2. Lewis was well aware of the dangers of autobiography: "To admire Satan, then, is to give one's vote not only for a world of misery, but also for a world of lies and propaganda, of wishful thinking, of incessant autobiography." C. S. Lewis, *A Preface to Paradise Lost* (Oxford: Oxford University Press, 1967 [1942]), p. 102.

3. The correction made by Alister McGrath to Lewis's chronology of his conversion, the change from 1931 to 1932, should be taken as standard. See McGrath, *C. S. Lewis—A Life*, p. 158.

4. "[W]hatever also may be true, the popular scientific cosmology at any rate is certainly not. I left that ship not at the call of poetry but because I thought it could not keep afloat. Something like philosophical idealism or theism must, at the very worst, be less untrue than that." C. S. Lewis, *They Asked for a Paper: Papers and Addresses* (London: Geoffrey Bles, 1962), p. 164.

5. The crucial difference between idealism and Christianity for Lewis was that the latter allowed the transcendent also to be particular. See Franklin Arthur Pyles, "The Influence of the British Neo-Hegelians on the Christian Apology of C. S. Lewis" (diss., Northwestern University, 1978), p. 16.

6. Because the summary that follows has been used by others, I need to say that I formulated and published it in my earlier book on Lewis, *C. S. Lewis: Then and Now* (New York: Oxford University Press, 2001), pp. 22–24.

7. Gaston Bachelard, *The Poetics of Space*, trans. Marie Jolas, foreword by Etiene Gilson (New York: Orion Press, 1964). George Sayer comments, "The attic became at once the center of life for the boys. Here they were not just brothers, but friends exploring a common and lively world, a world largely enunciated by Jack while Warren looked on with admiration as his little brother wrote story after story and drew picture after picture." George Sayer, *Jack: C. S. Lewis and His Times* (San Francisco: Harper & Row, 1988), p. 19.

Chapter 2

1. Since Lewis is dealing in this chapter of the book with religion in general, I am surprised that he stresses the uniqueness of the person and work of Christ and does not allow, as he does in other places, that the desire for and effects of a deliverer or sacrificial savior, while critical to Christianity, appear as well in the history of religions.

2. It is worth noting that in this book Lewis, to an unusual extent, employs or implies biblical texts. He refers to specific texts thirty times and at other times to the Bible more generally. Indeed, it could be said that his treatment of the problem of pain is really a commentary on the sayings of Jesus regarding what is possible for God and on the relation of human suffering to God's love in Hebrews 12:6. In my opinion, Lewis wants to deal with the problem less in relation to the philosophical

tradition and more in relation to suffering created in the lives of Christians by their experiences of pain.

3. It is not my purpose in this first part of the book, which draws attention to reasonable assumptions that supply groundings for Lewis, to point out, as I shall in the third part, that Lewis treats Christianity as providing a set of principles that need repeatedly and in and for changing circumstances to be applied. But here we have a striking instance of this method. Lewis extrapolates from the Genesis account of the Fall the principle that humans choose disobedience, but he then goes on to present an entirely different narrative, what he calls his own "picture" (71). It is an adaptation of an evolutionary understanding of human emergence that has three stages: a preconscious or innocent stage, a conscious stage in which humans become aware of their relation to their Creator, and a fallen stage in which humans move from self-consciousness to self-preoccupation or pride.

4. I think it is important to notice that Lewis identifies pain with evil. It differs from evil in that, unlike evil, it does not require undoing (117). Although he does not develop the point, it implies that pain, since it is evil, cannot be caused by God.

5. While some working in animal ethics may find Lewis's understanding of the relation between human and animal awareness to be not full or positive enough, especially his hierarchical view of kinds of beings, it is important to stress that he wrote vigorously against cruelty to animals, especially vivisection, and saw cruelty to animals as consistent with what he finds objectionable about modernity. He says, for example, "objective superiority is rightly claimed for man, yet that very superiority ought partly to *consist in* not behaving like a vivisector: that we ought to prove ourselves better than the beasts precisely by the fact of acknowledging duties to them which they do not acknowledge to us." C. S. Lewis, *God in the Dock: Essays on Theology and Ethics* (Grand Rapids, MI: William B. Eerdmans, 1970), p. 226.

6. Lewis identifies more with the second than with the first of these versions also because the principle of the resurrection of the body counters the modern separation of the physical from the spiritual, so that the widespread Christian eschatological assumption of a spiritual continuation is more modern than Christian. He says, for example, "By teaching the resurrection of the body it [Christianity] teaches that Heaven is not merely a state of the spirit but a state of the body as well:

and therefore a state of Nature as a whole." C. S. Lewis, *Miracles: A Preliminary Study* (New York: Macmillan, 1947), p. 161.

Chapter 3

1. "What we call bad things are good things perverted." C. S. Lewis, *A Preface to Paradise Lost* (Oxford: Oxford University Press, 1967 [1942]), p. 66.

2. An important but subtly introduced interest of Lewis's should be noted. As I shall point out in the third part of this book, Lewis included, as a crucial component of his work, the need to apply continuing or universal moral and doctrinal principles to particular and changing circumstances. It is interesting that Screwtape's relation to Wormwood is also patterned on this way of working. The problem of Screwtape's use of this method is that the principles he applies in order to direct or correct Wormwood are wrong or inadequate.

3. "We all have Naturalism [or materialism] in our bones and even conversion does not at once work the infection out of our system. Its assumptions rush back upon the mind the moment vigilance is relaxed." C. S. Lewis, *Miracles: A Preliminary Study* (New York: Macmillan, 1947), p. 161.

4. While Lewis's focus is on individual personhood, he is not an individualist. However, when he speaks about the larger reality adumbrated by Christianity, it is not so much the church as the community of believers generally, as in *Mere Christianity*. Consequently, a church is an actualization or application of a principle of this community and is partial, mixed, and constantly both changing and needing to be changed.

5. Alister McGrath attributes Lewis's ideas about war to a deficiency in his worldview. He says, "Lewis's mental map of reality had difficulty accommodating the trauma of the Great War." Alister McGrath, *C. S. Lewis—A Life: Eccentric Genius, Reluctant Prophet* (Carol Springs, IL: Tyndale House, 2013), p. 51. I think Lewis's view of his world accommodated the trauma of war but did not grant war the defining or determining status that many of his contemporaries, both literary and theological, did.

6. It is also why Screwtape says, earlier, that all pleasures are made by the Enemy; "all our research so far has not enabled us to produce one" (44).

7. Recall Lewis's description of Belfast, especially its noise, in *Surprised by Joy*.

Chapter 4

1. "In his view, the enemy was not, however, limited to Hitler or the Germans, but included all the violently anti-Christian forces that were threatening to destroy the Europe that he knew and loved. He always disliked the black-and-white view of the war, that England was right and Germany wicked and wrong." George Sayer, *Jack: C. S. Lewis and His Times* (San Francisco: Harper & Row, 1988), p. 162.

2. See Peter Mandler, *The English National Character: The History of an Idea from Edmund Burke to Tony Blair* (New Haven, CT: Yale University Press, 2006).

3. I do not know whether Lewis read the work of E. B. Tylor, the first to hold a chair of anthropology at Oxford University. Tylor puts the matter in similarly stark terms, namely, the distinction between two worldviews, materialist and religious, saying that contemporary religious people are more like ancient people than they are like their materialist neighbors. Lewis echoes this view when he says, "Christians and Pagans had much more in common with each other than either has with a post-Christian. The gap between those who worship different gods is not so wide as that between those who worship and those who do not." C. S. Lewis, *De Descriptione Temporum* (London: Cambridge University Press, 1955), p. 7.

4. "Acts of thinking are no doubt events; but they are a very special sort of events. They are 'about' something other than themselves and can be true or false. Events in general are not 'about' anything and cannot be true or false.... Reason is given before Nature and on reason our concept of Nature depends." C. S. Lewis, *Miracles: A Preliminary Study* (New York: Macmillan, 1947), pp. 17, 23.

5. Lewis is quite clear and consistent on this point: "Of course it should be pointed out that, though all salvation is through Jesus, we need not conclude that He cannot save those who have not explicitly accepted Him in this life. And it should (at least in my judgment) be made clear that we are not pronouncing all other religions to be totally false, but rather saying that in Christ whatever is true in all religions is consummated and perfected." C. S. Lewis, *God in the Dock: Essays on Theology and Ethics* (Grand Rapids, MI: William B. Eerdmans, 1970), p. 102.

6. This fourth part of the book tends, as it proceeds, to turn somewhat sharply away from a general to a Christian audience and, in its concluding chapters, to become sermonic. While there is nothing objectionable about a sermonic tone, it seems at variance with the tone of the previous parts, and his audience is projected as more constricted: "we Christians," for example (208). This allows for an altered view of the "natural." Toward the end the natural, rather than forming a base upon which religion generally and Christianity particularly can be warranted and clarified, is less positively construed. In this part he identifies self-centeredness, the desire to take advantage of others, and the tendency to exploit the whole universe with the "natural life" (178). Aligned with this shift is the kind of standing that Lewis gives to the Christian principles or doctrines that he sets forth. In the first sections he primarily appeals to a general audience, and in the third part he announces that in the rest of the book he will "look at the whole picture as it will be *if* [my emphasis] Christianity is true" (75). But in the fourth part he asserts Christian doctrinal principles as axiomatic.

Chapter 5

1. This point, that ethics and morality are not dependent on religion generally or on Christianity particularly, seems to be very important to him. He says, in his essay "On Ethics," "The idea... that Christianity brought a new ethical code into the world is a grave error." C. S. Lewis, *Christian Reflections*, ed. Walter Hooper (Grand Rapids, MI: William B. Eerdmans, 1967), p. 46. George Sayer comments, "Jack would reply that Christian ethics were far from unusual and, in fact, were common to most religions and embraced by most high-minded men in all civilizations. He maintained that Christianity is not a new ethic, but a way of obeying the old traditional ethic." George Sayer, *Jack: C. S. Lewis and His Times* (San Francisco: Harper & Row, 1988), p. 182.

2. "Thus no thorough going Naturalist believes in free will: for free will would mean that human beings have the power of independent action, the power of doing something more or other than what was involved by the total series of events." C. S. Lewis, *Miracles: A Preliminary Study* (New York: Macmillan, 1947), p. 7.

3. "What we learn from experience depends on the kind of philosophy we bring to experience." Ibid., p. 3.

4. Martin Irvine, *The Making of Textual Culture: "Grammatica" and Literary Theory, 350–1100* (New York: Cambridge University Press, 1994).

5. "Every writer, if he possibly can, bases himself on an earlier writer.... This is one of the things that differentiates the period almost equally from savagery and from our modern civilization.... Though literacy was of course far rarer then than now, reading was in one way a more important ingredient of the total culture." C. S. Lewis, *The Discarded Image: An Introduction to Medieval and Renaissance Literature* (Cambridge: Cambridge University Press, 1964), p. 5.

Chapter 6

1. Lewis puts his interest in narrative spatiality this way, while commenting on the interest of readers in action and suspense: "For I wanted not the momentary suspense but that whole world to which it belonged." C. S. Lewis, *Of This and Other Worlds*, ed. Walter Hooper (London: Collins, 1982), p. 27.

2. It is not surprising that Lewis, given his long-standing interests in myth, should employ this plot pattern, since it is often associated with myths, as Joseph Campbell argues in his *The Hero with a Thousand Faces* (New York: Parthenon Books, 1949).

3. William Shelton, "Free Space: An Account of the First Soviet Space Walk Performed by Alexei Leonov on March 18, 1965, during the Voskhod 2 Mission," *Parabola: The Magazine of Myth and Tradition* 27, no. 2 (1993): 67–70, at 70.

4. See C. P. Snow, *The Two Cultures* (Cambridge: Cambridge University Press, 1959).

5. In my contacts with academics, I have met more scientists with knowledge of and appreciation for the humanities than humanists with a corresponding grasp of the natural sciences.

6. Lewis distinguishes two kinds of imagination, positive and negative or spiritual and diseased, in his essay "On Three Ways of Writing for Children," in *Of This and Other Worlds*, pp. 64–65.

7. In the concluding conversation with Ransom, the Oyarsa matches Weston's sense of being on the verge of something new and immense by suggesting that "[g]reat things are on foot" (142).

8. While Lewis is not explicit on the point, the ties between science, colonialism, and imperialism in the modern West are clearly drawn.

9. More could be said about walking as a narrative technique. For example, it is used by Lewis not only to allow the terrain of Malacandra to reveal itself but also to contrast Ransom with Devine, who is amazed and puzzled that Ransom walks so much (18).

10. Lewis adds a "postscript" to the narrative that is amusing and effective. It consists of extracts from a letter that Ransom has sent to him pointing to inadequacies in Lewis's account. This invention counters the possibility that Lewis as the teller is in a superior position relative to Ransom. Among the matters Ransom mentions is that the three kinds of inhabitants of Malacandra are not homogeneous, that differences exist within the kinds. Lewis, in other words, shifts primacy from the teller to Ransom who is himself, as mediator, secondary to the world to which he bears witness.

11. Lewis points out the important role in medieval literary culture of triads and of mediating middle factors. C. S. Lewis, *The Discarded Image: An Introduction to Medieval and Renaissance Literature* (Cambridge: Cambridge University Press, 1964), p. 74.

12. "It is as though there are plain, primary, first-order ways of thinking and speaking that have to be restored to people before they can make sense of the Christian literature." Paul L. Holmer, *C. S. Lewis: The Shape of His Fiction and Thought* (New York: Harper & Row, 1976), p. 94.

13. While not necessarily causal, there is, in my opinion, a substantial relation of this complex location or identity not only with counterparts in the New Testament but also with Lewis's deeply felt dual identity with England and Ireland, as I suggested in the introduction.

14. For Lewis this contrast seems to have been important in that he associates the Platonists with continuities and the Aristotelians with distinctions.

15. C. S. Lewis, *The Allegory of Love: A Study of Medieval Tradition* (New York: Oxford University Press, 1958 [1936]), pp. 90–93. It can be said, I think, that Bernardus Silvestris is as important for *Out of the Silent Planet* as Dante is for *Perelandra*.

Chapter 7

1. "I have come to regard as the greatest of all divisions in the history of the West that which divides the present from, say, the age of Jane Austen and Scott.... Between Jane Austen and us, but not between her

and Shakespeare, Chaucer, Alfred, Virgil, Homer, or the Pharaohs, comes the birth of machines." C. S. Lewis, "De Descriptione Temporum," in *They Asked for a Paper: Papers and Addresses* (London: Geoffrey Bles, 1962), pp. 17, 20.

2. Lewis singles Dante out for praise as a medieval writer who countered the tendency to separate cosmological and devotional writing by unifying them. See C. S. Lewis, *The Discarded Image: An Introduction to Medieval and Renaissance Literature* (Cambridge: Cambridge University Press, 1964), p. 120. This commendation of Dante and his use of Dante in this novel and in other places reflect Lewis's own attempt to bridge this and similar divisions and contraries in modern culture.

3. Lewis imputes an important role to Thomas Hobbes in the formation of modern ideas, primarily the basically antagonistic character of human societies and, as here, death as the principal human antagonist and survival as the principal human desire.

4. However, this moment in the novel implies approval of capital punishment, and killing criminals cannot be placed in the same category as warfare, which can be justified as defense of noncombatant inhabitants from destruction. True, Weston interprets himself as a representative man, a person at the cutting edge of society's advancement, so that he is more than a particular person. But he is also an individual. Not every reader will be willing, I should think, to take the necessity of Weston's execution for the plot of the novel as a persuasive argument for capital punishment.

5. "Good, as it ripens, becomes continually more different not only from evil but from other good." C. S. Lewis, *The Great Divorce* (New York: Macmillan, 1946), p. vi.

6. In *The Problem of Pain* Lewis presents his own version of the Fall as occurring at this crucial moment in the development of the species, when self-consciousness turns toward self-preoccupation and pride. He saw this process as reflected in the development of the human individual and the particularly treacherous stage in that process of growing self-awareness.

7. Little help for such a formulation can be drawn from Lewis, since for him the masculine is, in principle, superior: "whether the male is, or is not, the superior sex, the masculine is certainly the superior gender." C. S. Lewis, *A Preface to Paradise Lost* (Oxford: Oxford University Press, 1967 [1942]), p. 113. While it is legitimate and even important to dis-

tinguish sex from gender, human sexuality is a major arena of gender articulation and, by making the masculine principle superior, Lewis has certainly stacked the deck in projecting what he takes to be the normative relation of men and women to one another.

Chapter 8

1. "[T]he purpose of education is to produce the good man and the good citizen, though it must be remembered that we are not here using the word 'good' in any narrowly ethical sense. The 'good man' here means the man of good taste and good feeling, the interesting and interested man, and almost the happy man." C. S. Lewis, "Our English Syllabus," in *Rehabilitations and Other Essays* (Oxford: Oxford University Press, 1939), p. 81.

2. It is difficult to overstate the high estimation of culture and its role in Lewis's work. Culture needs constant attention, and a major mistake in modernity is the assumption that culture is whatever happens to be the case: "One of the most dangerous errors instilled into us by nineteenth-century progressive optimism is the idea that civilization is automatically bound to increase and spread. The lesson of history is the opposite; civilization is a rarity, attained with difficulty and easily lost. The normal state of humanity is barbarism, just as the normal surface of our planet is salt water." Ibid., p. 82.

3. It should be pointed out that Lewis infers this social norm from the textbook, and he does this by asserting that when people, like the authors, contend against objective values they usually do so on the basis of values that they do not themselves declare. Lewis then infers that it is primarily the welfare of the society that militates against ascribing any public standing to value judgments. Lewis then proceeds to argue that the criterion for the good that rests on what is good or useful for the society cannot sustain itself.

4. Lewis's point that the breadth and depth enjoyed by this epistemological view is due to its support of or usefulness for a morally questionable way of being in the world is, in my opinion, unusual and illuminating.

5. While attention to *The Abolition of Man* belongs in this part of the commentary, since it deals, as does the fictional trilogy, so heavily with science and because it is, like the science trilogy, so directed toward the critique of formative ideas in modern culture, it is clear also

that this book rests heavily on what, in the first part, I called reasonable assumptions. That is, Lewis does not appeal, in this major statement of his position, to religion in general or to Christianity in particular.

6. While I am reluctant to say that one of the three constitutive aspects of Lewis's work, reasonable assumptions, cultural critiques, and applied principles, is more important than the others, I do think that this reasonable assumption or assertion, namely, that we are or become persons in and through the relations that we have in and to our world, is central to his project as a whole.

Chapter 9

1. The high position held by Ransom relates to Lewis's reiterated interest in what is called "theosis," an understanding of sanctification that includes the possibility of humans taking on godlike qualities—a possibility that Lewis holds out in "The Weight of Glory" and toward the end of *Mere Christianity*. This suggests his agreement with Athanasius who, in his "On the Incarnation," says that God became man so that man could become God. Although Lewis does not present himself as a theologian, it is possible, in my opinion, to trace central characteristics of his theology to similar emphases in Eastern Orthodoxy.

2. "Either there is significance in the whole process of things as well as in human activity, or there is no significance in human activity itself. . . . If the world is meaningless, then so are we; *if we mean something, we do not mean alone*." E. M. Tillyard and C. S. Lewis, *The Personal Heresy: A Controversy* (London: Oxford University Press, 1939), p. 30.

3. Lewis is explicit that Bracton College takes no undergraduates. This emphasizes its character as a research institution but also, perhaps, its abstraction from responsibilities to the society and its vulnerability to takeover.

4. Lewis posits an interesting progression from scientific methods to theoretical materialism and the transmission of materialism to studies of human life by way of the social sciences. Lewis sees the consequences of this progression for the humanities to be their exclusion and trivialization in academic culture. While that account continues to be relevant to academic culture, it must also be said that the humanities, by deferring to the social sciences, have also been affected by the domi-

nance of theoretical materialism carried into them by the influence of Freud and, even more widely and deeply, of Karl Marx.

5. This point, that materiality cannot provide on its own an adequate worldview, is basic for Lewis: "We know what it [thinking] is like far better than we know what matter is like. Thought is what we start from: the simple, intimate, immediate *datum*. Matter is the inferred thing, the mystery." C. S. Lewis, *Christian Reflections*, ed. Walter Hooper (Grand Rapids, MI: William B. Eerdmans, 1967), p. 64.

6. Lewis implies an important point concerning academic culture's assumption that change is advance or improvement. This identification is taken over from evolutionary theory. While Lewis accepted evolutionary explanations, he was cautious about overextending them: "But we must sharply distinguish between Evolution as a biological theory and popular evolutionism or Developmentalism which is certainly a Myth." Ibid., p. 83.

7. Lewis often appears to be enjoying his depiction of some academic personalities. Filostrato, with all of his desire to define personhood as mental, is often referred to as fat.

8. Community in this context sounds like the desire to consume exhibited by the Father Below in *The Screwtape Letters*.

9. It is worth noting that St. Anne's is described as a kind of place more commonly found in Ireland than in England.

10. Some of these characteristics, especially the grouping of diverse and even dissimilar intelligent and educated people, suggest a resemblance to the Inklings.

11. Of special interest is Lewis's treatment of Bultitude. The extended description of the bear's thoughts and feelings, suggesting a kind of mind and even identity, is unusual and, in my opinion, convincing and commendable (303–5).

12. For a discussion of Lewis's use of Logres, see David C. Downing, "*That Hideous Strength*: Spiritual Wickedness in High Places," in *C. S. Lewis: Life, Works, and Legacy*, ed. Bruce L. Edwards, vol. 2 (Westport, CT: Praeger, 2007), p. 65.

13. "Donne, the poet whom Lewis habitually associated with the 'Saturnine' spirit, is overcome as husband and wife at last embrace each other's fertility." Michael Ward, *Planet Narnia: The Seven Heavens in the Imagination of C. S. Lewis* (Oxford: Oxford University Press, 2008), p. 52.

Chapter 10

1. The recent study by Sanford Schwartz establishes formal ways in which the three novels are related. The first of these concerns the structure of the books. Schwartz shows that in all three novels Lewis provides a central section and then creates similarities that relate in parallel fashion the chapters that stand on either side of that center so that the opening and closing chapters are similar to one another, as are the second and the penultimate, continuing in that manner to the center. The second formal factor is a progression in the dominant themes, from materiality to vitality and finally to spirituality, each of which can be identified with a particular writer or thinker: H. G. Wells with the first, Henri Bergson with the second, and Charles Williams with the third. See Sanford Schwartz, *C. S. Lewis on the Final Frontier: Science and the Supernatural in the Space Trilogy* (New York: Oxford University Press, 2009).

Chapter 11

1. For Lewis it is not enough for a Christian only to affirm principles or doctrines. Principles need always to be embodied or actualized: "For the truth is that when you have stripped off what the human heart actually was in this or that culture, you are left with a miserable abstraction totally unlike the life really lived by any human being." C. S. Lewis, *A Preface to Paradise Lost* (Oxford: Oxford University Press, 1967 [1942]), p. 64.

2. Lewis seems to imply that the Creation itself is a performance, an application or actualization drawn from a repertoire: "Another result of believing in Creation is to see Nature not as a mere datum but as an achievement." C. S. Lewis, *Reflections on the Psalms* (London: Geoffrey Bles, 1958), p. 83.

3. In his theory of reading Lewis advances the principle of receptivity as basic. See his *An Experiment in Criticism* (Cambridge: Cambridge University Press, 1961). One is tempted to say that reading and other kinds of encounters, such as those that occur to us while walking, require and warrant receptivity because encounters of all kinds are, for Lewis, textual.

4. If Lewis understands Christianity as providing a set of principles that can and should be applied to differing situations, the distinction between a principle and an application of it is required but often difficult to make. Certainly the atonement, that the relation of human beings to

themselves, others, the world, and God has been altered, is a Christian principle that cannot be separated from its particular application in the person and work of Jesus Christ. Although it can be found variously applied in the myths of other religions in which Lewis took an interest and although he also seems intrigued by the variety of explanations of what could be called the economy of the atonement, that is, why and how the person and work of Christ altered the relation of humans to themselves, their world, and God, I do not think that he implies a Christology that makes the Christian account of the atonement one actualization among many of a religious principle.

5. I think that uncertainty remains regarding the status of law relative to grace in Lewis's work. Grace is a principle that is applied variously in differing situations, but at times law also holds for him the status of a principle. He seems to assent to the idea expressed by some of the Psalmists that God's laws have "'*emeth*' truth, intrinsic validity, rock-bottom reality, being rooted in His own nature, and are therefore as solid as that Nature which He has created." Lewis, *Reflections on the Psalms*, p. 61.

6. Care should be taken here, lest the reader assume that for Lewis people who lack religion in general or Christianity in particular are by necessity immoral. The negative consequences of disbelief presented in the narrative are characteristic of disbelief in modernity and not of disbelief in general.

7. Corbin Carnell insists that Lewis does not allow for immediacy in humans' relations to God: "For Lewis there are not *im*mediate experiences of God, for all that we know of God comes through some created thing: language, art, people, history, rituals. God may reveal Himself directly to angels without using the things He has made, but Lewis does not believe He deals in this way with human beings." Corbin Scott Carnell, *Bright Shadow of Reality: C. S. Lewis and the Feeling Intellect* (Grand Rapids, MI: William B. Eerdmans, 1974), p. 135. Recalling the use by Lewis of Rudolf Otto's theory of religious experience, I am not so sure that this matter in Lewis is as clear as Carnell thinks it is.

Chapter 12

1. Paul Holmer puts it nicely: "More properly, the self is a relation, not a thing. The personality is neither godlike and truly original, nor simply an effect and made only by externals. It is both made and maker, debtor

and giver." Paul L. Holmer, *C. S. Lewis: The Shape of His Fiction and Thought* (New York: Harper & Row, 1976), p. 86.

2. "In the ninth canto Spenser explicitly classifies Eros, Storge, and Philia as 'three kinds of love.'" C. S. Lewis, *The Allegory of Love: A Study in Medieval Tradition* (New York: Oxford University Pess, 1958 [1936]), p. 339.

3. Lewis dwells on this distinction, particularly with respect to the works of Charles Williams. Christians are expected to practice both the "affirmation of images" and the "rejection of images," both the Beatrician and the ascetic ways. "But souls are none the less called to travel principally the one way or the other." C. S. Lewis, *Arthurian Torso: Containing the Posthumous Fragment of the Figure of Arthur by Charles Williams* (New York: Oxford University Press, 1969), p. 151.

4. Lewis says in a letter to Jane T. Spens (January 8, 1935) concerning this book, "His central contrast—that agape is selfless and Eros self-regarding—seems at first unanswerable; but I wonder if he is not trying to force on the conception of love an antithesis which it is the precise nature of love, in all its forms, to overcome." C. S. Lewis, *Collected Letters*, vol. 2, ed. Walter Hooper (New York: HarperCollins, 2004), p. 153.

5. Some of the dynamics of university life that are noticeable, if not determining, today may well have been already obvious to Lewis, who seems not to have felt fully a part of the university community. While he had rooms in college, he lived in Headington, and he valued highly a group of close friends, not all of them academics, the well-known Inklings, to which he, of all its members, gave the most attention.

6. Both in England and in America the recent upsurge of interest in Jane Austen, arguably traceable to the character of Mr. Darcy as played by Colin Firth in one of several film versions of *Pride and Prejudice*, secures the validity of Lewis's point.

7. Lewis has deep reservations about an interest in heavenly rewards. He sees such an interest as often selfish, and in his book on the Psalms he even characterizes it as not religious at all: "For the truth seems to me to be that happiness or misery beyond death, simply in themselves, are not even religious subjects at all. . . . [They] have no more to do with religion than looking after one's health or saving money for one's old age." C. S. Lewis, *Reflections on the Psalms* (London: Geoffrey Bles, 1958), p. 40.

Chapter 13

1. Lewis sharply distinguishes his own evaluation of London from that of Charles Williams: "On many of us the prevailing impression made by London streets is one of chaos; but Williams, looking on the same spectacle, saw chiefly an image—an imperfect, pathetic, heroic, and majestic image—of order." C. S. Lewis, *Arthurian Torso: Containing the Posthumous Fragment of the Figure of Arthur by Charles Williams* (New York: Oxford University Press, 1969), p. 105. While Lewis's negative attitude toward cities seems here to be a matter largely of taste or perspective, it is so frequently encountered in his work to be taken as basic and as qualifying his usually positive attitude toward human development and construction.

2. See Michael Ward, *Planet Narnia: The Seven Heavens in the Imagination of C. S. Lewis* (Oxford: Oxford University Press, 2008), p. 181.

3. American readers may be familiar with William Faulkner's moral placement of characters in his Yoknapatawpha stories. White men, who are principally associated with power in this questionable society, are centrally positioned in it while women, children, and African Americans, who are morally stronger but socially weaker, are located at its periphery.

4. The distinction between principles and their application seen in his fictional version of divine creation can also be seen in Lewis's lack of hesitancy in adopting evolutionary theories for the origins of the universe and of human beings.

5. Another positive note appears in the account of the origins of language, namely, that mirth, as well as justice, becomes possible when speech arises.

6. Lewis discusses the nature of *emeth* or truth in his *Reflections on the Psalms* (London: Geoffrey Bles, 1958), p. 83.

7. This is what I take Lewis to mean when he says, in *A Grief Observed*, "Indeed, it's likely enough that what I shall call, if it happens, a 'restoration of faith' will turn out to be only one more house of cards. And I shan't know whether it is or not until the next blow comes." C. S. Lewis, *A Grief Observed* (New York: Seabury Press, 1961), p. 33.

8. If the specific principles that operate in the Narnia Chronicles are actually creedal, it is interesting to note that the creeds, when it comes to Christology, include as principles specific items of the biblical narratives, especially the birth, suffering, death, and resurrection of Jesus. For this reason, it seems to me, Lewis is more constrained when imaginatively

deploying Christological principles than he is when constructing his versions of origins and endings, because the creeds do not specify the details as to how these things did and will occur.

Chapter 14

1. "That is, I believe that the primary moral principles on which all others depend are rationally perceived." C. S. Lewis, *Miracles: A Preliminary Study* (New York: Macmillan, 1947), p. 34.

2. "The ultimate ethical injunctions have always been premises, never conclusions." C. S. Lewis, "On Ethics," in *Christian Reflections*, ed. Walter Hooper (Grand Rapids: William B. Eerdmans, 1967), p. 55.

3. "Though we ought always to imitate the procedure of Christ and His saints, this pattern has to be adapted to the changing conditions of history." C. S. Lewis, "Modern Man and His Categories of Thought," in *Present Concerns* (Boston: Houghton Mifflin Harcourt, 1987), p. 61.

4. "We know what it [thinking] is like far better than we know what matter is like. Thought is what we start from: the simple, intimate, immediate *datum*. Matter is the inferred thing, the mystery." Lewis, *Christian Reflections*, p. 64.

5. "With Darwinism as a theorem in Biology I do not think a Christian need have any quarrel." Lewis, "Modern Man and His Categories of Thought," p. 63.

6. "In love, in virtue, in the pursuit of knowledge, and in the reception of the arts, we are doing this. Obviously this process can be described either as an enlargement or a temporary annihilation of the self. But that is an old paradox: 'he that loseth his life shall save it.'" C. S. Lewis, *An Experiment in Criticism* (Cambridge: Cambridge University Press, 1961), p. 138.

7. "The man who is contented to be only himself, and therefore less a self, is in prison." Ibid., p. 140.

8. "The account of the self is that its capaciousness, its roominess, its capabilities determine the account that is given of the world." Paul L. Holmer, *C. S. Lewis: The Shape of His Fiction and Thought* (New York: Harper & Row, 1976), p. 89.

Conclusion

1. Lewis to Warnie Lewis, February 18, 1940, in *C. S. Lewis Collected Letters*, vol. 2, ed. Walter Hooper (New York: HarperCollins, 2004), p. 351.

2. Although we should remember that Lewis did not consider himself to be and did not try to be a theologian, there is a good bit of theology, both implicit and developed, in his work. I have said that I do not think he can be called an Evangelical, as that designation has been formed in the American context, or neo-orthodox; the question arises as to what recognizable form of theology his own seems most to resemble. At first, I thought the answer was Reformed, and I still think that it is a more likely candidate than the two listed above. But taking into account his interest in "theosis," as in the sanctification of Ransom, his tendency to define Christianity in terms of the ecumenical creeds, his emphasis on cosmology, his use of "Life" to describe God in *Mere Christianity*, his strong stress on relationships and love, and his positive theological anthropology, I would begin, if I were to explore his theology more fully, with its possible similarities to Eastern Orthodoxy.

3. Lewis was, to be sure, well aware of the statement of Jesus in the synoptic Gospels concerning the dependence of finding oneself on losing oneself, but it is not clear to me what role that biblical saying had in his development of a theory of personal identity based on acts of giving oneself to others by means of attention, appreciation, and care. It is interesting to note, for example, that Matthew Arnold, in "Literature and Dogma," took this saying of Jesus, despite its apparently contradictory quality, to be one of the most profound statements ever made. The maxim also had cultural standing.

4. "[Literature] communicates in such a way that, when successful, it creates new capabilities and capacities, powers a kind of roominess in the human personality. One becomes susceptible to new competencies, new functions, new pathos and possibilities." Paul L. Holmer, *C. S. Lewis: The Shape of His Fiction and Thought* (New York: Harper & Row, 1976), p. 20.

5. Interestingly, few thinkers in the past can be more associated with this understanding of textuality and reading than two highly influential figures of whom Lewis seems to have had very little good to say, namely, John Calvin and Francis Bacon.

INDEX

Abelard, Peter, 93, 211
addiction, 173, 238, 258, 260–61
adolescence, 248, 254, 257–58
American readers, 5, 9, 12, 232, 251, 266, 291n3
analogy, 31, 54, 103
angels, 68
animals, 62, 63, 64, 88, 173–74, 184, 205, 210, 227, 238, 242, 262, 278n5, 287n11
Anselm, St. 23, 211
apocalypticism, 168
Aquinas, St. Thomas, 103
Aristotle, 88, 138, 283n14
Arnold, Matthew, 13, 225, 293n3
astronomy, 142
atonement, doctrine of, 93, 94, 204, 211, 212, 242, 260, 261, 268, 288–89n4
Augustine, St. 21, 58, 62, 67, 242
autobiography, theory of, 22, 23, 276n2

Bachelard, Gaston, 30
Bacon, Francis, 293n5
Barfield, Owen, 27
Barth, Karl, 268
Bergson, Henri, 27, 30, 88, 90, 104, 262
Bernard of Chairvaux, St., 21, 101
Bible, 5, 16, 29, 58, 221, 277n2
  Genesis, 150, 168, 240, 241, 255, 258
  Job, 240, 241, 255
  Isaiah, 51
  Matthew, 52
  Mark, 52, 93, 149, 243
  Luke, 52
  John, 210
  Romans, 87
  Philippians, 260
  Hebrews, 55
  Revelation, 210, 246
Blavatsky, Helena, 25
Boethius, 82
Buber, Martin, 165
Buddhism, 25
Bunyan, John, 21
bureaucracy, 69, 70, 178, 230

Calvin, John, 106, 217, 268, 271–72, 293n5
Calvinism, 55, 87
Cambridge University, 3, 6, 12, 22, 169, 230
capital punishment, 101, 284
Carnell, Corbin, 275n1, 289n7
Catholicism, 10, 16, 217, 226
celebration, 218
Christology, 28, 49, 51, 93, 259, 260, 280n5, 289n4, 291–92n8
Church of England, 11
cities, 24, 37, 127, 244
Coleridge, Samuel Taylor, 13, 154
competition, 33, 79, 101, 116, 123, 131, 132, 198, 228, 230
courage, 82, 240
creation, doctrine of, 53, 67, 204, 240, 241, 242, 243, 246, 255, 258, 268, 288n2, 291n4
Crowley, Aleister, 110

Dante, 141, 145, 284n2
Daoism, 164
Darwinism, 91, 125, 218, 292n5
  social, 79, 138
Davidman, Joy, 39
Descartes, René, 173, 190, 191, 197
de Saussure, Ferdinand, 129
determinism, 27, 98, 114, 173, 180–81, 270, 272
discernment, 263–64
Donne, John, 189, 287n13
Durham, University of, 154

Eagleton, Terry, 12
Eastern Orthodoxy, 286n1, 293n2
ecclesiology, 28, 226–27, 275n3, 279n4
Eliot, T. S., 5, 74, 188
enchantment, 239
eschatology, 64, 108, 150, 233, 243, 245, 266, 268, 278n6
Evangelicalism, 11, 16, 28, 259, 268, 293n2
exclusive disjunctions, 49, 93

Fall, theory of, 57, 69, 153, 258, 266, 278n3, 284n6
Farrer, Austin, 271
Faulkner, William, 291n3
First World War, 13, 33, 35, 42, 73, 75, 111, 182, 189
fortunate fall, 146, 152, 153, 174, 199, 217
free will, 172, 181, 242, 271, 281n2
Freud, Sigmund, 97, 113

gender, 17, 151–2, 230, 248, 250, 284n7
Germany, 12, 85
gift-giving, 234–35
Golding, William, 74
Gospels, 29, 49, 52, 80, 210, 212, 259, 293n3
Graves, Robert, 5
Greece, 3, 4
Greene, Graham, 74, 111
Greeves, Arthur, 23, 37
group identity, 180, 184, 230

Headington, 3, 29
Hegel, G. W. F., 30, 137, 225, 254, 270
Hobbes, Thomas, 198, 218, 284n3

Holmer, Paul L., 292n8, 293n4
homosexuality, 33, 176, 249
human agency, 54, 61, 97, 99, 113, 180
Hume, David, 44, 198
humility, 77, 101, 102, 103, 176

idealism, 27, 35, 78, 86, 114, 115, 123, 129, 245, 254, 255, 267, 269
imagination, 15, 25, 32, 33, 208, 247, 261
impartation, of grace, 94, 105, 261
imperialism, 142, 164, 194, 196
imputation, of grace, 94, 105
Incarnation, 49, 50, 104, 146
India, 26, 237
Inklings, 6, 287, 290n5
intuition, 28, 48, 55, 88, 89, 113, 135, 148, 163, 174, 197, 209, 262
Ireland, 3, 4, 223, 275n1, 283n13, 287n9
Irvine, Martin, 117
Israel, 48, 93

James, William, 24, 115
Jenkin, A. K. Hamilton, 37
Jesus Christ, 50, 55, 80
joy, 26, 34–36, 76, 110, 222
Joyce, James, 5
Jung, Carl, 175, 262

Kant, Immanuel, 110, 261, 262
Kirkpatrick, William, 4, 26

Lawrence, D. H., 5, 151, 233
Leavis, F. R., 13, 276n6
Leonov, Alexei, 124
Lévi-Strauss, Claude, 129
Lilith, 206
Locke, John, 191, 241
London, 25, 179, 205, 236–37, 241

MacDonald, George, 4, 27, 51, 94
Malvern, 24, 25, 32
Maritain, Jacques, 10
Marx, Karl, 268
materialism, 27, 32, 35, 72, 74, 90, 114, 115, 116, 124, 172, 186, 193, 194, 245, 254, 268, 269, 271
McGrath, Alister, 270n1, n3, 279n5
mediation, 94, 134, 138, 156–57, 168, 188, 216, 283n11
Milton, John, 66, 68, 71, 80, 145, 152
Moore, Mrs. Janie, 4, 38–40, 73, 78
Morris, William, 4
myth, 4, 5, 25, 36, 275n2

narcissism, 239, 273
narrative theory, 21, 121, 168, 282n1
neo-orthodoxy, 268, 293n2
neutrals, 173, 185
Nygren, Anders, 221

objectivity, in value theory, 155, 162
Origen, 93, 211
Otto, Rudolf, 45, 46, 48, 110, 114
Oxford University, 3, 5, 6, 7, 12, 22, 27, 32, 33, 37, 39, 41, 88, 110, 140, 169, 178, 230, 256

pacifism, 100
pantheism, 92
Paul, St., 21, 81, 87, 106, 260
Pelagianism, 242
personal identity, 17, 85, 107, 110, 113, 155, 132, 180, 181, 185, 192, 197, 198, 22, 223, 227, 237, 241, 264, 272
personhood, 98, 155, 157, 270
Plato, 37, 133–34, 138, 233, 283n14
pleasure, 34, 75, 77, 80, 127, 143, 147–48, 222, 230
prayer, 73, 82, 105
Prichard, H. A., 28, 88
pride, 58, 81, 101, 106, 115, 238
promising, 96, 99, 136, 238
Protestantism, 16, 60, 226
psychology, 57

racism, 17, 249
Rackham, Arthur, 26
rational choice theory, 158
reading, theory of, 117, 123, 224, 259, 292n6
reason, 14–15, 44, 55, 262
resurrection, doctrine of, 148
Richards, I. A., 13
Richardson, Samuel, 66
romantic love, 79, 232–33
Romanticism, 34, 35, 36, 45, 68, 110, 117, 145, 152, 225, 272
Ross, W. D., 28, 88

Sagan, Carl, 15
sanctification, 135, 141, 147, 149
Schleiermacher, Friedrich, 45, 46
schools, public, 32, 154–56
Schwartz, Sanford, 288n1
scientific method, 142, 160–61, 190
Second World War, 6, 9, 10, 73, 85, 145, 205, 249
self-consciousness, 74, 150, 151, 197, 241, 272
sex, 76, 79, 98–99, 133, 148, 151, 231–33
Shaw, G. B., 233
Silvestris, Bernard, 138–39
Snow, C. P., 125
social ethics, 11, 96–97, 157
sociology, 170–71
Socratic Club, 6, 66
soteriology, 94, 259
spatiality, 30, 31, 121, 122, 123, 205, 213, 225
Spencer, Herbert, 79. 198
structural linguistics, 129, 151
subjectivity, in value theory, 155, 162
sublime, 46, 110, 224
subtlety, 69, 73, 74, 146

temporality, 14, 77, 78, 81, 151, 195, 196, 205, 212
textuality, 117, 123, 223–24, 282n5
theosis, 56, 286n1, 293n2
Thomism, 10
transposition, 51, 148
Tylor, E. B., 114, 270, 280n3

urbanization, 111, 191, 244

Victorian period, 111, 140, 195
vitalism, 90, 137, 233

walking, 130, 131, 136, 141, 273, 283n9, 288n3
Ward, Michael, 237, 252
Weber, Max, 69
Wells, H. G., 123
Wheaton College, 10
Williams, Charles, 290n3, 291n1
Woolf, Virginia, 74
Wordsworth, William, 27, 34, 46, 110
worldviews, 28, 29, 31, 35, 65, 72, 110, 115, 116, 117, 137, 144, 161, 172, 264, 271, 280n3, 287n5

Yeats, W.B., 4, 5